DATE DUE

OCT 2002

DISCARD

BROCKTON PUBLIC LIBRARY

The Minority Quarterback

THE
MINORITY
QUARTERBACK

And Other Lives in Sports

IRA BERKOW

Ivan R. Dee

CHICAGO 2002

THE MINORITY QUARTERBACK. Copyright © 2002 by Ira Berkow. All rights reserved, including the right to reproduce this book or portions thereof in any form. For information, address: Ivan R. Dee, Publisher, 1332 North Halsted Street, Chicago 60622. Manufactured in the United States of America and printed on acid-free paper.

Library of Congress Cataloging-in-Publication Data:
    Berkow, Ira.
       The minority quarterback, and other lives in sports / Ira Berkow.
          p. cm.
       Reprint of columns and feature stories originally published in The New York times between 1981 and 2000.
       Includes index.
       ISBN 1-56663-422-9 (alk. paper)
       1. Minorities in sports—United States—Miscellanea.   2. Athletes—United States—Miscellanea.   I. New York times.   II. Title.
    GV709.5 .B47 2002
    796'.08—dc21

                                                                    2001047578

For Ian

Contents

PIVOTAL PLAYS

A KALEIDOSCOPE OF SPORTS

Foreword

❦ THE LOOK in Michael Jordan's eyes when he was seeking to make a new career for himself in baseball was different from when I had last seen him. I sat with him now in front of his locker in the cramped clubhouse of the Birmingham Barons Class A baseball team on a late afternoon in May of 1994. The look in Michael Jordan's eyes was different now from when he had won his last of three straight NBA championships, just a year earlier, as the nonpareil star of the Chicago Bulls basketball team.

He wasn't succeeding at baseball—a prodigious endeavor even for this remarkable athlete, for he was thirty-two years old and hadn't played baseball since high school. He seemed not nearly as confident—his batting average was around .200—his eyes not sparkling as they once had and as I remembered them when he was lighting up the basketball world, and beyond, for the Bulls.

There was also the aspect of sadness in his eyes for the still-fresh memory of the random murder of his father, James Jordan. In the Birmingham clubhouse that late afternoon, Jordan spoke about his father and about his father's wish one day to see his son play professional baseball. James Jordan thought his son could succeed at it, too. Michael said that every day when he woke up he saw his father's face before him, and spoke to him.

For Michael Jordan, for all the high-flying Air Jordan hype, was at bottom a dutiful son, a daring young man, a vulnerable human being. Even for one of the world's most celebrated stars, when it rained, it poured.

So it is that, oddly enough, memorable moments for someone writing about sports and sports personalities often occur away from the playing field. The sports feature stories and columns that I have pursued for the *New York Times* have generally found another side to the athlete or the person whose life has been touched, transformed, enriched, or, as in some cases, damaged in the sports world.

There's the baseball player who still seeks a dream of one day starring in the big leagues, and has played on so many professional teams, in so many leagues, that he has worn out more luggage than a carnival troupe.

There's the quarterback who, after being knocked unconscious in a National Football League game, woke up in a completely dark room, strapped to a gurney. He didn't know where he was or what had happened. He thought he had died and been buried. He quit football shortly after that harrowing experience.

There is Arthur Ashe who, knowing he had precious few months left to live, sought to make the world a better place, starting with his moving advice to his small daughter.

The pieces selected here have a variety of mood and subject matter, from the humorous (as I perceived the humor—what's a knee-slapper to me might be a yawn to the next guy) to the thoughtful to the tragic. The sports world that I have been privileged to experience has broad dimensions. It goes from the ballpark to the boxing ring to, well, Woody Allen's film-cutting studio, where we talked about his passion for sports, his admiration for the prowess of athletes, their artistry, and the "burning genius" of some like the former New York Knicks basketball player Earl Monroe: "When he takes off and races the length of the court, he resembles an animated cartoon character whose feet never touch the ground."

My work brought me in contact not only with the famous and the widely known but also with the little known and some of the infamous. From Michael Jordan and Muhammad Ali and Pee Wee Reese to Marge Schott and John Riggins and Angel Cordero to the

Russian boxing champion who disappeared in Brooklyn without a trace and the high school football star who seemed to have everything but hanged himself from a tree.

One of the most intriguing stories I have ever worked on was that of Marcus Jacoby, a teenage white boy who dreamed of playing quarterback in college and accepted a scholarship to Southern University, an historically black institution. I spent a good part of nine months working on the story, much of it in Baton Rouge, Louisiana, the locale of the college as well as Jacoby's hometown. This was one of a fifteen-part series that ran over a period of three months in the *New York Times*—the paper called it "the most ambitious journalistic project in its history." In April 2001 the series was awarded the Pulitzer Prize for "National Reporting."

My assignments at the *Times* in the twenty years I have been with the paper have been divided between feature stories and column-writing. And while newspaper editions are essentially momentary, the experiences of people endure.

I. B.

New York City
January 2002

The Minority Quarterback

GREEN

DIAMONDS

Fergie Jenkins's Twist in the Road

IN THE MORNING, Ferguson Jenkins had noticed that the hose to the large red vacuum cleaner was missing, but he paid little attention to it, never once imagining what terrible use it might be put to.

Then in the late afternoon, around five o'clock, the phone rang in the kitchen of his ranch house in Guthrie, Oklahoma. The date on the calendar on the wall was Tuesday, December 15, 1992, two days after Jenkins's forty-ninth birthday. Jenkins was outside, smoothing the red clay in the driveway with a shovel, when his ranch foreman, Tommy Christian, answered the phone.

"Sheriff Powell!" he called to Jenkins from the doorway.

"Sheriff Powell?" Jenkins recalled thinking. "What can he want?" The last time he had spoken to Doug Powell was two years earlier, after a robbery at the Jenkins ranch.

From the driveway, Jenkins could see that the sun, weak all day, was disappearing behind the hills and two man-made lakes on his 160 acres. It was getting cool as a wind picked up in this isolated area of the plains, about eight and a half miles north of Guthrie, the nearest town, and about forty miles north of Oklahoma City.

Jenkins was wearing a green windbreaker, green baseball cap, jeans, and work boots. This is a working farm, with eight horses, fifty-two head of beef cattle, and sixty acres of wheat, and Jenkins dresses for it. So did his fiancée, Cindy Takieddine, who lived with him, his adopted twelve-year-old son, Raymond, and his three-year-old daughter, Samantha, the child he had with his wife, Maryanne, who was seriously injured in a car crash in December 1990. Her death in January 1991 came just four days after the announcement that Fergie, as everyone calls him, had been named to baseball's Hall of Fame.

The election had been the culmination of a nineteen-year career in the major leagues, mostly with the Chicago Cubs and Texas Rangers, in which Jenkins won 284 games, was a 20-game winner seven times, won the National League Cy Young Award in 1971 and the American League Comeback Player of the Year Award in 1974, and then finally retired in 1983.

Jenkins is a big man. At 6 feet 5 inches and 225 pounds, he is about 20 pounds heavier than in his playing days, but he carries his weight well, with a graceful, slope-shouldered walk. Having learned that the sheriff was on the phone, he entered the two-story redwood house, walked past the Christmas tree that Cindy had decorated for three days, took the receiver, and was told that the sheriff wanted to see him in Guthrie. Within fifteen minutes, Jenkins arrived in town in his pickup.

"I have some horrible news, Mr. Jenkins," said Sheriff Powell. "And there's no easy way to tell it. Cindy Takieddine and Samantha Jenkins were found dead of carbon monoxide poisoning. They were found in a Bronco pickup on a rural road near Perry."

"No, you're wrong, sheriff," said Jenkins. "You're wrong. I'm picking up Samantha at 5:30 at her day-care nursery." He looked at his watch. "In about ten minutes."

"It was a positive I.D., sir. And a note was left."

"Call the day-care center," said Jenkins. "You'll see; Samantha's there."

Powell called the center for Jenkins, and put the call on a speakerphone. Samantha Jenkins was not at the nursery.

"Mr. Jenkins was devastated," recalled Powell. "This was one of the hardest things I've ever had to do as sheriff, or deputy, in

6

Logan County. Mr. Jenkins is highly admired here. He's been a model citizen and always willing to speak at civic or school or church groups. As famous as he is, that's how down to earth he is. He rode up to Perry with my undersheriff to identify the bodies, about thirty miles. All the way there and all the way back he never said a word."

It was back in Powell's office that he learned that Cindy, a tall, forty-four-year-old blonde, had stopped at the day-care center and picked up Samantha, whom she had dressed at home that morning in a green party dress with white sash and white stockings and black shiny shoes, saying it was for a Christmas party at the nursery school. But no party was scheduled.

Before Cindy and Samantha left home that day, Jenkins went to town to buy groceries. It was the last he saw them alive. "There were no arguments," recalled Jenkins. "We were civil to each other."

"She didn't look or act no different," said Christian, the foreman.

After picking up Samantha at the day-care center, Cindy drove to the deserted road. She affixed the vacuum cleaner hose to the exhaust pipe of the Bronco, ran it up through the back window, sealed the window with the duct tape she had taken from home along with the hose, and, with the ignition still running, climbed into the back seat and held Samantha in her arms. The coroner's report estimates that this happened around noon.

A few hours later, a pumper on a nearby oil rigging spotted the car, with two bodies slumped in the back seat, and he phoned the police.

On the day after Christmas, twelve days after the tragedy, Ferguson Jenkins loaded his pickup truck with unwrapped Christmas presents and returned them in Guthrie to Wal-Mart, Sam's Wholesale Outlet, and Anthony's Clothing Store. They included a jogging outfit and sweaters for Cindy. For Samantha there were Cabbage Patch dolls, a Minnie Mouse towel set, a Beauty and the Beast towel set ("She loved Beauty and the Beast," said Jenkins), coloring sets, a large box of crayons, a sweater that had Santa Claus and reindeer and the word "Christmas" across it, and matching socks.

When Jenkins returned home from the stores, his three daughters from his first marriage, to Kathy Jenkins, were in the house. The girls, Kelly, twenty-two, Delores, twenty-one, and Kimberly, fifteen—all in college or high school—had come down from their home in Chatham, Ontario, where Jenkins was born and raised, to celebrate Christmas with their father, as they did every year. But this year they had also come to go to the funeral of their three-year-old half-sister.

Jenkins's eighty-six-year-old father, who is in a nursing home in Chatham, had not made the trip for the funeral. "Said he couldn't take it," said Jenkins. It was his father, Ferguson Jenkins, Sr., to whom Jenkins dedicated his induction into the Hall of Fame and who sat proudly in attendance in a wheelchair. Jenkins had told the gathering at Cooperstown: "My father was a semipro ballplayer and he played in the Negro leagues, but he didn't make the major leagues because he was limited by history"—the color barrier in big-league baseball that existed until 1947.

"But he has outlived that history," Jenkins continued. "I always told him that anything I do in baseball, I do for the two of us, and so now I feel I'm being inducted into the Hall of Fame with my father."

Jenkins's mother, Delores, has been dead for several years. She had become blind after complications while giving birth to her only child. "I remember she always walked with a white cane and always made sure that my baseball uniform was sparkling clean and my baseball shoes were polished," Jenkins has recalled. "I'm not sure how she knew, but she never let me out of the house to play ball unless I was all in order."

Jenkins grew up playing baseball and hockey and basketball, and was often the lone black in those leagues in Chatham. "I heard 'nigger' a lot," he recalled, "but I was always determined to make people respect my abilities. I always wanted them to say,

'Hey, watch that black guy, he's good.' And I did get into some fights, mostly in hockey, and lost a few teeth. But I came out of it."

He left home after signing a contract with the Philadelphia Phillies when he was eighteen, having just graduated high school, "a tall, skinny kid of 155 pounds," he said. "My father was a cook on shipping lines in the Great Lakes, and my mother was home alone a lot. I've always felt kind of guilty leaving her, but I knew I had to pursue my career." Three years later, at the end of the 1965 season, he was called up to the Phillies as a relief pitcher. In his first game he replaced the veteran Jim Bunning, whom, he re-called, he had badgered for pitching help.

"How do you grip the ball? How do you throw your slider?" Jenkins would ask Bunning. The next season Jenkins was traded to the Cubs, and Leo Durocher made him a starter. Jenkins learned his craft well while pitching in Wrigley Field, the smallest ball park in the major leagues.

With the often lackluster Cub teams, he pitched in bad luck. He still shares a record for the most 1–0 losses in a season—five, in 1968, in games against pitchers that included Bob Gibson and Don Drysdale. Still, he won the Cy Young Award in 1971 with a 24–13 record, leading the league in complete games with 30, innings pitched, 325, and strikeouts, 304. He won 20 games six straight seasons for the Cubs, and then fell to 14–16 in 1973. The Cubs responded by trading him to Texas in a move that stunned him and much of baseball.

The next year, 1974, Jenkins won twenty-five games and the American League's Comeback Player of the Year award. Like his former teammate Ernie Banks, he never played on a pennant-winner. He came close, however, during the 1969 season when the Cubs, leading for much of the season, faded in the stretch as the Mets won the National League's East Division, and then the pennant and World Series.

Jenkins was traded to Boston in 1976, traded back to Texas in 1978, released after the 1981 season, and then signed as a free agent by the Cubs. He pitched two more seasons and then retired, two months short of his fortieth birthday. He caught on as a pitching coach in the Rangers' organization, where he spent several years with their Oklahoma City Class AAA team before being given his release three years ago.

Jenkins was always one of the most gentlemanly of ballplayers and was thrown out of a game only once, when he threw a few bats onto the field in a pique. "Fergie, I'm sorry," said the umpire, "I'm going to have to ask you to leave." Jenkins had one other incident of greater notoriety. In August 1980 he was arrested in Toronto on a charge of carrying in his luggage small amounts of hashish, marijuana, and cocaine. He was suspended by baseball commissioner Bowie Kuhn but soon was reinstated by an arbitrator who said that Kuhn could not rule on Jenkins before the courts did.

But while Jenkins was found guilty of possession of drugs in December 1980, no police record exists. At sentencing in the Ontario Provinicial Court, Judge Jerry Young told Jenkins: "You seem to be a person who has conducted himself in exemplary fashion in the community and in the country, building up an account. This is the time to draw on that account." Judge Young then wiped the slate clean for Jenkins.

It was while he was with the Oklahoma City team that he found that ranch house. He and Maryanne, whom he had met and married while with the Cubs, had loved the house at first sight, he said. Both liked the solitude it afforded and the beauty of the landscape there. Her son, Raymond, by a previous marriage, was then eight, and his father had died and Jenkins had adopted him. "I call him Fergie usually," said Raymond, a bright, good-natured youth, "unless I want something. Then I call him Dad."

Ray, who had known only cities, had to make adjustments to farm life, and did, getting to learn how to care for and ride horses, and, at paternal urging, to paint posts too, not always with pleasure. Adjustments for him, and for Jenkins, would grow increasingly harder when Maryanne was injured in a car accident near their home, and, after a month in intensive care, died of pneumonia. Samantha was then six months old.

When Cindy Takieddine, divorced and working as a secretary in a law office in Los Angeles, read about Jenkins's election to the Hall of Fame, she called the Cubs to try to locate him, to congratulate him. She managed to get his home phone number. She had met him when he was a young player with the Cubs and she was nineteen. They had struck up a friendship, though Jenkins says it was never a romance, and he hadn't seen her in about fifteen years. When she learned from Jenkins on the phone that his wife had died, she offered to come with a girlfriend to Guthrie on her vacation and help him any way she could. He accepted.

"They cooked, they took care of the house and they watched over the kids," Jenkins recalled. The girlfriend soon went back home, but Cindy stayed and they fell in love. Six months ago they became engaged. He said she started feeling pressure from friends about marriage. "It'll happen, just not right away," Jenkins told her. Meanwhile, she was a great mother and, essentially, a great wife, Jenkins said. She traded her white slacks for farm overalls. She was a talented decorator around the house, putting, as the foreman, Christian, called it, "the woman's touch on it, with all them frills and friggles." He added, "And she was always a lady."

Cindy kept the checkbook in order and looked over the endorsements and the personal-appearance schedule for Jenkins, who flew periodically to card shows, fantasy camps, and speaking engagements. She grew to be a loving and concerned mother to Raymond and developed a close bond with Samantha. Cindy also seemed to take to farm life and was active in classes in town, particularly ceramics. She made angels and deer heads and a Santa Claus for Christmas that was placed on the mantel above the fireplace in the living room.

"There were some spats between Fergie and Cindy, sure; what couple doesn't have spats on occasion?" said Lemoyne Hardin, a family friend. "But it was pretty clear that they got along just fine."

A lot of mail came to Jenkins, much of it asking for autographs, and sometimes Cindy would open it up, see that it was from a woman, and throw it away. When Jenkins found out, he said that was not right, that it was his personal property. If she wanted to open his mail, he would be happy to do it with her.

Tension seemed to increase when a sports reporter from Cincinnati called the Jenkins home in early December and Cindy answered. He asked whether it was true that Jenkins had accepted a job as a pitching coach in the Cincinnati Reds organization. Cindy had known nothing about it, and it angered her.

"Cindy knew I was talking with front-office people," said Jenkins. "But I hadn't told her about the Reds, hadn't shared it with her. But I hadn't signed the contract. I still have the contract, unsigned." At his kitchen table recently, he took out a briefcase and two pink contracts, and showed them still unsigned.

"I told her that baseball had been my life, and that I still had a dream of one day being a pitching coach in the major leagues," he said. "But I said nothing is certain yet, I hadn't made any definite decision about baseball. But she was concerned. She said she was nervous about having to spend eight months alone at the ranch, and she wasn't sure how she could manage the place. I told her that she could come visit me wherever I was. It appeared I'd be with the Reds' minor league club in Chattanooga and that things would work out. Not to worry. I think that's what troubled her. I think so. I don't know for sure. I never will."

Jenkins sighed. "I sit here and I seem calm," he said. "But my mind is racing ninety miles an hour. The other night I woke up about three in the morning and came down here and just looked around. I said, 'Why? Why? Why did she have to do it? Why if she's unhappy, chop off her life like that? And take the baby with her?' Okay, be angry at me, but don't punish the baby."

After Jenkins had returned the Christmas presents, he remembers "getting short" with his daughters. The suicide and homicide, the Christmas season, all of it was bearing down on him, "smothering me," he said. "I apologized to my kids," he said. "I told them,

'Your dad's just not having a good day.' They understood, I think. I said to myself, 'Fergie, get a grip.'

"But I knew I needed help, needed to talk to someone. I thought of calling 911. But then I thought about a chaplain I'd met in the hospital where Maryanne had been. I needed answers, and I thought a clergyman might know. I called and told him it was urgent. He said to come right over. We talked for about three hours.

"He told me that God will not put more pressure on an individual than he can handle. Well, I don't want any more pressure. I don't want any more grief, any more sorrow. I really don't know how much more I can take. But talking to him was a big help. And I had talked to a priest, too. He told me he thought that Cindy had had a chemical imbalance. But I'm going to be going to some support groups now. I think it's important."

Jenkins is a Baptist and says that despite his agonies he has maintained a belief in God. "People tell me that God has his reasons," he said. "I'm hoping somewhere down the road he lets me know. I certainly can't figure it out."

The suicide note that Cindy left on the front seat of the Bronco provided no answers for him either, he said. He took out the letter that was written in pen on the back of a lumber-company receipt. It read:

"My last statement. My name is Cindy Backherms Takieddine. My address is in my purse. Contact Ferguson Jenkins. He can claim the bodies.

"Fergie said opening his mail is a gross invasion of his privacy—truly immoral. But ruining someone's life and telling them to get out the best way they can—that's immoral. I am to leave with what I came with. I was betrayed.

"I cannot leave and go away without Samantha. I love her more than life itself and cannot envision my life without her. She has been my child for almost two years.

"To all those who love me and Boog please forgive me—I had no way out." Boog was Cindy's nickname for Samantha.

"We had been talking," said Jenkins. "We talked a lot. We

13

worked things out a lot. I never wanted her to leave. I never said that. I don't understand what she meant by betrayal. I just don't know. I've got so many questions. And no answers."

Jenkins was now on the white porch overlooking his property, as the sun, on an unseasonably warm day, reflected on the lakes and the cattle that were grazing, and on the horses. "My uncle Coleman said I should blast the house, that it's unlucky," he said. "I even thought of it. But this is my home, where I'm going to stay. And I'm going to have a priest bless it." Jenkins ran a hand against his greying temple and looked out at the farm that he loves so much. "It's much quieter now with just me and Raymond," he said. "But we're trying to make it, trying to get things done. And I'm trying to be his dad as much as I can."

Jenkins said he still isn't sure about the Reds job, and who will stay with Raymond if he does go. "I still have things to figure out," he said.

Later that evening, in the dark, he drove for dinner into town to a pizza parlor with Raymond. The lights from the pickup truck reflected on the red clay farm road. Raymond seemed to be doing all right. His father talked now about the computer game Raymond had been promised for Christmas if he did well in school, in the seventh grade. He had produced a 96 average and received the game. Raymond talked about the computer game and what he wanted to do when he grew up. "Probably mess with computers," he said. Jenkins smiled.

"Oh, Raymond," said Jenkins after a moment, "it's supposed to start getting cold and rainy tomorrow. I think you'll have to take the horses into the barn."

"Okay, Fergie," he said, quietly and respectfully. "I'll remember."

Father and son sat, lost in thought. Jenkins, in his green baseball cap, was silent behind the wheel. The only sound in the night was the rattling of the truck on the road.

[1993]

Jack Lazorko
Doesn't Pitch
Here Anymore

🐾 MAYBE you've never heard of Jack Lazorko, the thirty-seven-year-old right-handed pitcher who is as compact as a tugboat and is called "Il Bulldog" in Italy, "El Bulldog" in Latin America, and "Zork" in the States. Maybe you've never seen him play, his dark brows over intense hazel eyes, armed with an assortment of pitches from forkballs to knuckle curves to sliders to fastballs that dip and fastballs that rise—none of which will blow anyone away, as he describes it, but all of which are invariably around the plate and always carry a purpose.

While he is hardly a household name, fans in hundreds of the most unlikely towns around the world plus a legion of people in baseball—from players to executives—know him, or of him. After all, he played for or with or against many of those in baseball. Maybe most of them.

"Sometimes," he said, "it feels like all of them."

Few baseball careers have been anything like Jack Lazorko's, who was born in Hoboken, New Jersey, and grew up in River Edge to the north, and who has called so many places home since then that, he says, he has single-handedly kept mapmakers in business. Maybe you haven't followed his career for the past sixteen years as he played for nine major league organizations and seventeen of their teams, and maybe a dozen more teams in the Caribbean and Mexico and South America and Europe. This year alone he has worn the uniform of the Yankees (in spring training) and of the Norfolk Tides, the Mets' Class AAA team. When a call was made recently to the Tides' executive office, it was asked whether Jack Lazorko was there.

"Not anymore," came the reply. Gone after seven games.

It is, in a nutshell, the story of Jack Thomas Lazorko's baseball life.

"I've been released by more teams in more leagues in more countries and in more languages than anyone in the history of baseball," Lazorko said one day last week. "And I'm the only man to have been released by both the Mets and the Yankees in the same year—within four months!" He shakes his head and smiles wryly. "Unbelievable."

Unbelievable because, as he said recently at his home in Rockwall, Texas, "I always seem to be the eleventh man on a ten-man pitching staff."

He is currently unemployed. Again. But that could change tomorrow. Or the next day. He is ready. He says he has learned to pack in ten minutes, and that's for a six-month trip, if necessary. He asks two questions of his new team: "What color spikes do you wear?" And "What color sleeves?" He has in his closet piles of various colored baseball shoes and piles of sweatshirts. In his attic above the garage are several dozen suitcases, hanging bags, and equipment bags. One day last May his wife and children drove into the garage, and the seven-year-old, Mitch, noticing that the foldable stairs to the attic had been pulled down, said, "Oh, Daddy's got a job."

"But this year might be the turning point, when I start to think of something else, a normal job, maybe like coaching," said Lazorko. "It's come to that."

Lazorko has played at all levels of amateur and professional baseball, from rookie league to the major leagues. He has played in the United States and Canada and Mexico and Latin America and Europe, for teams ranging from the El Paso Diablos to the Tulsa Drillers to the Phoenix Fire Birds to the Wichita Aeros to the Asheville Tourists to the Sun City Rays (in the Senior League) and on to, among others, the Calgary Cannons, Edmonton Trappers, Los Mochis (Mexico) Caneros, Santurce (Puerto Rico) Crabbers, Valencia (Venezuela) Magallenes, and Parma (Italy) Angels. Just recently he joined a team called the Hollywood Legends, which played and won a weeklong European tournament in Belgium.

Maybe you weren't aware of Jack Lazorko's brief pitching stints in the major leagues in parts of five years in the 1980s with Milwaukee, Seattle, Detroit, and California (twice) as a spot starter, middle reliever, and infrequent closer—and that it took him three years to notch his first victory in the big leagues (he has five victories against eight losses, two saves, and a 4.22 earned run average in sixty-nine games). The last time he appeared in the major leagues was in 1988, with the Angels.

Maybe you didn't see him pitching with his customary aggressiveness in the dead heat of Managua, Nicaragua, where he and his teammates were protected from antsy local fans by soldiers bearing machine guns, or hurling in the midnight sun in Skelleftea, Sweden, just a three-hour bus ride from the North Pole. And maybe you haven't seen him throwing in recent days at a screen with a roped-off strike zone in his small backyard here, in this bedroom community just northeast of Dallas, hoping for one more chance at the big leagues, or Japan, or somewhere.

"Every year we say, 'This year, this year won't be crazy like the last one,'" said Brenda, his wife of fifteen years. "And every year turns out to be crazy, like the last one, only more so."

"Every year we start out with a plan," Lazorko said. "We have Plan A, Plan B. . . . This year we're on Plan Double Z, and the summer has only just started."

"A lot of people think ballplayers have it made," said Brenda. "They don't realize that only a relative handful do. And they don't realize the stress involved. Jack has played for sixteen one-year contracts. Every time he pitches, his livelihood is on the line. It's got to a point when I'm at a game where I hate to hear the organ play. I know Jack's coming into the game and my stomach starts to churn."

Brenda is a petite blonde with an even disposition, which she has needed, and with the inner strength of a tiger, something that has also been required.

"Oh, the times we've had," she said. "Like twice we've bought Christmas trees in places, once in Puerto Rico, once in the Dominican, and we've been sent somewhere else, and we had to sell the trees. Then there was the time we were on a road trip in Hawaii with the Edmonton team and Jack got the call to the big leagues for the first time, to go immediately to play for the Brewers in Baltimore. Well, we had one suitcase, and Jack took it. I had to buy another suitcase to get home with the kids."

Brenda Nanney and Jack Lazorko met when they were in college together in 1978 at Mississippi State. He graduated that year with a degree in business administration. The next year Brenda, who got a degree in fashion merchandising, went to visit Jack in Sarasota, Florida, where he was playing in his second professional season.

"As soon as I got there, he was sold to Asheville," she said, speaking of his move from the Houston Astros organization to that of the Texas Rangers. "Right then I should have known."

In the first five or six years of their marriage, they moved fifty or sixty times. "Then we just started to lose count," she said. "It seems that every time I unpacked everything, we were traded or sold. It was like a bad omen. Even when we were in one place for a while—like we were in Tulsa for a full year—I still kept all my cosmetics in the bag."

This spring training Lazorko snared a tryout with the Yankees, after many appeals, including some to his former teammate at Mississippi State, Yankee Manager Buck Showalter. "Jack," said Showalter, "is a survivor." Reggie Jackson came by the clubhouse and noticed the name taped to the locker. "This can't be the same

Lazorko who pitched for Seattle years ago," he said. "Yeah, Reggie, that's me," said Lazorko, from behind Jackson. Lazorko was released by the Yankees in March.

In April he sent letters and visited teams and called managers and general managers and player personnel directors nationwide and in foreign lands looking for a job. His phone bill for the month was $249. At the end of May he caught on with the Mets and was sent to pitch for the Norfolk Tides. After two games he was released.

"I got belted a little in the first game, where I gave up two runs in two-thirds of an inning," he said, "but I was a little rusty, not having pitched in a game in two months. But Clint Hurdle, the manager, threw me in the next day and I gave up just one hit. The next thing I know, it's hit the road, Jack."

He is always so close, he feels. So close to reaching his dream of having a fulfilling career as a major league pitcher. This, he says, is more important even than the big bucks he would receive. He sees players he played with in the minor leagues, pitchers like Tom Henke and Ron Darling and Tom Candiotti, among others, making millions of dollars. The most he ever made was $125,000, when he pitched for Edmonton on a major league contract. In contrast, in his early years in the minors his first contract was for $500 a month in A ball, around $1,500 in AA ball, but as much as $15,000 a month in Class AAA. But in his lean years, "to make ends meet," he said, he had to pitch winter ball and, on the side, sell radio advertising, storm windows, and meat from the back of a truck.

In recent years, though, Lazorko has earned a regular, if generally modest, living (especially when you factor the expenses for his peripatetic existence) for Brenda and their three children, eleven-year-old Jake, seven-year-old Mitch, and three-year-old Nicky—all of whom travel with him.

The Lazorkos lived in Italy last season, renting a fourth-floor walk-up in Parma, where he made $90,000 and was named the most valuable player in the Italian League as well as in the championships, which Parma won. He pitched and won the last two games on the same day.

"Traveling the way we have, the kids have got an education you wouldn't believe," said Brenda.

Back in Texas, where Brenda was raised and where, Lazorko said, one can conveniently catch nonstop flights to almost anywhere in the world, the Lazorkos live in a nicely appointed two-story brick house on a street appropriately named Meandering Way. Lazorko has been careful with the money he has earned, and has been able to buy the house as well as keep up a college fund for his children. "And we've managed to save some—not a lot," said Lazorko. "But I'm going to have to find a job soon. These kids drink a lot of milk."

So Lazorko was on the telephone trying to sell himself and his pitching arm to a rather reluctant clientele. "Oh, he's not in?" said Lazorko, in the kitchen, the American League Red Book and the National League Green Book, loaded with team phone numbers, on the table before him. "Well, could you tell him Jack Lazorko called? Would he mind calling me back? He'll know what it's about it. Thank you."

Lazorko shrugs, checks another number.

"We want to go with younger guys," he hears from some people he calls. Or: "We're full right now." Or: "We don't have any spots open." Or: "I'll take your number and I'll call if somebody goes down." That's exactly why the Mets called in May. "To be brutally honest, we just needed an arm," said Gerry Hunsicker, the Mets' director of player personnel. "Some guys went down with injury, we had a few other things happen, and Jack had been calling me, so I told him, 'Okay, but it might not be for very long.'

"Jack's a good guy to have on a ball club. He gives you everything he's got. I knew him when he was in college. I coached against him when I was at Florida International University. That was twenty years ago. I remember him as a kid with a strong arm. A pretty good-looking pitcher with an above-average fastball and definitely major league potential. But the realities now are that we got kids we're developing. Kids with a future ahead."

Buck Showalter said: "At this stage for Jack, he needs pinpoint location where he can throw the breaking ball for strikes at will, and he just has to be a cut above the others. I like Jack, and I've always loved his attitude. But I felt his stuff came up just a little short."

Lazorko said: "If I get lit up whenever I go out there, that's one thing. Then I know it would be time to hang 'em up. But that doesn't happen. I keep guys in the ball park, I keep runners on base, and I'm one of the best fielding pitchers in the game."

Brenda does not discourage her husband in his pursuit. And the kids, apparently, have not suffered. Jack tutored them in Italy, and Jake spent his ninth birthday climbing the Matterhorn with his folks and his tenth birthday climbing one of the pyramids in Egypt, until a security guard told him it wasn't allowed.

"Everyone has his level of frustration," said Lazorko. "Some guys who play fifteen years in the big leagues are frustrated that they haven't made the Hall of Fame. Some guys who played ten years never got in a World Series. We had a great college team and eight guys were drafted by big league teams, but only one of us ever made the Show. How do you think those other guys felt? And me? I still love the challenge of setting up the batters and getting them out."

But something else gnaws at him. "I just want a little more, just to prove that I was a real, contributing big-league player, and not a fringe guy."

It is nighttime, and warm. The black Texas sky is sugared with stars. Crickets are in harmony. Jack Lazorko has switched on the garage lights, and they throw a gentle glow on his backyard. Diagonally, the yard, from the corner of where the red-brick garage meets the house, to the now-shadowed gray picket fence and the roses that line it, is just a little more than sixty feet six inches, the distance from the pitcher's mound to home plate. At the far end is the screen, a backstop, and just below the roped strike zone is a large netted bag that catches most of the balls that he throws. "What's great about this is that I can keep my arm in shape, and I don't need a catcher," said Lazorko.

He is wearing a dark-blue Yankee T-shirt and grey Yankee shorts and rubber-soled cleats. He is standing on the concrete walk in the corner, where he has placed a pitching slab. Behind him is his living room, and through a picture window his wife can be seen sitting in a leather chair watching television. A leather bag of some 125 baseballs lies on the patio table near him.

He begins to throw, slowly at first, stretching his stocky body. Then he begins to throw harder, testing his assortment of pitches, almost but not quite skinning his knuckles on the bricks of the garage wall.

This is his routine when he is, as he says, "between jobs." He pitches to batters in his imagination, batters he is familiar with, like most of the lineup of, say, the Oakland A's, whom he had been watching earlier on television. And he throws in what he calls "situations." "Otherwise," he said, "you're just throwing and not thinking."

He's pitching now to Rickey Henderson with a man on, and going inside with a fastball and low and away with his slider. Next, Mark McGwire is up. Lazorko throws a curve. "Uh, oh," he said, "I hung that one. Home run." And he grunts. He is sweating now, plucking up one ball, deciding what to pitch, and letting go. This is work. This is pleasure. This is Jack Lazorko's life.

"If I were called up, I could pitch tomorrow," he said, breathing deeply after throwing a high hard one. "Tomorrow."

He took another ball from his bag and looked down to get the sign, with, maybe, Ruben Sierra at bat in his mind's eye.

"I just need the opportunity, is all," he said. He wound up and threw. The ball thumped against the shadowed screen—for a strike.

[1993]

A World Away
from the Series

❦ A PALE MOON, like an eavesdropper, had appeared above the modest redwood ranch house here in Hico, in central Texas. In the cool early evening, Mitch Williams, in that now familiar scraggly beard and sweatshirt, jeans, and black cowboy boots, sat on the deck and looked out over the broad, flat six hundred acres he owns, which, he says, when giving directions to it, is "in the sticks, four miles from paved roads."

It was here that Mitch Williams came immediately after the World Series. It was here he came to get away. To get away from the madness and taunts and death threats and police protection that his performance in the World Series had generated. To get away "from blowin' that last game," as he described it, to get away from "achin' inside."

The tranquility here, the isolation, the peacefulness is what the man known as Wild Thing craved.

When the Philadelphia Phillies returned home from Toronto after losing the sixth and final game to the Blue Jays, they returned with only twenty-four of their twenty-five players. Mitch Williams wasn't on the flight back. Williams, who had come in in the ninth inning to protect a 6–5 lead, had thrown the last pitch of the World Series, the one that Joe Carter hit for a home run with runners on first and second in the bottom of the ninth inning, giving the Blue Jays an 8–6 victory.

"Can't hear planes, trains, cars—nothin'," said Williams, on his deck Thursday, just five days after the last World Series game. "Can't hear nothin' except when the river is runnin'. Then you can hear the river." As darkness descended, however, one could hear only crickets.

How has he slept since that last game? "Slept better the last four days than I have all year," he said. "The reason?" He smiled. "I'm down here."

He hadn't slept well in the week before, especially after two phone calls to the Phillies' office threatened Williams's life after Game Four, which he also "blew," as he said. In the house he had rented for the season in Moorestown, New Jersey, he was up most of the night. "We were scared," said his fiancée, Irene Iacone, who, with her three-year-old son, Damon, is with Williams on the ranch. "Every time he heard a creak—and that housed creaked a lot—Mitch was up and looking around, looking out the window. He had that 9-millimeter pistol at arm's reach all night."

Two local policemen patrolled the house that night, one in front and one in back. When the team flew to Toronto, Williams received permission from his manager, Jim Fregosi, to skip the workout so he could get some sleep in the hotel room.

In his hotel room after the last game, when, as Iacone recalls, his eyes were red from pain, from holding back tears—"Oh, he felt so bad, and every time I looked at him I began to cry, and he tried to console me"—he called Iacone's sister and boyfriend, who were staying in their house. He was told the windows had been broken by rock throwers. "While we were on the phone with them," said Williams, "the police were arresting people outside the house."

And when the Phillies returned to Philadelphia after the last game, Williams and Iacone and Damon were on a flight to Dallas. "If it had just been me, I'd have gone back with the team," Williams said. "But this was Irene's first year with me, and I didn't want to put her through all the things I know we were going to hear, stuff I'd hear at times all year—'You bum.'"

So Williams, the 6-foot-4-inch, 205-pound left-hander, went back to Texas, to the place with the wrought-iron fence at the entrance with the nameplate "3 & 2 Ranch." "Appropriate name, isn't it?" he had said with a smile.

He is aware, meanwhile, that that last pitch, on a 2-and-2 count to Carter, will likely place him in baseball's hall of infamy. He knows about Ralph Branca's pitch to Bobby Thomson that cost the Dodgers the pennant in 1951. He listened when someone told him that Branca had gone to a priest afterward and asked, "Why me, Father?" And the priest had supposedly said, "Because the Lord felt you were strong enough to carry the burden."

"I've always believed that God will never give somebody something they can't handle," said Williams, drinking a soft drink from a can. "I feel I can handle this. I said in the clubhouse after the game, if there's anybody here who can handle it, it's me. I'd rather this be put on my shoulders than any of my teammates."

It was remembered that immediately after the home run, Phillies first baseman John Kruk, Williams's good friend, hugged him in the clubhouse. What did Kruk say to him? "Nothing," said Williams. "What could he say?"

Fregosi told him, "Mitch, if it hadn't been for you all season, we wouldn't have got this far." And when the other players tried to stand and shield him from the news media at his locker after the game, he would have none of it. "I'm going to face the music," he said. And he sat there answering questions from wave after wave of reporters. It was an impressive, and moving, moment.

"I wasn't going to sit there and make excuses. I lost the game, and I said so. I know that the reporters have a job to do, and that is to cover us in the games. I respect that. And I also know that the last thing a guy wants to do is stick a microphone in my face after I've just blown the World Series. But they have their job, and I have mine."

Williams said it was the hardest thing he has ever had to do as a ballplayer. He talked about the "terrible pitch" that catcher Darren Daulton had called for: a fastball high and away, and he had thrown it low and inside. "I just jerked the ball," he said. "Carter thought it was a slider. That's how bad the pitch was."

Williams said that with two men on—he had given up a walk and a single—he had gone through several scenarios in his mind, but none with the actual result. "I thought about Carter hitting a double-play ball, or him hitting a fly ball and the runners advancing to second and third, but then there would be two outs. I had no doubt that I was going to save the game. But he hit the hell out of the ball, and I said, 'Wow, I hadn't thought about that.'"

When did Williams know the pitch was gone for a home run? "As soon as he hit—I dropped my head," said Williams. "I didn't even look. I walked to the dugout. I didn't even hear the crowd screaming. Nope, none of it."

He said he wasn't aware that Carter had jubilantly jumped as he ran down the base line. "I remember I jumped about nine feet in the air when I pitched the last out to clinch the pennant," he said, about his saving the sixth game of the playoffs against the Braves. "All the tension and all the excitement was pent up for so long, for 162 games of the season, and then it was all released at that one moment. It was wonderful." The feeling would not last long. "It's amazing how much difference one week can make," he said.

He said he was convinced that he could handle the consequences of that pitch, and that this place, in Texas, was the best place to get all of that out of his mind. "But," said Iacone, "I'm sure some of those thoughts pace through his head."

Why did he feel above all others on his team that he could handle the agony of this defeat? "Because of six hundred games in the big leagues," he said. "I'm a closer. My job is to come into the game when it's on the line. I said before the playoffs, 'My job hasn't changed.' And I've said all along, 'You have to have a short memory to be a closer.' Nothing you did yesterday has any bearing on what you do today, or tomorrow. And when that last game was over, I said that the next game is what's important. Even if the next game is next year."

As he spoke, he was anything but Wild Thing—a name derived from a pitcher in the comedy movie *Major League,* who, like Williams, had a blazing fastball but constant control trouble. Williams, this night, appeared a sensitive, reflective young man, one who turns twenty-nine in three weeks.

Williams has been pitching in clutch situations since at least when he graduated from high school in West Linn, Oregon, in 1982 and signed a professional baseball contract at seventeen with the San Diego Padres. Four years later he was pitching in the big leagues with the Texas Rangers. He was traded to the Chicago Cubs before the 1989 season—he made the All-Star team that year—and then in 1991 was traded to the Phillies.

Some fans have said that there is no way Mitch Williams can return to pitch for Philadelphia, even though he has one year remaining on his contract, in which he earns $3.5 million a season. There was speculation that the Phillies' front office had questioned whether Williams could again pitch effectively for the team. A column by Hal Bodley in *USA Today* was headlined: "Time for Williams to Leave Phillies." But Williams doesn't want to leave Philadelphia.

"Why, because of a handful of fans?" he said. "I love it there, love the situation, the ownership, the players, the pitching coach, the manager. It's where I want to be. I've never been on a team where everyone is so team-oriented. No me, me, me, I, I, I, like most teams. If Kruk, for example, gets punched out four times in a game and we win, he's ecstatic. That's the way it was down the line. There was no quit in that team, no quit in any of us."

"As bad as I felt," Williams said about the end of the World Series, "Darren Daulton came over to me in the clubhouse and said, 'All year I've been tellin' hitters what's comin', and wouldn't you know, in a World Series someone finally believed me!'" I appreciated that. We had just lost the World Series and the guys were concerned with picking me up.

"I was achin' inside at that time, and they knew it. I felt I had let my teammates down in a crucial situation of the sixth game of the World Series. But they know I tried with everything I had. It just didn't turn out."

Williams's eyes appeared to moisten a little as he spoke, though it might simply have been the reflection from the porch lights, now turned on because it had grown dark. "There shouldn't be tears," he said. "I mean, a ball game is a ball game. Sadness is when someone like Dennis Byrd is possibly paralyzed in a football game. But winning or losing a ball game, that's just the nature of the game."

He said his perspective comes from his parents, who divorced when he was twelve but with whom he remains close. His father, Jeff, is a machinist in Oregon, and his mother, Larrie, works in a company's shipping department. "We were a lower-middle-class family, and I know that a lot of people in this world work a lot harder than I do, and without the recognition and earning the kind of money I do," he said. "I've been blessed that I play a game for a living. I mean, I know that I could be out digging ditches."

Meanwhile, there was farm work to do. Along with his brother, Bruce, a former minor league pitcher who tends the ranch when Williams is away, Williams will feed the five horses, the fifteen head of cattle, and the two goats. The brothers will plow the field to plant hay. They might also go fishing for bass and prepare to hunt deer when the season opens this week. And Williams is getting ready to marry Iacone in New Jersey on December 26.

He said he had received phone calls from a number of people, including Bill Giles, president of the Phillies, and Lee Thomas, the team's general manager. "They asked me how I was doing," said Williams. "I said, 'Fine, I'm doin' fine.'" He grew quiet now and took a sip of his soft drink. He looked out into the darkness. "I love it out here, it's so quiet," he said. "And look at that moon—a full moon—beautiful, isn't it?"

[1993]

The Strange Tale
of Eric S.

❦ THE PATIENT had not appeared for breakfast, and so at 8:05 A.M. on March 16, according to the log of the Rancho L'Abri Drug and Alcohol Treatment Center in Dulzura, California, a civilian assistant named Keith Langhorn "entered room #6 of the lodge to check on Eric S."

"Observed patient lying on his bed and noted no rise and fall of chest," Langhorn noted. "Went for help from graveyard staff member Brent S. We checked the pulse and tried to wake patient. No response. Noted eyes were dilated and body cold. I left staff member with the body to call executive director, who instructed me to call medical director. Instructions given to call 911. Which was done immediately. Checked for heartbeat. None detected."

Shortly after, on that sunny Wednesday morning in the quiet farming village about thirty-five miles from the heart of San Diego, the fire department arrived, and then the sheriff. But the man with longish dark hair and a dark mustache who wore a white T-shirt and white briefs could not be revived. He lay on top of the blanket on the bed in the small, simple room, his hands on his chest, a few pieces of luggage in a corner, jeans and a shirt tossed on top of a dresser, and a .22-caliber revolver loaded with five bullets under his pillow. He wore one piece of jewelry—a wedding ring.

And Eric Vaughn Show, who just two years earlier had ended

his eleven-year major-league pitching career with the Oakland A's after pitching for ten years with the San Diego Padres, and who had started games in the 1984 National League Championship Series against the Chicago Cubs and the World Series against the Detroit Tigers, was pronounced dead. He was thirty-seven years old.

An autopsy released soon after by the coroner's office said the cause of death was inconclusive, that is, there was no observable trauma or wounds to the body. A toxicology report would be coming in about two weeks. But in statements to the center's staff, Show had said that he was under the influence of cocaine, heroin, and alcohol. He said he used four ten-dollar bags of cocaine at about seven that night, Tuesday night. "Didn't like how I felt," he said, adding that he then ingested eight ten-dollar bags of heroin and a six-pack of beer.

The questions about Eric Show's death are no less difficult to answer than the ones about his life. Why was he so hard on himself, such an apparently driven individual? Why was he so compulsive, or at least passionate, about almost everything he undertook?

Show (the name rhymes with cow) was known as a highly intelligent, articulate man with broad interests that ranged from physics—his major in college—to politics to economics to music. "Eric didn't fit the mold of the typical ballplayer," said Tim Flannery, a former Padre teammate of Show's. "Most ballplayers were like me then; we had tunnel vision. We weren't interested in those other things."

Show was a born-again Christian who regularly attended Sunday chapel services as a player and sometimes signed his autograph with an added Acts 4:12, which discusses salvation as coming only from belief in Jesus Christ.

He was an accomplished jazz guitarist. Sometimes after games on the road, he would beat the team back to the hotel and play lead guitar with the band in the lounge.

He was a member of the right-wing John Birch Society, a fact the baseball world was surprised to learn in August 1984 as the Padres moved toward their first and only division title.

And he was a successful businessman with real estate holdings, a marketing company, and a music store, all of which kept him in expensive clothes, with a navy blue Mercedes and a house in an affluent San Diego neighborhood.

But other elements seemed to intrude. And ultimately the contradictions of the best and worst in American life became a disastrous mixture that defeated him.

For most baseball fans, Eric Show was a decent pitcher who had once been lucky enough to make it to the World Series. But to the people who were close to him, he was, in the end, someone they did not fully know. "He led several lives, apparently," said Arn Tellem, his agent at the time of his death.

To Joe Elizondo, his financial consultant, and Mark Augustin, his partner in a music store, and Steve Tyler, a boyhood friend from Riverside, California, where both were born and raised, Show was a charming, devoted friend and a caring man. "He would give you the shirt off his back," Elizondo said. "And he did. I once told him how much I liked a shirt he was wearing, and he said, 'Here, it's yours.' He'd stop a beggar on the street and learn he was hungry and run to a diner and bring back a hot meal for him."

To others, though, Show could seem selfish or arrogant.

And there were the drugs. Some said Show's drug problems began when he took injections to relieve pain in his back after surgery, and he sought more and more relief. Others wondered if he had been taking drugs before he reached the major leagues. He may also have begun taking drugs simply because he liked the challenge of being able to handle the dreaded substance. After all, his job was to accept challenges and, being a professional athlete, to overcome them often. And during the early and mid-1980s, Show's first years as a major leaguer, numerous players were using cocaine, including his teammate Alan Wiggins, who liked to argue with Show and later died of AIDS.

Show, who stood 6 feet tall and weighed 185 pounds as a player but was listed in the last year of his life at 165 pounds, had been in and out of several rehabilitation centers in recent years. He had been in L'Abri for a month, from February 12 to March 14. The average stay is forty-five days, or until a person's insurance runs out. But Show appeared "anxious" to leave the center on March 14, according to the report of a staff member, although he was urged to stay. The center is a voluntary refuge, and Show got his way, and departed.

Apparently he eventually headed for a seedy section of downtown San Diego, where he bought drugs and went on a binge. By 11 P.M. on Tuesday, March 15, Show had returned to his home, a two-story, four-bedroom, tan and green stucco house on a cul-de-sac, and called the rehabilitation center. He said he had been "using" and wanted to return to the center. Would someone come and pick him up? A van arrived forty-five minutes later.

"I'm weary," he said when he arrived at the center. He said he had vomited a few times after taking the heroin. "I have to lie down," he said. Not long after, he was dead.

His death evoked memories of two strange scenes in Show's life, one in 1992 and the other last year.

In the spring of 1992, Show was in training camp in Arizona with the A's. He had signed a two-year contract with them in late 1990 and had managed only a 1–2 record with them in 1991. Following several mornings in which he had reported late for workouts, he showed up with both hands heavily bandaged.

He explained that he had been chased by a group of youths and had had to climb a fence, and had cut himself. But what was not reported was that the police later told club officials that Show had been behaving erratically in front of an adult bookstore, and had fled when officers approached. They finally caught him trying to climb a barbed-wire fence.

Last July he was caught by the police when running across an intersection in San Diego and screaming that people were out to kill him, and then begged the police to kill him. He was hand-

cuffed, and while in the back seat of the police car he kicked out
the rear window. He was taken to the county mental hospital for
three days of testing. Show had admitted "doing quite a bit of
crystal methamphetamine."

It was one more startling development, one more contradic-
tion for an athlete who, in reference to his John Birch member-
ship, once said: "I have a fundamental philosophy of less
government, more reason, and with God's help, a better world.
And that's it."

Actually, it wasn't it. Show, as a John Birch member, also denied that he was a Nazi or a racist. In fact, he had a Hispanic financial adviser, a Jewish lawyer and agent, and black friends in
baseball and his music world. People from his first agent, Steve
Greenberg, to Tony Gwynn, a black teammate, agreed that he was
no bigot. "He joined the Birch Society because he thought it
would provide answers to how the world works," Tellem said. "He
was always looking for answers."

Show once said, "I've devoted my life to learning." Asked what
he was learning, he replied, "Learning everything." He read vora-
ciously, spent hours in museums, and had long, heartfelt discus-
sions with anyone who would meet his intellectual challenges.

The intellect was apparent at Ramona High School, where he
was a star student and pitcher. The sense of risk was evident to his
friends, who remembered him climbing a sixty-foot sheer cliff and
then waving his shirt in defiance.

But in his home there was heartbreak. His parents divorced
while he was still at Ramona. And between the son and the father,
Les, an engineer who suffers from Alzheimer's disease, there was
constant conflict.

"He had a very difficult father," said Jack Smitheran, Show's
baseball coach at the University of California in Riverside. "He
was extremely involved, extremely result-oriented. One time he
stuck his head in the dugout and began talking to Eric. I don't
know what he said, but it was after Eric had thrown a bad inning.
I told him to leave."

In college, Show met his wife, the former Cara Mia Nieder-house, whose given name was chosen by her father, for the song. She was soft-spoken, with reddish-brown hair. Friends described her as "cover-girl beautiful." They met when he was playing in a college summer league in Kansas. He was a senior; she was a college junior who was home on vacation.

There were no children in their sixteen-year marriage, which lasted until his death. Cara Mia tried to set "boundaries," Elizondo said, and always allowed him back into the house. But like Show's college friends, she was unable to control his behavior.

When he left college in 1978, Show was signed by San Diego, and within three years, on the strength of a good fastball and a sinker, he was wearing the Padres' uniform. In his first full season, in 1982, he was 10–6. Two years later he was 15–9 as the Padres surprised everyone by beating the Cubs in the playoffs and making it to the World Series, where they lost to the Tigers.

Like the other starting pitchers on the Padres, Show was awful in the post-season, giving up seven home runs in eight innings. Derisive fans took to calling him "Long Ball Show." But his post-season failure was quickly overshadowed by other events in his career. On September 11, 1985, he gave up a single to Pete Rose, allowing Rose to break Ty Cobb's all-time record of 4,192 hits. While the crowd in Cincinnati roared, and play halted for twenty minutes, Show sat on the mound. Some thought it was disrespectful, but Show said he had nothing else to do.

It was one incident, and there were others. Jerome Holtzman, a baseball writer for the *Chicago Tribune,* recalled a game in which Show threw only slow pitches. "They were all nothing balls, and he got clobbered," Holtzman said. "I was amazed." Holtzman went to the Padres' manager, Jack McKeon, and asked about the performance. "Eric was experimenting," McKeon told Holtzman, with a shrug. "That's Eric."

"Guys know he marches to his own drummer," Flannery said during Show's days with the Padres. And while Flannery said "we just chuckle at him and leave him alone," Show irritated some

34

players, sometimes pouting visibly on the mound when an out-fielder didn't get to a ball he thought should have been caught.

In 1988, Show was 16–11 for San Diego, the most victories he ever had in a season. The next June he suffered a lower back injury and had surgery to remove a disk. To pitch despite pain, Show began taking cortisone shots. Some said they believed that was the beginning of Show's drug problems, and that he sought more and more relief.

In the fall of 1990, after an 8–6 season, Show was released by the Padres. By then there had been instances of erratic behavior: late arrivals, confrontations with management, and screaming matches with other players. The A's, who had rehabilitated veteran pitchers from other teams, took a chance and signed him to a $1.6 million contract for two years. But there were problems, and as-sorted unexplained injuries in his 1–2 season of 1991. And then in the spring of 1992, baseball bid him goodbye.

"We tried to get help for him through our employee assistance program," Sandy Alderson, the A's general manager, said. "And we did. But it obviously didn't work."

Still, Show seemed to continue trying to get free of the addiction. Mike MacIntosh, the San Diego Police Department chaplain, recalled how Show had called him around Christmas and wept on the telephone, pleading for help. And just a few days before he died, Show wrote a tender letter to his wife, saying he hoped to draw a line between the part of his life that was, and the part of his life that would follow. He talked about a comeback in baseball and said he was working on a new pitch—a "cup ball" that would work as a change-up.

And then, on that last Tuesday night, when Show went back to the rehabilitation center for the last time, Elizondo recalled that Cara Mia and Eric had embraced and she had said gently, encour-agingly, "Go get 'em, honey."

At the Acheson and Graham Garden of Prayer Funeral Home in Riverside, Eric Show lay in an open green casket while outside an unexpected downpour struck the building. A Padres' baseball cap and a baseball had been placed beside Show, along with a guitar and a picture of Steve Tyler and him when they were boys. A cross hung around Show's neck.

Dave Dravecky, who had been a John Birch member with Show in 1984, delivered the eulogy, talking about how Show had helped him deal with the loss of his pitching arm to cancer. Elizondo spoke about how warm and passionate Show had been as a friend. All the members of Show's family were there, except for his ailing father.

Cara Mia had requested that Romans 7:5–25 be read. "For the woman which hath an husband," it says at one point, "is bound by the law to her husband so long as he liveth." And: "But I see another law in my members, warring against the law of my mind, and bringing me into captivity to the law of sin which is in my members."

And: "O wretched man that I am! Who shall deliver me from the body of this death?"

"He tried, oh, he tried so desperately," his sister Leslie Cifelli said. "But he couldn't free himself."

It was recalled at the funeral that Show had a deep yearning to learn, experience, and reach out. Show once related the following incident to a friend: On a clear night when he was seven, he took his mother's hand and pointed to the heavens. "Mom, there's something out there beyond those stars and that moon," he said, "and I'm going to find the answer."

Perhaps, now, he has.

[1994]

The End of Gil McDougald's Silent Seasons

❦ IT IS A silent summer for Gil McDougald; they are all silent summers.

Once, summertime for Gil McDougald, a standout Yankee infielder in the 1950s, was full of the sweet sounds of baseball—balls being struck, the chatter and laughter of teammates, the roar of the crowd. He can no longer hear those sounds, although, says his wife, Lucille, "He can hear them internally."

Gil McDougald is deaf. He gradually lost his hearing during his playing days, after a freak accident in batting practice in which he was struck by a batted ball. Ironically, this occurred just two years before the famous incident in which he cracked a line drive off the right eye of Herb Score, a Cleveland Indians pitcher.

Until that moment against Cleveland, in the first inning of a game in Municipal Stadium on the night of May 7, 1957, Score appeared on the way to becoming one of baseball's best pitchers ever, and McDougald seemed to have a long career ahead of him. "I heard the thud of the ball hitting his head and then saw him drop and lie there, bleeding, and I froze," McDougald recalled. "Someone hollered for me to run to first. When Score was taken off the field on a stretcher, I was sick to my stomach. I didn't want to play any more."

But Casey Stengel, his manager, insisted he continue. "He said, 'You're getting paid to play.' And while that seems harsh, it was right. It's like getting right back on a horse after you've been thrown. But I said that if Herb loses his eye, I'm quitting base-ball."

McDougald remembers that Score's mother called and told him it wasn't his fault, that it was just an accident. He called Score in the hospital, to apologize, to offer his heartfelt best wishes, and kept in regular touch with him.

Score returned to action the next season, his eye healed. But in many ways, neither McDougald nor Score was ever the same again. After the Score incident, fans in cities that the Yankees visited began to boo McDougald. "Some people would holler, 'Killer,'" he said. "Funny thing is, as bad as I felt, I went on a hitting spree. I can't explain it."

Yesterday, Old-Timers Day at Yankee Stadium, McDougald, now sixty-six years old, chose not to attend, even though the theme involved his years as a Yankee. It was the forty-fifth anniversary of the beginning in 1949 of the Casey Stengel era, and the first of Stengel's record five straight World Series championship teams. McDougald was a member of three of them. He played superbly in those garlanded baseball days as a feared clutch hitter and a regular second baseman, third baseman, and shortstop, wherever Stengel felt he needed him on a particular day. In McDougald's fifty-three games in eight World Series over his ten-year career, he started every game at one of those three positions.

"It is too frustrating and too exhausting for Gil to be around the other players and trying to understand all the banter and the reminiscences," said Lucille McDougald. "He was content to watch it on television at home."

It was during batting practice one afternoon that McDougald himself had been struck by a batted ball. He was standing behind a screen at second base talking with the Yankee coach, Frank Crosetti. "I saw a ball lying on the ground nearby and reached to

38

pick it up, my head going just beyond the screen," he said. "Just then Bob Cerv hit a ball that hit me in the ear. I collapsed and everyone came running over. They carried me off the field and I was out of action for a few games.

"The doctors told me I'd be all right. Well, I wasn't. The blow had broken a hearing tube. At first it just affected one ear, my left. One time I'm getting needled by some fan at third base and I turned to Rizzuto at short and said, 'Too bad I didn't get hit in the right ear, then I wouldn't have to hear this guy.'"

But the hearing got progressively worse, although it had nothing to do with his leaving baseball after the 1960 season, at age thirty-two. "I just got tired of the travel and the attitude of the baseball people," he said. "I started at $5,500 a year with the Yankees, and then was making $37,500 at the end. But they acted like they owned you and that they were giving you the moon and stars."

He had a family with four children at the time, and felt he needed more money to support it and saw a way to do it through a business of his own. He had already begun a dry cleaning business and it was doing nicely. "Some of my teammates, and others asked, 'How can you quit baseball?' No one thought I'd follow through. But I found it was easy."

Because of his loss of hearing, McDougald says he hasn't answered a telephone in ten years. Because of the handicap, he sold his share in the building maintenance company he owned, which employed 2,200 people on the East Coast, and he was forced into early retirement.

"When I couldn't use the phone, it became a real pain in the neck," he said. He keeps an interest in baseball, however, and while he watches some of it on television, he says he doesn't miss the voices of the announcers—except for his old teammates, Phil Rizzuto and Tony Kubek. "The others just talk so much that it wears you out," said McDougald. "I'd just as soon watch the action and draw my own conclusions."

And what does he see? "I see a lot of guys making a million

dollars," he said, and laughed. "There are some very good ballplayers, but some of the things they do are pretty funny. Like if a pitcher throws close to a batter, he faints. When he wakes up, he charges the mound."

McDougald sat at the kitchen table in his sprawling, twenty-two-room Spanish colonial house in Spring Lake, New Jersey, where he lives with his wife and, depending on who happens to be staying or visiting, some or all of his seven children, seven grandchildren, and one great-grandchild. He and Lucille adopted three of their children, of mixed races, later in life through Catholic Charities. "We had four children to begin with, and then when they all grew up and left the house, Lucille and I started getting lonely," he said, "so when we were about forty years old we set about to adopt the other kids."

In a white short-sleeve pullover and blue jeans and white sneakers, he appears as trim as in his playing days. Indeed, at 180 pounds, the 6-foot McDougald weighs about the same as when he played for the Yankees, from 1951, when he came up to the majors with Mickey Mantle, through 1960. He hit over .300 twice and finished with a solid lifetime batting average of .276. "He was a money player," said Saul Rogovin, who pitched for the White Sox in that era. "He would hurt you in the late innings."

Through the window behind McDougald is another large, white, columned house like his and, just beyond that, the ocean, sparkling in the morning sunlight, the waves hitting the beach with a sound of which McDougald is now unaware. There remains an angularity to his ruddy face and body, and one is reminded of that odd, open, wide stance of his at the plate, head cocked to one side, like, well, like he was listening to a faraway sound.

"An awkward man, a wonderful man," Stengel said about him.

McDougald laughed now, recalling Stengel, and mentioned a particular move the manager used to make: "Casey always knew when a man was ready to pinch-hit or not. And I could read him like a book. He'd come by on the bench and stand and look you right in the eye. Like he'd stop in front of Bobby Brown, and he'd say something like, 'Bauer,' or 'Woodling, grab a bat.' Still looking at Brown. Casey was a hunch manager. No statistics for him. He'd look at a guy and get the feeling. It was funny."

There is no problem, to be sure, with McDougald's speech, and he responds when questions are written out for him, or, on occasion, when he reads lips, which is laborious for him: "You have to concentrate so hard that it begins to give you a headache," he said.

Sitting with Lucille at the kitchen table, McDougald recently tried to field a visitor's question. He knit his brow, trying to read the lips. "What did you say?" he said. Lucille said, slowly, "He said, 'Did Stengel ever give you advice about hitting?'"

He recalled a moment in the fifth game in his first World Series, against the New York Giants in 1951. The bases were loaded and he was about to bat. Stengel called him back to the dugout. "Casey said, 'Hit one out,'" McDougald said with a laugh. "And wouldn't you know, I went up to the plate and did. It was in the Polo Grounds, I hit a fly ball that carried about 260 feet down that short left-field line, just one of those Chinese homers, but it cleared the fence." At the time, it was only the third bases-loaded home run in World Series history.

McDougald batted .306 during that regular season of 1951, the only Yankee batter to hit .300 or better, and was named the American League's rookie of the year, playing second base and third, ahead of either Jerry Coleman or Bobby Brown. He also hit fourteen homers, one more than another rookie on the team, Mickey Mantle.

"I remember our first spring training together, and you couldn't believe the publicity for Mickey," he said. "He was in the newspapers and magazines more than the president. From that point forward, his life was never his own. That's what stardom does. It was like what I saw with Joe DiMaggio. Nineteen fifty-one was his last season as a ballplayer, and I don't think I saw him come down to eat in the hotel one time. He stayed in his room because he'd be so bothered by people.

"Mickey was a nineteen-year-old kid from Oklahoma. New York seemed like a huge place to him. I was different. I was from San Francisco, twenty-two years old, and had a year of college. He began hanging out with Billy Martin, and every night was a party. I roomed with Hank Bauer, and it wasn't the same for us.

"But Mickey had different pressures than me, being the star he was. I saw him on television recently and he talked about the drinking helping to relieve the pressure. It was very sad for me, knowing Mickey as I do, liking him, seeing what's happened."

He remembers the wild things some of his teammates did, including Ryne Duren, the pitcher. "Once I saw him drink two bottles of vodka out of both sides of his mouth," said McDougald. "I thought, 'He's crazy.'" Duren is an alcoholic who later rehabilitated and now counsels others about their drinking problems. "I saw Ryne at a golf tournament a few years back," said McDougald, "and he looked beautiful."

McDougald shied away from other activities, such as dinners and banquets, because he found them frustrating and somewhat embarrassing because he was unable to hear. "I'd just sit there like a dummy," he said. Over the years he had grown more disturbed as the hearing began to wane. And when his family gets together, he still grows impatient with not being able to share in the conversations—"especially the jokes," he said—and so may retire upstairs where he can work on business interests he retains, or check the stock market, in which he remains active, or view television or read a book or magazine or newspaper, seeking to "keep up with the world." Or he may practice his putting on the small artificial green in his den.

McDougald still regularly plays tennis and golf. In a recent, genial dialogue with Ottilie Lucas, the blind wife of his nephew, they debated handicaps. She said she'd rather be blind than deaf because with loss of eyesight she is more sensitive to the world around her and so appreciates it more. McDougald argued that he'd rather be deaf than blind. "If I was blind," he said, "I couldn't play golf."

At one point McDougald considered getting a hearing implant, but it wouldn't do much good, he was told, since he can occasionally hear sounds but the sounds are fragmented, and he can make no sense of them.

He remains in touch with some of his old teammates, like Rizzuto and Yogi Berra, and remembers his biggest thrill being his first game in Yankee Stadium. "The ballpark seemed so big to me," he said, "and the roar of the crowd was overwhelming."

He even occasionally gets a note from Herb Score. "He pitched again after I hit him, but he was never the same again," said McDougald. "I could see him recoiling after he threw, rather than following through as he had before. But he's done very well as an announcer for the Indians, and I'm glad to see it."

McDougald had done well too, succeeding in business and then, for seven years, coaching the Fordham University baseball team while still active in his business. He quit coaching baseball when he could no longer hear the crack of the bat.

"You know, there used to be a sportswriter for the *New York Times* named John Drebinger, who covered the Yankees," said McDougald. "He wore a hearing aid. We'd mock him all the time and play tricks on him. He'd come over in the clubhouse and we'd be moving our lips, as if we were talking. He'd beat that squawk box in his ear, then he'd turn it up. And then we'd all start laughing. He'd say, 'Why you dirty so-and-so's.'" And McDougald laughed.

"And now it's happened to me," he said. "But you go on, you learn to live with it. You make your adjustments. There's still a lot to live for, and love."

Gil McDougald turned and looked out of the window, his face to the rays of sun that streamed in, silent and welcome, like the summertime.

43

Six months later . . .

THERE WAS a tension at breakfast that Gil McDougald tried not to acknowledge, a tension that had been building since November. That was when he had undergone the operation to insert a cochlear implant behind his right ear with the hope of being able to hear again.

McDougald, silver-haired at age sixty-six, but still looking trim in his tan turtleneck, sat in a booth in the East Bay Restaurant on First Avenue with his wife, Lucille, and one of their daughters, Denise Costigan, one of their seven grown children, in fact. The McDougalds had taken the nearly two-hour train ride from their home in Spring Lake, New Jersey, and would be going across the street to Bellevue Hospital. There McDougald would be programmed for a hearing apparatus and would learn if this operation, a relatively recent and delicate procedure, was a success or not.

"When I sent out my Christmas cards I wrote that it would be wonderful if the procedure was a success and Gil could hear again," Lucille McDougald was saying. "I showed him the card before I sent it out. He said, 'You can't say that. You have to accept the fact that there are no guarantees with this operation. It's like baseball. You can't get too excited, otherwise you'll blow the whole thing.' I said, 'I'm the author of this card, and I'll say what I want.'"

McDougald laughed. "So many people have called and written that they are praying for me that I'm concerned," he said. "I mean, if the procedure doesn't work, they'll blame me for their loss of faith."

McDougald had come to this point after an article last summer had described his silent life, in which, as Lucille described it, he heard the roar of the crowd "only internally." The article described how McDougald, unable to talk on the telephone anymore, had to sell his share in the building maintenance business he owned; how he stopped attending functions with old friends and old ballplayers—some, like Yogi Berra and Phil Rizzuto and Mickey Mantle, were teammates during his career—because he was unable to participate in the jokes and give-and-take; and how, at family functions, McDougald would leave the table in frustration at being unable to hear the conversation.

Several doctors contacted him and told him about the implant surgery and about Dr. Noel Cohen, head of otolaryngology at New York University Medical Center. Reluctant at first to subject himself to further disappointment, McDougald finally called Dr. Cohen.

Cohen determined that McDougald was a good candidate for the operation because he retained a tiny bit of residual hearing of tones. But McDougald postponed the operation until the winter. "I didn't want to give up my summer of golf," he said. "I had waited this long, I could wait a little longer."

"Everyone," said Cohen, with a smile, "has his priorities."

The implant is a receiver that is wired to an electrode, which stimulates the cochlea, an organ in the inner ear. The implant cannot restore normal hearing because it does not amplify sound, instead converting sound into electronic signals. Its effectiveness varies from patient to patient.

After the operation, Cohen pronounced the implant a success. But it would take about six weeks for McDougald to heal, and then he had to visit an audiologist, Betsy Bromberg, at neighboring Bellevue, for an evaluation of his hearing and to have the apparatus programmed. How well would this work? Would McDougald be able to hear?

In the office, McDougald sat at a desk with a computer on it. Bromberg sat across from him. His wife and daughter sat within arm's length. A small microphone was set behind his ear, and a transmitter with a magnet was placed over the site of the implant. A cable was extended from the microphone to a speech processor the size of a hand calculator that can be worn on a belt or placed in a breast pocket.

Then Bromberg began the test that would determine how

much McDougald's hearing had improved. She covered her mouth with a sheet of paper so he could not lip read. "Tell me," she said, "what you hear?"

She said, "Aah." He hesitated. "Aah," he answered. She went, "Eeeh." He said, "Eeeh."

"Hello," she said. "Hello," he said. "I'm going to count to five," she said. "Do you hear me?"

"Oh yeah!" he said. "Wow! This is exciting!" His wife and daughter stared, hardly moving.

Bromberg wrote down four words on a pad of paper and said them: "football," "sidewalk," "cowboy," and "outside." "Now, Gil," she said, "I'm going to mix up the word order and cover my mouth, and you tell me the word I say."

"Cowboy," she said. "Cowboy," he said. "Outside," she said, "Outside," he said. And then he began to flush. Tears welled in his eyes.

"This is the first time in . . ." Lucille said and then choked up, unable to finish her sentence. "It's unbelievable."

"It's a miracle," said Denise. Both began crying.

Bromberg said, "It's okay. Everybody cries at times like this." And then mother and daughter embraced. And they hugged Gil. And they hugged Bromberg, and hugged the director of the unit, Susan Waltzman, who had been observing.

"It's great," said McDougald. Then he sat down. "I have a problem," he said. "My voice, gee, it sounds terrible."

"You haven't heard your voice in about twenty-five years," said Bromberg. "You'll get used to it."

She went through some more adjustments and then gave Mc-Dougald a lesson in how to operate the various components. She told him how he will have some problems, especially in trying to hear a companion on a busy street, or someone at the far end of a noisy dinner table, or someone in another room. In time he might also be able to hear on the telephone.

"It's really a surprise," said McDougald. "I mean, I really didn't expect . . ." He paused, trying to find the words to express his feeling. "They've turned the music on," he said.

Last night the McDougald household was bursting with children and grandchildren. "Everyone," said Lucille McDougald, "has come to watch grandpa hear."

[1994, 1995]

Larry Doby Emerges from the Shadow

❦ LARRY DOBY remembers clearly his first day in the major leagues, that day fifty years ago when he broke the color barrier in the American League. It was eleven weeks after Jackie Robinson had played his first game for the Brooklyn Dodgers in the National League. Doby remembers the excitement of that day when he became only the second black player in the major leagues—he had hardly slept in four nights leading up to it—and he remembers the dismay.

Saturday, July 5, 1947, a sunny morning in Chicago: Lou Boudreau, the manager of the Cleveland Indians, took the twenty-two-year-old second baseman into the visiting team's locker room in Comiskey Park and introduced him to the players. Each of Doby's new teammates stood at his locker and looked over the young black man who had just been purchased by the Indians' owner, Bill Veeck, from the Newark Eagles of the Negro National League. Doby and the manager went from player to player.

"Some of the players shook my hand," Doby recalled recently, "but most of them didn't. It was one of the most embarrassing moments of my life."

As major league baseball and the nation prepare for a season of homage to the integration of the game, virtually all of the attention is centered on Jackie Robinson, which is understandable, since he was the first. Jackie Robinson commemorative coins, a Jackie Robinson video, a Jackie Robinson seminar. "And that's the way it should be," Doby said. "But Jack and I had very similar experiences. And I wouldn't be human if I didn't want people to remember my participation."

Doby went through much the same kind of discrimination and abuse that Robinson suffered—not being allowed to stay in the same hotels and eat in the same restaurants as the white players, hearing the racial insults of fans and opposing bench jockeys, experiencing the reprehension of some teammates. But while Doby will be honored at the All-Star Game—which, coincidentally, will be played in Cleveland on July 8—and at an Indians game a few days earlier, he in some ways seems the forgotten man.

"Jackie Robinson, of course, deserves all the credit he gets," Boudreau said last week. "But I really don't think that Larry gets the credit he deserves for being the pioneer in the situation he was in."

When the then-6-foot-1-inch, 185-pound Doby stepped onto the field before that first game with the White Sox, he stood silently in Cleveland uniform number 14, glove in hand, for what he recalled as five or ten minutes. "No one offered to play catch," he said. Finally, he heard Joe (Flash) Gordon, the All-Star second baseman, call to him, "Hey, kid, let's go." And they warmed up.

Doby, a left-handed batter, was called in to pinch-hit in the seventh inning and after "hitting a scorching drive foul," according to a news-agency report, he struck out. But he was officially a big-leaguer, one who the following year would help the Indians win the pennant and the World Series. He became the first black player to hit a home run in a World Series, made six straight American League All-Star teams, and, at one time or another over a thirteen-year career, led the American League in homers, runs batted in, runs scored, and slugging average as well as strikeouts. When he retired in 1959, he did so with a .283 career average and 253 home runs.

About Robinson, Doby said: "I had the greatest respect for Jack. He was tough and smart and brave. I once told him, 'If not for you, then probably not for me.'"

Robinson and Doby were followed into the big leagues in 1947 by three other blacks: Henry Thompson and Willard Brown, who joined the St. Louis Browns in late July, and Dan Bankhead, who came up to the Dodgers in August. Thompson and Brown lasted for only a few weeks (though Thompson returned in 1949 to play several years with the New York Giants) while Bankhead pitched the rest of the season for the Dodgers.

Roy Campanella joined the Dodgers in 1948 and Don Newcombe made it in 1949. Today, major league baseball estimates that about one-third of its players are black or Hispanic, but in 1950, three years after Robinson and Doby broke the color barrier, only five major league teams had been integrated. By 1953 there were twenty blacks on seven of the sixteen teams. And it was not until 1959, when the Boston Red Sox played Pumpsie Green, that every major-league club had a black player.

Lou Brissie, who pitched for the Philadelphia A's beginning in 1947, recalled: "I was on the bench and heard some of my teammates shouting things at Larry, like, 'Porter, carry my bags,' or 'Shoeshine boy, shine my shoes,' and, well, the N-word, too. It was terrible." Brissie, who was from South Carolina, had been shot and left for dead in Italy during World War II. He pitched with a large steel brace on his left leg and instinctively felt an identity with the young black player. "He was a kind of underdog, like me," Brissie said.

Doby has not forgotten the abuse: the "N-word" being used every day, the calls of "coon" and "jigaboo," the times he slid into second base and the opposing infielder spit in his face. "I never sought sympathy or felt sorry for myself," Doby said. "And all that stuff just made me try harder, made me more aggressive. Sometimes I'd get too aggressive, and swing too hard, and miss the pitch."

But he cannot forget the sense of loneliness, particularly after games. "It's then you'd really like to be with your teammates, win or lose, and go over the game," he said. "But I'd go off to my hotel in the black part of town, and they'd go off to their hotel."

Doby is now seventy-two, his hair sprinkled lightly with grey. He is huskier than in the old photos of him breaking in with the Indians. He works for major league baseball, handling the licensing activities of former players. Wearing a tie and suspenders and an easy smile and forthright manner, this father of five, grandfather of six, and great-grandfather of three reflected on his years as a ballplayer as he sat recently in a sunny twenty-ninth-floor room at the baseball commissioner's office in Manhattan.

"When Mr. Veeck signed me," Doby said, "he sat me down and told me some of the do's and don'ts. He said, 'Lawrence'—he's the only person who called me Lawrence—'you are going to be part of history.' Part of history? I had no notions about that. I just wanted to play baseball. I mean, I was young. I didn't quite realize then what all this meant. I saw it simply as an opportunity to get ahead.

"Mr. Veeck told me: 'No arguing with umpires, don't even turn around at a bad call at the plate, and no dissertations with opposing players; either of those might start a race riot. No associating with female Caucasians'—not that I was going to. And he said remember to act in a way that you know people are watching you. And this was something that both Jack and I took seriously. We knew that if we didn't succeed, it might hinder opportunities for other Afro-Americans."

Doby had been leading the Negro National League in batting average, at .415, and home runs, with fourteen, when he was signed by the Indians. He began as a second baseman but was switched to the outfield, where he would be assured of starting. But he was unaccustomed to playing there, and in an early game, in center field, and with the bases loaded, he misjudged a fly ball in the sun and the ball hit him on the head. It caused his team to lose the game.

After the game, Bill McKechnie, an Indian coach who had befriended Doby, said to him, "We'll find out what kind of ballplayer you are tomorrow." Doby recalled that McKechnie smiled. "It was a challenge and a kind of vote of confidence," Doby said. "The next day I hit a home run to win the game."

Doby appreciated Gordon and McKechnie and the catcher, Jim Hegan, in particular, who would seek to salve his disappointments and perhaps take a seat next to him after he had struck out or made an error. "They were tremendous," Doby said. "But there were others who don't remember, or don't want to remember, some of their actions. And sometimes I'd see them later and they'd say, 'Hey, Larry, let's go have a beer.' I thought, 'When I needed you, where were you?' I forgive, but I can't forget. I politely decline their invitations."

Doby spent his grammar school years in Camden, South Carolina. He recalls seeing the white people riding in fringed horse-drawn buggies through the black neighborhood, and tossing dimes and nickels at the small black children. And then they would rub the children's heads for good luck. "My grandmother warned me never to pick up the money," Doby said. "She thought it was undignified.

"And then I always tried to act in a dignified manner. When I was in the major leagues, some people thought I was a loner. But, well, when Joe DiMaggio was off by himself, they said he just wanted his privacy. And midway through the 1948 season the Indians signed Satchel Paige, and they made him my roommate. Well, he was almost never in the room. I'm not sure where he went. But he was a character and he enjoyed being perceived that way. He'd come into the clubhouse and clown around, and did some Amos 'n' Andy stuff. I didn't think it was right—at least, it wasn't right for me."

Eddie Robinson, the Indians' first baseman when Doby broke in, said by telephone from his home in Fort Worth: "I thought it took a lot of courage for Larry to go through what he did. He handled himself quite well." But when Boudreau put Doby at first base to start the second half of a doubleheader on Doby's second day in the major leagues, Robinson would not let him use his glove. "I didn't want anyone else playing my position, and it had nothing to do with black or white," Robinson said. As Doby recalls, the Indians were able to borrow a first baseman's glove for him from the White Sox.

Doby had been the only black player on the Eastside High School baseball, football, and basketball teams in Paterson, New Jersey. He went briefly to Long Island University and Virginia Union before being drafted into the navy. He first learned of Jackie Robinson's signing with the Dodgers' organization when he was on a Pacific Island in 1945. "I wondered if I might have a chance to play in the big leagues, too," Doby said. "Until then, I thought I would just go back to Paterson and become a high school coach."

Doby talks often at schools and discusses the changes in American life. "I know people are critical and say that not enough progress has been made in baseball, or sports in general, particularly in the coaching or administrative levels," he said. "And I believe there has not been enough progress made either. But when you look at other elements of American society, sports stacks up pretty good. If Jack and I had a legacy, it is to show that teamwork—the ability to associate and communicate—makes all of us stronger."

In 1978, Doby was named manager of the White Sox, taking over for Bob Lemon midway through the year. He held the position for just eighty-seven games, posting a record of 37–50.

"I was the second black manager in major league history," Doby said, "after Frank Robinson." Frank Robinson managed the Indians starting in 1975.

"Funny thing," Doby said, with a smile, "I followed another Robinson."

[1997]

The Odd Bond
at Second Base

🐾 THE WHITE BOY was thirteen or fourteen years old, and his brother was about sixteen, when, with dusk descending on that summer day in Louisville, Kentucky, in the early 1930s, the older boy shouted a racial slur at six black kids, telling them, "Get off this street!" With that, the six black kids took chase after the white boys, and the two white kids ran with everything they had and made it safely home.

How did he feel about his older brother's action, the now seventy-eight-year-old man named Harold (Pee Wee) Reese, was asked recently. Reese, recuperating from surgery for lung cancer a few weeks ago, rubbed a greying eyebrow in the living room of his winter home in Venice, Florida, as he thought about the incident involving him and his brother, Carl Jr.

"I thought it was stupid," he said. "I mean, to throw out a threat like that when there were six against two!"

Reese, the former star shortstop for the Brooklyn Dodgers and a member of baseball's Hall of Fame, smiled, for of course there was much more to it than the numerical equation.

Some fifteen years after that childhood incident, Pee Wee Reese became a pivotal figure in the acceptance and support of a rookie teammate, Jackie Robinson, who broke the color barrier in the major leagues in 1947. Looking back now, fifty years after Robinson's historic breakthrough into the so-called national pastime, two moments in particular stand out between Reese and Robinson. Reese, in a cream-colored short-sleeve shirt, green pants, and tan buck shoes, his hair grey, his arms creased with age and the flesh not as tight as in his Dodger days, and a slightly tired look in his eyes from a radiation treatment in the morning, thought back upon those years.

The first of the two incidents occurred at the beginning of spring training in 1947, when Robinson had been called up to the Dodgers from Montreal, Brooklyn's top minor league team, on which Robinson had starred during the 1946 season. A petition was drawn up by a group of mostly Southern Dodgers players that declared they would not take the field with a black man.

"I'm not signing that," Reese told the ringleaders, who included Dixie Walker, Kirby Higbe, and Bobby Bragan. "No way."

Reese, the soft-spoken but respected team captain, with a Southern upbringing, perhaps surprised the petition-carriers. "I wasn't thinking of myself as the Great White Father," Reese said. "I just wanted to play baseball. I'd just come back from serving in the South Pacific with the navy during the Second World War, and I had a wife and daughter to support. I needed the money. I just wanted to get on with it."

But there was more to it than the money. And Reese's refusal to sign the petition, many believe, meant the end of the matter. Robinson played, and endured vicious abuse from opposing teams, from beanballs and spikings to racial epithets and spitting. Robinson had promised Branch Rickey, the owner and general manager of the Dodgers, that for at least his first two years in the major leagues, he would hold his tongue and his fists, no matter the provocation. And one day—it was probably in Cincinnati, Reese recalled, in 1947 or 1948—the attack was so nasty that Reese walked over to Robinson and put his hand on the black man's shoulder.

"Pee Wee kind of sensed the sort of hopeless, dead feeling in me and came over and stood beside me for a while," Robinson recalled, as quoted in the forthcoming biography *Jackie Robinson* by

Arnold Rampersad (Alfred A. Knopf). "He didn't say a word but he looked over at the chaps who were yelling at me through him and just stared. He was standing by me, I could tell you that." The hecklers ceased their attack. "I will never forget it," Robinson said.

Over the years, Reese became perhaps Robinson's best friend on the Dodgers, though there were others who were reasonably close to him as well, including the white players Carl Erskine, Gil Hodges, and Ralph Branca and, of his black teammates, Junior Gilliam in particular. But Reese's attitude, including that defining gesture of solidarity on the field that they were, in the end, teammates and brothers under the skin, did not come from a save-the-world mentality.

"Something in my gut reacted to the moment," Reese said. "Something about—what?—the unfairness of it? The injustice of it? I don't know."

Reese's son, Mark, a forty-year-old documentary filmmaker, has wondered where that gut reaction from a man brought up in Southern mores came from. "I think it might have something to do with that hanging tree in the middle of the town of Brandenburg, Kentucky," Mark Reese said. Brandenburg is about thirty-five miles south of Louisville, and a few miles from Ekron, where the Reese family lived on a farm and where Reese's father, Carl Sr., became a railroad detective.

"When my dad was a boy of about nine or ten years old," Mark Reese said, "he remembers his father pointing out a tree in Brandenburg with a long branch extending out. It was there, his father told him, that black men had been lynched. I believe it was an important thing for my dad, because many times when we visited relatives in Brandenburg, he would point out that tree to me, and tell me about the lynchings. He never made a big point about the significance, but there was definitely an emotion in his voice, an emotion that said to me, anyway, that it was a terrible thing that human beings did to another human being, and only because of the color of their skin. And I imagine that when his dad told him the story, there was a similar emotion."

Pee Wee Reese shrugged at this interpretation. It is his innate manner to play down himself and, apparently, his contributions, particularly in the area of Jackie Robinson, where, he feels, he might only be a deflection from the limelight that Robinson deserves. In the book, *Baseball's Great Experiment,* a thorough study of the black entry into baseball, the author Jules Tygiel quotes Reese telling Robinson sometime before Robinson's death at fifty-three in 1972, "You know I didn't go out of my way to be nice to you." And Robinson replied, "Pee Wee, maybe that's what I appreciated most."

"I seem to remember a conversation along those lines," Reese recalled in his home here. "Sounds right." He laughed.

He recalled the first time he learned about Robinson. "I was on a ship coming back to the States from Guam, in the middle of the ocean, and was playing cards. Someone hollered to me: 'Hey, Pee Wee, did you hear? The Dodgers signed a nigger.' It didn't mean that much to me and I kept playing cards. Then the guy said, 'And he plays shortstop!' My God, just my luck, Robinson has to play my position! But I had confidence in my abilities, and I thought, well, if he can beat me out, more power to him. That's exactly how I felt."

It turned out that Robinson, in his first year as a Dodger, would play first base, and then for the next several years move to second base and team with Reese for one of the brightest double-play combinations in baseball, as the Dodgers won pennant after pennant.

Just as Reese does not give himself undue credit, he seems clear-eyed about others. And while Robinson has been raised in some circles to a near deity, Reese saw the man within. "Jackie was a great player, a great competitor, and pretty fearless," Reese recalled. "He had only a fair arm but made up for it at second base by never backing down when a runner came barreling in. And he'd do some things that I wondered about. He would actually taunt some pitchers. He'd shout at them from the batter's box to just try to throw at his head! I told him: 'Jackie, quiet down. They might take you up on it. And if they're still mad, they might throw at me, too!'" Reese laughed. "And after the two years were up in which he had promised Mr. Rickey that he'd turn the other cheek, he became a guy who would stand up for himself. And he could be a tough bench jockey, and he might plow into a guy who was in his way."

One time, after Robinson had been in the league for a few years, he groused to Reese that the pitchers were throwing at him because they were racists. "No," Reese replied. "They aren't throwing at you because you're black, Jackie. They're throwing at you because they just don't like you." Robinson smirked and then smiled. Reese could say such things to Robinson because of their friendship, and because Robinson knew where Reese's heart—and mind—were. After all, it was Reese who was the first Dodger in Robinson's first spring training camp to walk across the field and shake his hand. "It was the first time I'd ever shaken the hand of a black man," Reese said. "But I was the captain of the team. It was my job, I believed, to greet the new players."

But greeting, and associating with, a black man was something different, to be sure. "When I was growing up, we never played ball with blacks because they weren't allowed in the parks. And the schools were segregated, so we didn't go to school with them. And there'd be some mischief between blacks and whites, but, as I remember, it was just mischief. It wasn't hatred, at least not from me."

And it was Reese who first sat down in the clubhouse to play cards with Robinson. When Dixie Walker later took Reese aside and said, "How can you be playing cards with him?" Reese recalls that he replied, "Look, Dixie, you and Stell"—Walker's wife—"travel with a black woman who takes care of your kids, who cooks your food, who you trust—isn't that even more than playing cards with a black?" And Walker said, "But this is different."

But not to Reese.

Today, Reese, at 5 feet 10 inches, weighs 165 pounds, after losing nearly 15 pounds in a week's stay in the hospital after the surgery for lung cancer (he quit smoking cigarettes about ten years ago). A third of his lung was removed. Doctors believe they have cut the cancer out, but Reese must continue to undergo radiation treatments. He is strong enough, however, to be back playing golf and on Saturday celebrated his fifty-fifth wedding anniversary with his wife, Dotty.

After his playing days, he coached with the Dodgers for one year, in 1959, then broadcast ball games for CBS and NBC and was a representative for the Louisville Slugger bat company. But for Reese, now a great-grandfather, there remain some painful physical reminders of an athletic career. He has an arthritic thumb, perhaps the result of his youth as a marbles champion, from which he derived his nickname. And Reese walks with a slight tilt because of trouble with his knees—he has had one knee replacement and may need a second. The injuries are a result, probably, of a major league career in which he made eight All-Star teams and batted .269 over sixteen seasons, ten of those seasons with Robinson. Reese was considered one of the smartest players in the game (remember when he took the cutoff throw from Sandy Amoros and wheeled in short left field as though having eyes in the back of his head and fired the ball to first base to double off the Yankees' Gil McDougald to help preserve for Brooklyn the seventh and deciding game of the 1955 World Series?).

At Robinson's funeral, in Manhatttan on October 27, 1972, Harold (Pee Wee) Reese, a son of the South, was one of the pallbearers. "I took it," Reese said, "as an honor."

[1997]

Schottzie's Owner Is Like None Other

✌ SHE WAS in a hurry as she strode to the elevator behind the press box, trailed by her small party and the smoke from the cigarette clenched between her teeth. This was in Riverfront Stadium, home of the Cincinnati Reds. The woman, with her salt-and-pepper hair cut short, was sturdily built and wore a white-and-red sweater and fire-engine red slacks—the colors of her team—and brown loafers.

At the elevator she turned her back to the steel door and kicked it with repeated thuds. Very shortly, the elevator door slid open. "Hello, Mrs. Schott," said the elevator operator, looking concerned.

"What took you so long?" she said to him in a kind of raspy voice.

There were times when Marge Schott, owner of the Reds, kicked so hard for the elevator—it was her signal—that the heel of her shoe fell off. Sometimes her kicks destroyed the electronic sensory device of the elevator. Such scenes took place regularly over several summers, and now Schott, sitting several weeks ago behind the cluttered desk in her stadium office, recalled them. "I'm very impatient. Sometimes women are that way." She smiled and nodded in agreement with herself.

The remarkable behavior of Margaret Unnewher Schott, sixty-three years old, doesn't stop at the elevator door. The recent disclosure of a deposition taken in a suit filed against her by a former employee revealed that she has made racially and ethnically demeaning comments, including use of the word "nigger."

The controversy over her remarks has plagued her now for several weeks and, for many, has transformed her image from that of a quirky eccentric known best for parading her St. Bernard around Riverfront Stadium into a mean-spirited, insensitive woman. It has also drawn scrutiny from her fellow owners and others in and out of baseball. Hank Aaron has publicly called for her suspension, as has Abraham H. Foxman, national director of the Anti-Defamation League of B'nai B'rith, who said Schott had "tainted and sullied baseball."

There are strong indications that baseball's executive council will seriously review the situation at its next meeting, on December 7, and could fine or suspend her. Peter O'Malley, the Los Angeles Dodgers president, was quoted in the *Los Angeles Times* as saying: "If the statements attributed to Marge Schott are accurate, I believe Mrs. Schott should resign as chief executive officer."

In an interview last Wednesday, Schott rejected much of this newly publicized portrayal, and yet acknowledged, wittingly or otherwise, some of the substance that has prompted it. "I'm not a racist; I've never meant any harm," she said. "I'm so sick of all this. It's discouraging. I wish they'd stop all this falseness."

In her deposition she either acknowledged, or did not deny, using words like "nigger" and "Jap" and terms like "money-grubbing Jews." "But if and when I've used them," she said last week, "it was only kiddingly." They were "joke terms," she said. She denies calling Eric Davis and Dave Parker, two former black players, "million-dollar niggers."

"Of course nigger is a demeaning word," Schott continued. "But I know that blacks call it to each other, too. I've been in the business world for twenty-four years and never had any problem with discrimination. I've got a Jewish manager in my car dealership who is like a son to me. And it hurt when it was reported that I called Eric and Dave nigger this or nigger that. I love Eric. It hurt me when they booed him here. I love his parents, really good people. I called Eric the other day and explained to him that it wasn't true. I tried to call Dave too, but haven't reached him yet."

While only one of her forty-five front-office employees is black, Schott said that that wasn't the whole story. "Look on the field; you see black players for the Reds," she said. "They're part of the organization, too."

Regardless of the backlash she has encountered, she has continued to use some of the terms that have gotten her into trouble. Recently she pointed out gifts to a visitor in her office that she said she had received from "the Japs" while in Japan touring with a group of Reds players. She made the comment without a seeming concern or understanding of its pejorative implications.

When speaking about a visit last week from Bill White, the president of the National League, she recalled that she used the word "Jap" in talking with him. "Bill said to me, 'Marge, will you quit that!'" She laughed. "I said, 'Bill, I didn't know it was so bad. But I'll stop.' I didn't mean to insult the Japanese; I love them. I have great respect for the way they've come back in the world."

In her deposition she also acknowledged keeping a Nazi swastika armband in her home. When asked about that last week, she explained: "It was a gift I got several years ago from a worker in one of my car agencies. He took it off a dead German. It's what they call, what, 'memorabilia'? It's no big deal. I keep it in a drawer with Christmas decorations."

Earlier this month, recalling that she had family members in Germany who had suffered during World War II, she said: "Hitler was good in the beginning, but he went too far."

The controversy around Schott was stirred by the former team controller Tim Sabo, who sued Schott last year for $2.5 million. In the suit, Sabo, who is white, contended that one of the reasons he was dismissed was that he did not approve of her use of racial and religious slurs. Sabo's case was dismissed on the ground that Ohio's "at-will" doctrine of employment allows an employer to fire or hire as he or she sees fit. But some of her statements in the deposition sounded racist, bigoted, arrogant, stupid, or callous, or all of the above.

Those who have worked closely with Schott in baseball say that while she is capable of being "very, very charming when she wants to," she can also be vicious, vindictive, and surpassingly ignorant, especially when it suits her purpose.

A widow of 24 years, Schott runs a major league baseball team with a 123-year history that today may be as famous for its mascot, her St. Bernard named Schottzie, as it is for any of its players. She recently fired her third general manager in eight years, Bob Quinn, and a manager she liked, Lou Piniella, recently quit in disgust. She fired Quinn just two seasons after he helped engineer a World Series championship. Actually, her lawyer gave Quinn the bad news. "I can't fire people face to face," she said. "I'm a wimp about it."

Quinn, who spent three seasons with the Reds, had won praise for his 1990 feat. And he had been hailed by peers and press alike for the trades he made in the months leading up to the 1992 season.

The Reds began the 1992 season as a strong contender in the National League West, but a series of injuries to key players made it hard for them to compete with Atlanta. Still, Cincinnati finished with a very respectable ninety victories. Some baseball people, like John Schuerholz, the general manager of the Atlanta Braves, were stunned at Quinn's dismissal. "Bob Quinn did the best job of any G.M. in baseball," he said.

Two days before Quinn's firing, Piniella, the field leader of the 1990 championship team and for the following two seasons as well, did what many had expected. He resigned. "I just didn't want any more," he said. "I left there on good terms. I honored my contract. I just didn't want to be renewed." What Piniella didn't want any more of was an organization that too often reflected its owner, either by being idiosyncratic, or eccentric, or worse.

Before the disclosure of her deposition, Schott was viewed by some as a grande dame, the queen bee of the Queen City. The populace appreciated a certain rough-hewn charm in her, and even considered her a civic hero because she purchased her hometown team in 1984 when there was a threat of its being sold to outsiders and possibly being moved. Schott had been a limited partner in the Reds since 1981 and became the president and chief executive officer after the purchase. "I bought the team with my head and not my heart," she said. "It was Christmastime, and you know how women are at Christmas. You buy things and charge it."

Yet despite this expenditure, she is often portrayed as cheap, even though her player payroll has risen from $15 million in 1990 to $37 million last season. She has been accused of selling employees day-old doughnuts ("That's ridiculous," she said). But she admits having charged Piniella for donating three bats from the Reds for a charity (she is, to be sure, active in several charities of her own choosing), and she once made Quinn pay his way to the All-Star Game.

Schott's dog was part of the reason for Piniella's leave-taking. Actually, Piniella had to deal with two dogs, since the original Schottzie died in 1991 at age eight, and Schott bought the second dog, sometimes called Schottzie 02, last spring. It was dismaying for Piniella to see a dog have the run of the field during practice, and he was insulted to have to pose for pictures wearing a baseball cap with the stuffed likeness of Schottzie's large face on the brim.

Schottzie 02, while adored by the owner, is often reviled by many others in baseball, including a number of players from the Reds, who have complained about dog excrement littering the field during warm-ups. One Cincinnati pitcher, Tim Belcher, grumbled last season about Schottzie 02 bothering him while he was warming up. It is an embarrassment, say many of the players. A travesty, a joke. "Look," said one, "it's just not professional to have a dog running around the field when you're out there working. It's wacky."

"I get their chewing gum on my shoes," Schott said of the players. "They should be happy I don't have a horse, right?"

64

"Our club," said one former Reds executive, "was a laughing-stock in the league."

White, the National League president, once called a team executive of the Reds and asked, "What do you think I should do about the dog?"

"At the very least put her on a leash," the executive replied.

So far, Schottzie 02 has remained unleashed.

Despite all the criticisms of her quirkiness, Schott has presided over a team that was losing money when she bought it and that now operates in the black. Profits last year were estimated conservatively at $15 million.

She weathered the stormy Pete Rose years, in which she was virtually a bystander as Rose battled gambling problems that concluded with his banishment from baseball. "I like Pete a lot," she said, "and my greatest thrill in baseball was the night he broke the hit record." After Rose surpassed Ty Cobb's hit record in 1985, Schott presented Rose with a Corvette. "And I learned later that he sold it," she said. "That hurt me. Women do get hurt a lot."

Schott generally keeps a distance between herself and the decisions of her baseball people. She does not pretend to know baseball and would be hard pressed to define a sacrifice fly or a squeeze play. She says her favorite play is the Wave, in which she participates from her box seat in Riverfront Stadium.

A few years ago, in salary negotiations with a player's agent, the agent mentioned Barry Bonds. "Who's he?" she asked. And on the day Don Baylor was hired by the Colorado Rockies as manager, she was asked if the development took the pressure off her to seek a minority manager. "Why?" she asked. "Is Baylor black?"

Her lack of knowledge about baseball, and her mistakes about things not directly connected to the sport, make some shake their heads. A few years ago there was a meeting of owners in a Chicago hotel and Schott arrived so early that she was seated for some time at the conference table before any of the other owners showed up. Later she was overheard speaking on a public telephone to her office. "Hey!" she said. "Why didn't you tell me there was an hour difference between Cincinnati and Chicago?"

But she has more to do, she believes, than just run a baseball team or study geography or time zones. She says she was just a spoiled housewife when her husband, Charles Schott, died and left her with a car dealership and a huge inheritance. Coming in without any real knowledge of the business, she learned it.

She also keeps a close watch on all the various odds and ends associated with the Reds. "I'm a saver," she said. Some have extended that description, calling her a hoarder. Those people refer to a large room in Riverfront Stadium that is filled with goods left over from various giveaway days: caps and batting helmets and bats and balls and, according to one source, candy bars that date back eight years and calendars of the original Schottzie that were printed in 1986 and 1987. And some of those items she still tries to sell. Her office, meanwhile, is a kind of cathedral to stuffed animals—many of them St. Bernards of various sizes and shapes, and many of them wearing Reds caps.

She regularly refers to being a woman in a man's world, and to having overcome slights and abuse. She talks about "the buddy system," and the "little boys club" that is the fraternity (with a sole sister) that makes up the group of major league owners. She was the only one of them, for instance, to abstain on the vote that ended the reign of Fay Vincent as commissioner of baseball. "I didn't like what some of them were doing," she said, "how seven teams for example were getting in bed with the Cubs on their superstation, and I didn't find out about this until late. So I thought, if they want to play their games with each other, let 'em. I don't want any part of it."

When she took over the team, some of the baseball men who were suddenly working for a woman hardly spoke to her. "And it took me a couple of months to get my own parking space at the ball park," she said. "The only one who talked to me was the elevator operator."

She tells people that she knows some employees try to take advantage of her. That may be why she charged Piniella for the bats (she didn't press the issue, and he didn't pay) or why she is niggling about sending her executives to some baseball meetings. ("All these men do there is play golf," she said.)

She still lives in the huge house on seventy acres in a leafy Cincinnati suburb left her by her husband. It is grey stone with turrets and slate roofs and, she was told by painters, "360 openings, which includes windows and doors." It looks like a castle.

"It's a man's house, isn't it?" she said as she walked around the large, rather dark, rooms. She still keeps the clothes from her husband in a closet. "People have asked why I don't move. I tell them I've gotten used to the place."

"When you're left alone, after your husband dies, there is insecurity," she said. "For any woman. But especially for me. You see, my father was Achtung-German. He used to ring a bell when he wanted my mother. When I was twenty-one and went to vote, he told me who to vote for. I said, 'Yes, daddy.' And I was that way with Charlie and Charlie's father. So men have influenced me a lot. And when I didn't have one to tell me what to do, it was hard to get my footing. I have. But there's still insecurity. I mean, it's still a man's world."

She walked into another room of the house and opened a secret door that was built during Prohibition in order to hide liquor. "Kids love to come here because of all the nooks and crannies in the house, like this one," she said. "I have a big Christmas party for kids every year. Charlie and I never had kids. Oh, we tried, but we couldn't manage it. We once had twenty-two St. Bernards here, though. Drove my husband nuts. I said, 'They're just pups. We'll get rid of them when they grow up.' He said, 'Grow up? They're up to my waist already!'" She laughed and lit up another cigarette.

"Then another time I began collecting bees. Had 'em all over the place. Had bottles and bottles of honey. Everything was sticky. That drove Charlie nuts, too. But I always felt guilty about not having children. It was a tragedy to us, my biggest heartache. I have four sisters and they had ten kids in eleven years. They're like rabbits. But since I never had kids—I don't know—maybe I want my ball team to be like family.

"If I could have a team of only sweet guys, I'd love it, but they probably wouldn't be able to play ball too well. And I want families to come to Reds games. We're still the lowest-price ticket in the major leagues. And we have hot dogs that cost only a dollar. People say, 'You sell hot dogs for a dollar? I can't believe it!' But how else could families afford a day at the ball park?"

As soon as she swung open the kitchen door, Schottzie 02 bounded up to greet her. "Hey little baby, hey little baby," she said, hugging the dog. Marge Schott handed Schottzie a biscuit and the dog ate it lustily. Schott watched and smiled. Then she returned to another room, one with heavy drapes and knickknacks on the shelves. "I don't hire maids because I have so much junk I'd never know what's missing," she said.

She sat down in a tall dark wooden chair in the large room and lit up another cigarette. She was alone. In the other room, Schottzie 02 was barking.

[1992]

He Pitched and Tied His Shoes with One Hand

❦ ONE LOOKS for turning points. How is it that he has come this far, this way? Maybe it was the time when Jim Abbott was five years old and came home from school, angry and tearful, and held up the steel hook a doctor had recommended he use for a right hand. "I don't want to wear this anymore," he told his parents. Other children were afraid to play with him and, in the way that small children can be cruel, called him names like "Mr. Hook." Even then he struggled not to appear different. He never wore the hook again.

Or maybe it was the time when he saw that his parents had learned to tie a shoe with one hand so they could teach it to him. He, unlike them, was born with just one hand, his left.

Or maybe it was when his father, in a park in Flint, Michigan, taught him to throw a baseball and then remove the glove ever so smoothly and swiftly from his right wrist and place it on his left throwing hand in order to catch his dad's quick throw back, and then switch the glove back again in order to throw. He developed the technique so skillfully that when he was pitching in high school, the story goes, the first nine batters on an opposing team tried to bunt for hits. He threw the runners out each time.

"That story has grown out of proportion," Abbott said. "It was only five or six batters."

Or maybe for Abbott, the twenty-five-year-old pitcher recently obtained by the Yankees in a trade with the California Angels, there was no single turning point. Maybe it was simply the concept that his parents, Mike and Kathy Abbott, had come to live by, that Jim, except for the strange fate of having been born with one hand—there is a stub with one small, fingerlike protrusion where the right hand would be—was as normal as any other kid, and should think of himself that way.

Four years ago, Abbott became the first and only one-handed pitcher in baseball history, and one of the elite who can throw the ball at speeds of up to ninety-four miles an hour. Abbott also accomplished something else that, while not singular, is rare. He went from the campus of the University of Michigan to the Angels, their first-round pick in the amateur draft. He has never spent a day in the minor leagues.

Abbott's parents were married at eighteen and had Jim when they were still eighteen. There was a time early on when they felt sorry for themselves, but they soon overcame the shock and influenced Jim not to feel sorry for himself, either. Kathy Abbott recalled that occasionally Jim drew stares from people. "Oh, yes, because of Jim's hand," she said. "I'd forgot about it."

"I never heard Jim ask, 'Why me?'" said his father recently. "And as he grew up, I watched the way he handled himself around people. He's always had a lot of friends, always laughed. Even when some people have said insensitive or cruel things. Like a reporter asking, 'Is anyone else in your family deformed?' But Jim is always a gentleman. I don't understand how he does it. His dad is now taking lessons from him."

"My parents kept me in the mainstream; they never shielded me," Abbott said, sitting recently with his wife, Dana, on a stuffed white couch in their ground-floor apartment in Newport Beach, California. Outside, near the window, stood a palm tree. Inside there was a small, decorated Christmas tree. Abbott said he felt blessed. "When we moved into a new neighborhood, my father said, 'Jim, go out and meet the kids. Say, I'm Jim Abbott. Ask to play in their game.'"

One can somehow still picture Abbott, now 6 feet 3 inches and 215 pounds and looking husky in a short-sleeve blue shirt, blue jeans, and worn running shoes, as that blond-haired, open-faced, seeking boy. He recalled that his parents always supported him but never pushed him, that they emphasized he should do whatever came naturally, and that he could just about realize whatever dreams he had, including, eventually, pitching in the major leagues.

"I will always be thankful to my parents for how they dealt with it," he said. "They were young. They were alone. There were no support groups. Really, I look back with admiration."

Pitching for a mediocre Angels team that, as it happened, often didn't play well behind him or hit well for him, he managed to post commendable statistics. Last season, for a team that tied for fifth place in the American League West, Abbott compiled a 2.77 earned run average, fifth best in the league, although his record was 7–15. The year before he was 18–11 with a 2.89 ERA. In his two previous seasons, his records were 12–12 and 10–14 (and in those fourteen losses his team scored a total of fifteen runs).

"He pitches his heart out every time," said Rod Carew, the Hall of Famer and the Angels' batting coach. "But he pitched with incredibly bad luck. He could win twenty games for the Yankees, easy. I'd put him in the category with Catfish Hunter and Nolan Ryan, some of the greatest pitchers I faced. And he's a terrific guy to be around. I hated to see him go."

On the bench, Angels players laughed among themselves how Abbott, with his cutting fastball and hard slider, broke five or six opponents' bats a game. And they would take pleasure in observing other players watch Abbott field a shot through the box, handling his glove so fast that it was nearly sleight-of-hand. "Did you see that!" players in the other dugout exclaimed. "Did you see that!"

71

Why, then, did the Angels trade Abbott? A contract dispute seems at the crux. Abbott was at the end of a one-year contract with an option. The Angels offered a four-year contract at $16 million. Abbott's agent, Scott Boras, had asked for a four-year deal for $19 million but made it clear that this was negotiable. At this point, it seems, Jackie Autry, who runs the team for her husband, the old troubadour-cowboy Gene Autry, and the general manager, Whitey Herzog, decided they would show Abbott and Boras who was boss and traded the pitcher for three Yankee minor league prospects.

"I was surprised," said Abbott. "I just thought I'd spend my whole career with the Angels. It's kind of easy to get it into your head that you're indispensable. And then suddenly I was traded and felt a real sense of rejection. And there were the concerns about coming to New York—just a big, looming city. As great a city as it is—and I've always loved to visit there—I wasn't sure. You hear a lot of horror stories. And I was concerned about Dana making the transition because she was born and raised in Southern California. But she seemed excited about it."

Dana Douty lettered in basketball and earned a degree in economics from the University of California at Irvine last year, shortly before she and Abbott were married. "Jim's such a fierce competitor that going to the Yankees will just be another challenge for him," she said. "He even hates it when I beat him in gin rummy."

"But I'm getting better," Abbott insisted.

"You are," she assured with a smile, "you are."

Despite his boyish looks, Abbott hardly seems one to be intimidated, even by New York City. "I like the team the Yankees are putting together," he said. "I like the players they've recently picked up, like Jimmy Key and Wade Boggs and Spike Owen and Paul O'Neill, and plus, of course, it's a privilege to play with guys like Mattingly—or should I call him Don?" He smiled. "Or Mr. Mattingly?" He was half serious.

"And I have no problem with anything I've heard about George

Steinbrenner. I mean, it sounds to me like he wants to have a winner in the worst way. I love that."

Abbott spoke about a phone call from Yankees Manager Buck Showalter. "You'll like the fans," Showalter told Abbott. "They stay for the whole game and hang on every pitch, and they know baseball. They'll cheer you when you do well and boo when you don't. But there's an excitement at Yankee Stadium that's different from Anaheim."

"The call pumped me up," said Abbott. And while he didn't want to say anything bad about the Angels, a team that "gave me a chance," he was nonetheless upset when he read something an Angels executive had said: "Oh, people are unhappy to lose Abbott only because he's a one-armed pitcher."

"I have an arm," said Abbott. "I don't have a hand."

Abbott is not the only one-handed player in major league history. There was Pete Gray, the one-armed outfielder for the St. Louis Browns in 1945. "I didn't grow up wanting to be another Pete Gray," said Abbott. "I grew up wanting to be another Nolan Ryan."

Abbott was always a good athlete, and sports has helped give him a sense of stature that he might not have had otherwise. He became a high school pitching sensation and then got a scholarship to Michigan, where he majored in communications and was so brilliant a pitcher (and a capable batter, too) that in 1987 he was named amateur baseball player of the year. In 1988, he won the Sullivan Award as the best amateur athlete in the country.

With all that, he is not pleased when, for example, people have come to him to autograph a baseball that Pete Gray had signed. While Abbott admires Gray, he doesn't want to be thought of as an oddity. Gray, for all his remarkable achievements and ability, was still kind of a sideshow in the major leagues, a wartime player used primarily to draw crowds, a player who would be introduced last to the fans in pre-game introductions. Gray batted .218 in his one year in the big leagues. Abbott is one of the finer pitchers in baseball, and, after four seasons, an established one.

"I just don't think all of this about me playing with one hand is as big an issue as everyone wants to make it," said Abbott. "I don't try to run from the attention about it, I just accept it."

Abbott received so much mail with the Angels—as many as three hundred letters a week—that the public relations department regularly piled it into shopping carts when he was on the road. Many of the letters were from children who were physically handicapped or disabled, or from parents of such children. "Some of the stories are unbelievable, so tragic," said Abbott. One letter came from an eight-year-old girl who had been attacked by a mountain lion and lost an arm. Another boy had lost an arm when fireworks exploded.

"I try to write them all back. But sometimes there's really not much I can say. I don't really believe in this stuff about ballplayers as role models. But if I can be of help to anyone, if anyone can take something from the fact that I'm a baseball pitcher, then fine. But when I'm out on the mound pitching, I'm pitching because I love it, because I like the challenge of trying to get people out. I'm not pitching because I want to prove anything to anyone."

In every city he travels to, parents bring their children to meet him. "There was this one boy, about seven years old, who came into the clubhouse with his parents," Abbott recalled. "He had only parts of two fingers on one hand. He asked me if kids were mean when I was growing up. He said they called him 'Crab' at camp. I said, 'Yeah, they used to say that my hand looks like a foot.' I said to him, 'Do you think that teasing is a problem?' He said, 'No.' I said, 'Is there anything you can't do?' And he said, 'No.' And I said, 'Well, I don't think so either.'

"Then I looked around the room and said to him, 'Look, I'm playing with guys like Dave Winfield and Wally Joyner and Dave Parker. I'm playing with them and I'm just like you.' I'd never said that before, that I was thrilled to be here and it didn't matter if I had two good hands. But I put myself into his shoes and remembered what I was like at his age. And I'm sure that kids need someone to relate to. But so do their parents. Most of the time I think it's my parents these people should be talking to, not me."

While there were surely grim moments in his background, much of it, he says, he has blocked out. Like, perhaps, his feelings of self-consciousness as he tried to hide the stub of his hand from view. Even now, perhaps subconsciously, his father said, he still sometimes does.

But Abbott, meanwhile, tries to look forward, not backward, which is why he has turned down numerous movie and book offers. "I'd hate to be held to what I said or thought when I was twenty-one years old," he said. "But anyway, a book on me would be boring. Like, 'Oh yeah, he pitched a great game.' Or, 'When he was losing with the Angels he got booed.' Not great literature."

It was near the end of day, the sun was setting behind the palm tree and the Christmas tree, and the Abbotts rose to get in some late Christmas shopping. They entered the apartment garage, where a set of his golf clubs in a red golf bag leaned against the wall. Abbott climbed behind the wheel of his cream-colored minivan. He was asked: Is there anything he can't do that he wished he could?

"Yes," he said, after a moment. "I'd love to play the piano."

[1992]

Trying to
Re-enter the Zone

W IN THE early morning sunlight, the baseball tossed into the cloudless blue sky looked like a mini-moon that had lost its way. It went up and up, sailing well over the head of the intended receiver, a middle-aged coach with a catcher's mitt. The strong, loose-limbed young pitcher who had thrown the ball watched the flight with some dismay. It was not the first time he had seen a ball take off as though it contained a maddening inner spring.

The young man and the coach were engaged in a casual long toss, separated by about 150 feet, in which a pitcher stretches his arm. They were alone last week on the outfield grass in a practice field of the St. Louis Cardinals' spring training complex in Jupiter, Florida. As the ball landed near the center-field fence, the young pitcher, Rick Ankiel, shrugged and called, slightly sheepishly, to the retrieving coach, "Too strong today."

Too strong, it turned out, for too many days. No one is quite sure what went wrong, but something went dreadfully wrong with Ankiel's pitching motion, as well as the circuitry in which the brain informs the arm of what it wishes it to do, consciously or subconsciously.

Ankiel's problems began in the playoffs last year and continued into this season. He would throw a ball over the catcher's head; pitches in games and even in warm-ups would slam with a terrible thud against the backstop, when they were not darting in the dirt five feet in front of the plate.

The habits and instincts of a lifetime abruptly vanished.

Later that day, Ankiel's Cardinal teammates of just a month ago battled the Cincinnati Reds at home in Busch Stadium. It would normally have been Ankiel's turn in the starting rotation. Just three years ago he signed a bonus contract out of high school for $2.5 million. He won the Carolina League Pitcher of the Year award in his first professional season, the Minor League Player of the Year award in his second, and then, last year in his third season, he won the National League Rookie Pitcher of the Year award.

Ankiel, a twenty-one-year-old left-hander from nearby Port St. Lucie, Florida, who can throw a ninety-five-mile-an-hour fastball, had made the journey from here to St. Louis brilliantly, but he would not make it on this day. And as a ballplayer, there is the possibility that he may never make it again.

The muscle memory, or simply the requisite concentration, of other ballplayers has similarly come unraveled. Most famously and astonishingly, Steve Blass, a veteran All-Star pitcher, woke up one morning in the early 1970s and could not find the plate. He never did. Von McDaniel was a rookie pitching sensation with the Cardinals in 1957, but the control he had confidently shown disappeared forever overnight the next season.

In recent times, second baseman Steve Sax and Chuck Knoblauch each discovered one day that he could no longer throw accurately to first base. And Mark Wohlers, an ace reliever with the Braves, began out of the blue to throw wildly; he went to the minor leagues and has made a comeback with the Reds, where this season he is 2–1 with a shaky 4.50 earned run average in relief.

Ankiel began this season with the Cardinals, but, picking up disastrously from last year's playoffs, he was wild in the first month of the season. The Cardinals sent him to their Class AAA

77

farm club in Memphis to try to regain his confidence and his control, but he continued throwing baseballs as if he had never held one before.

After three terrible starts with the Memphis Redbirds—in the last two he could not complete the first inning—he was sent to the Cardinals' extended spring training camp, where low-level minor leaguers work on their fundamentals before starting an abbreviated season. He will be here indefinitely, according to Walt Jocketty, the Cardinals' general manager.

Ankiel was put under the special supervision of Mark Riggins, the Cardinals' minor league pitching coordinator.

"I'm just trying to get it right," Ankiel said, in a kind of mantra, to reporters here. He displays a polite and pleasant disposition. His sandy hair is dyed with blond streaks, there is a small shrub of whisker on his chin, and his eyes are both playful and wary.

How does the arm feel? "Outstanding," he said, with a jaunty air that he often maintains.

How does he deal with this turn of events? "Day by day," he said.

Does he ever feel lonely on the mound, as some pitchers have testified? "Lonely?" he repeated. "No. The pitcher controls the game."

For good or bad?

He did not reply but gave a look out of the corner of his eye that said, suspiciously, What are you getting at?

Was he frightened about his future? Was he embarrassed at having to be sent here? These were matters, it was obvious, he would not talk about. But someone in the Cardinals organization who is close to Ankiel said, "If you built a building, and the building collapsed, how would you feel?"

The slide began for Ankiel when he opened the National League East playoff series against Atlanta last October 3. He had finished the season with an 11–7 record and led the team with a 3.70 ERA. Down the stretch drive in September, he responded beautifully to pressure, posting a 4–0 record and a 1.97 ERA.

Against the Braves in the first round of the playoffs, and against the Mets in the League Championship Series, in which he started one game and relieved in another, he walked eleven batters in four innings. He threw nine wild pitches, the majority of them flung ten feet over the batters' heads. In just one inning against the Braves, he threw five wild pitches, breaking a record for ineptitude that had stood since 1890.

When he was taken out in the first inning of his start against the Mets, Ankiel told Cardinals Manager Tony La Russa, "I can't feel the ball."

Ankiel won his first regular-season game against Arizona this spring, pitching well and in control. The next game, against Houston, he walked five, including three straight in the second inning, and struck out six in five innings.

The next game, Ankiel's last in the big leagues, was on May 11 at home against the Pirates. By the top of the fourth inning, he had thrown five pitches to the backstop. His first two pitches to the leadoff hitter in the fourth hit the backstop. At that point, La Russa removed him from the game. "He was upset when he left," La Russa said, "and I don't blame him." Later that day the Cardinals sent Ankiel to Memphis.

In the announcer's booth in the ballpark that day was Blass, now a television analyst for the Pirates. "It was chilling," Blass recalled. "He just had no idea what he was doing out there. And I saw him last year when he was one of the outstanding pitchers in the league.

"When you're on your game, your mind is locked into the game, into what you are doing, as Rick's was. Nothing else exists. Then when you start going bad, your mind plays different tricks. You hear everything going on in the ballpark. Things in the stands you never heard before, you hear now. And when you go into your motion, you lose all concentration. It's like you freeze before you release the ball. It's kind of a psychotic thing.

"Nobody knows how it starts and, for me, no one knew how to correct it."

79

Blass was asked if this kind of failure is more physical or mental. "It begins with the mental," he said, "and a loss of confidence. Then all your pitching mechanics become affected."

After last season, Ankiel said he believed that he was not following through enough when he released the ball. Then his footwork was analyzed, his grip scrutinized. Riggins suggested to Ankiel recently that he was dropping his elbow too low before throwing the ball.

A fan wrote that he should try pitching blindfolded. Someone else thought a CAT scan might produce some interesting results. How about hypnosis? Acupuncture? A St. Louis letter writer thought if he became a temporary minor league pitching coach he could get his mind off his own problems. "It would let him see the trees for the forest," the letter said.

Ankiel's agent, Scott Boras, had him spend time with Harvey Dorfman, a sports psychologist. Apparently they are still in touch. Dorfman has tried to get Ankiel to focus on executing one pitch at a time, regardless of the situation, be it a playoff encounter or a meaningless game.

A New York psychiatrist, Isaac Steven Herschkopf, whose patients have included professional athletes but not Ankiel, said sometimes a person suffers a significant loss but is unable to express his emotions verbally or even to comprehend their depth. The odd pattern of suddenly being unable to do something you have done with relative ease your whole life sometimes "emerges in a nonverbal situation," he said.

If Ankiel has endured such a significant loss, it might be the divorce of his parents, which occurred last summer, or the nearly six-year sentence in a federal prison that his father, Richard Sr., received in May 2000 after he pleaded guilty to two counts of conspiracy to possess cocaine and marijuana with intent to distribute. Although Richard Ankiel, Sr., has had a long history of encounters with the law, he and Rick have maintained a close relationship. He was Rick's coach on Little League teams and even called

Rick's pitches during high school games, to the consternation of the coaches.

Ankiel said his father remained a valued adviser as he made his way through the minors to St. Louis. "Sometimes after I'd had a bad outing," he said, "I'd call my dad and he hadn't seen the game, but he knew me so well that he'd say something like, 'You're hurrying your delivery.' And he was usually right."

Ankiel still speaks regularly with his father and, he says, "I talk with my mom every day. Every day."

The pitching coach of the Memphis Redbirds, Dyar Miller, said of Ankiel: "I think it would be good for Rick to open up a little bit. He's a good kid. He's just kind of hard to talk to about certain things. "He gives you the impression he wants you to think everything's okay. But deep down inside, there are some problems. And I think that's natural for a kid from his environment."

In a game, Miller said, it seems that Ankiel "suffers an anxiety attack, or whatever you call it."

The day before Ankiel and his coach did their long toss in the outfield, Ankiel, on a practice field alongside a scattering of palm trees, pitched in a simulated game on the practice field. Two minor leaguers took turns hitting. Some of the other young hopefuls in camp made it a point to sit in the dugout and watch. "Wow," said one, as a slider dipped in and the batter swung and missed. "You see that?"

Ankiel's pitching motion, smooth and graceful, is distinctive. His left knee rises almost to his chin, and his eyes peer over it for an instant like a small boy at a lunch counter. Then his arm whips out and the ball suddenly tears like a meteor toward the plate. Ankiel was having a good day; there was not a solid blow struck against him. When one pitch bounced in front of the plate, he hissed an expletive, but otherwise he showed little emotion.

Riggins stood watching a short distance behind Ankiel. "Beautiful," he said after another pitch. "There you go."

After several such innings, the simulated game was over.

Ankiel had thrown well. But Riggins and others had seen this before, in St. Louis and in Memphis, when Ankiel threw well in practice until he was thrust into a game situation. Then, as Blass had noted, Ankiel's "brain seemed to freeze."

What next for Ankiel? On Sunday, in an exhibition game against Montreal Expos minor league rookies, he pitched four innings of no-hit ball. On June 15 the St. Louis minor leaguers will begin play in rookie leagues in Tennessee and New Jersey. Ankiel may or may not join them. It depends on what chances the Cardinals are prepared to take with Ankiel, and what he is comfortable with. His career might very well hang in the balance.

Before Ankiel left Memphis for Florida, the Redbirds' manager, Gaylen Pitts, said: "He'd throw some pretty good pitches, then he'd get out of whack. Who knows who's got the key to the lock?"

Throwing in the sunny outfield here last week, Ankiel's face dripped with sweat as he and his lengthening shadow now pitched the standard distance, sixty feet six inches, to his squatting coach. Throwing mostly strikes, Ankiel's fastball time and again cracked like a pistol shot into the catcher's mitt. For those moments, at least, the key surely had been found.

[2001]

FIRST

AND GOAL

The Minority
Quarterback

 A LATE summer morning and the sun was already harsh on the dusty high school football field in Baton Rouge, Louisiana. The shirtless blond nineteen-year-old in shorts stained with sweat kept dropping back to pass, his hands at times so wet it was hard to grip the ball. He was throwing to a friend, working "up the ladder," as it is called, starting with short passes and ending long.

But his mind wasn't totally on his receiver. He could feel the eyes of the man in the dark glasses who sat in a car on the other side of a chain-link fence, a hundred yards away. The boy knew the man was watching. It had been subtly arranged. The National Collegiate Athletic Association does not allow tryouts, but if a college coach happens by a field where kids regularly throw the ball around, well, a coach may argue, where's the harm?

At that time, in July of 1996, Southern University, a football powerhouse among black colleges, desperately needed a quarterback, and the boy, Marcus Jacoby, badly needed a place to play quarterback. After half an hour, the man in dark glasses, Mark Orlando, Southern's offensive coordinator, had seen enough and drove off.

It had gone well. The boy was invited to the coach's apartment, where after a short visit he was offered a full football scholarship. The coach explained that the boy had a shot at the starting job, that the intended starter's poor grades had lost him his place on the team, and that the two backups did not have the coaches' confidence.

"Sounds good," Jacoby, who had been a star at Catholic High, one of Baton Rouge's schoolboy powers, recalled saying. "But I have to think about it—talk with my parents."

"Practice starts in four days," the coach responded. "We're going to need an answer soon."

Marcus Jacoby was unaware that if he accepted the scholarship, he would be the first white to play quarterback for Southern University. And he would be the first white to start at quarterback in the seventy-six-year history of the black Southwestern Athletic Conference. Jacoby had grown up in Baton Rouge, and yet he knew practically nothing about Southern, had never even been to the other side of town to see the campus. Until that July day he had spent his life surrounded by whites.

Southern's head coach, Pete Richardson, worked out of a modest wood-paneled office lined with trophies. In his three years there he had turned a laughingstock into a national force. Southern won eleven of twelve games his first year, 1993, and two years later it was the number one black college football team in the nation.

It is not easy for a black man to become a head coach. Despite his record, Richardson, fifty-four, has never had an offer from one of the 114 Division I-A colleges; only three of them have black head football coaches.

In college he played at the University of Dayton, hardly a major football school, and though he had limited natural talent, he reached the professional level, playing three years for the Buffalo Bills. He coached high school ball for a few years, then took the head coach job at Winston-Salem State in North Carolina. Finally, in 1993, he got his big break at Southern, which with its combined campuses is the largest historically black college in the nation.

"I can't get caught up with the thought that, 'Hey, why shouldn't I be at Notre Dame?'" he said in an interview. "I can't get sidetracked or go around with a chip on my shoulder." He is a stoical man and expected stoicism from his players.

That day in his office, the Jacobys said, they were impressed by his quiet intellect, the way he measured his words, his determination. Indeed, the president of Southern, Dr. Dorothy Spikes, often said that she had hired Richardson over better-known candidates not just because his teams had been winners but because of his reputation for integrity, for running a clean program.

Coach Richardson and the Jacobys discussed everything from Southern's rich athletic tradition to the engineering courses that interested Marcus, but for a long while they didn't mention the thing that worried the parents most. The quarterback is team leader. Would a black team accept a white leader? Would the black campus? The night before, at the Jacobys' home in the upper-middle-class white Tara section of Baton Rouge, talk had become heated. "What if they don't like Marcus?" Marian Jacoby had said, tears in her eyes. "What if there's some kind of . . . action?" Marcus had not been able to sleep he was so upset.

Now his father, Glen, an environmental engineer, asked the coach, "How are you going to protect my son?"

The room went silent, Glen Jacoby said later. "I realize that you're concerned," Richardson began, "but I just don't think it will be that big a deal. Sure, there will be some adjustments from all sides. But Marcus will have the backing of the administration as well as the coaching staff." Coach Richardson pointed out that there were other minorities on campus. He meant that of the 10,500 students, 5 percent were not black, but Mrs. Jacoby kept thinking about how it would feel to be in a stadium with her husband amid 30,000 black fans.

The coach didn't say it to the Jacobys, but no one knew better than he about the strain Marcus would feel being in the minority. As a successful black man, Richardson was used to the stares of surprise. "Walking into a place with a suit and tie on, you're always going to get that second look because you're not supposed to be there." When he coached at Winston-Salem, he drove a state government car. "Whites look at you and ask you what you're doing driving the state's car," he said. "You pull over to get some gas and people will address you the wrong way or policemen will look at you funny."

There was something else Richardson didn't say that morning: He was well aware how hostile Southern's fans could be to any newcomer, regardless of creed or color. Many had not wanted him hired. They felt he had come from too small a college; they had wanted a big name in black college football. They had even used race on him. Shortly after he arrived, a rumor started that Richardson's wife, who is light-skinned, was white, and that his white offensive coordinator was his wife's brother. None of it true, but Richardson didn't let it get to him. He knew the best answer was to win, and since he had done so, he was—as Southern's registrar, Marvin Allen, liked to point out—a campus god.

The coach thought he could make this Jacoby thing work. He wasn't sitting there fretting about whether Marcus could learn to be part of the minority. The first game was only six weeks away. As he would say later, he didn't have "ample time to find another black quarterback." Marcus would have to do what all good players did, what the coach himself had done: suck it up.

To reassure the Jacobys, the coach told them about his staff. Of six assistants he had hired when he started in 1993, two were white, one Asian. He was told Southern fans would never stand for that. But after his 11–1 debut season—the year earlier they had been 6–5—a popular T-shirt on campus featured a photo of the integrated staff, with the phrase "In Living Color."

The parents wanted to think about it overnight, but Marcus did not. He climbed into his Jeep, he said later, and went riding. He was getting his shot, finally. There was nothing he loved like football. As a boy, when he couldn't find a friend, he tossed footballs into lined-up garbage cans in his yard. His parents held him back in ninth grade so he would have time to grow and a better chance to play high school ball. After starring at Catholic, he went to Louisiana Tech, but there, prospects for playing were dim.

Now he envisioned a game night at Southern with a crowd cheering as he threw yet another touchdown pass. When he stopped at a red light, he lifted his head and at the top of his lungs screamed, "Praise God!"

From the Jacobys' home, Southern was a twenty-minute car trip, literally to the other side of the tracks. On the ride to the first practice, as he drove over the Hump—the small hill that is one of the barriers between Southern and white Baton Rouge—the momentousness of what he had done began sinking in. As he looked around, he began imagining himself playing a game, he recalled. "Would I see a white face?"

Southern's decision to sign a white quarterback made headlines, first locally, then nationally, and the reaction of some whites he knew startled him. When Jacoby called his girlfriend to talk about it, her mother answered. "The niggers over there will kill you," he recalled her saying. "There are bullets flying all over the place. It's a war zone." When his girlfriend got on the phone, she said, "Marcus, I don't want you to call me again." To many on the white side of town, who had never visited this campus bustling with middle-class black students on the bluffs of the Mississippi, it was as if Jacoby had voluntarily moved to the ghetto.

Like many white Americans, he knew there was still prejudice—though, he says, not at home. He had been raised to believe that, after generations of injustice, the country was now a fair place when it came to race—a level playing field, so to speak—and he had made a few black friends while playing high school ball.

The Jacobys were considered a little eccentric for Baton Rouge, having moved here from California when Marcus was three. His paternal grandfather was Jewish. His mother had attended Berkeley in the 1960s and still had some of the flower child in her. She was a fitness buff and had even tried putting her family on a vegetarian diet, stocking the refrigerator with so many oat products that Marcus's buddies asked whether they owned a horse. Marcus and his sister at first attended a private school, but their mother felt too many children there were spoiled by wealth. So she taught them at home for five years, until Marcus was a sophomore.

Friends and teachers at Catholic High remember him as hardworking, smart, and moralistic, with a strong Christian bent. "We'd make fun of his being so innocent," said John Eric Sullivan, one of his best friends. "By that I mean, he didn't do anything that most normal high school kids are doing. He'd be, 'Watch out, watch yourself,' when guys would be drinking. We'd say, like, 'Marc, relax, man.'" He told them he was waiting until he was twenty-one to drink.

The Southern coaches were impressed with his arm and had never seen a quarterback learn Coach Richardson's complex offense so fast. Jacoby stayed after practice to do extra throwing and often studied game films well past midnight. Southern at times uses a no-huddle offense, meaning the quarterback has to call plays rapidly right at the line, and Coach Richardson felt that of the three candidates, only Marcus Jacoby knew the system well enough to do that. Within days of arriving, he was first string.

That sparked anger among many of his new black teammates. For over a year they had been friendly with the two quarterbacks now relegated to backup, and they resented the newcomer, complaining that he had not earned his stripes. "He was *given* his stripes," said Virgil Smothers, a lineman. "There was a lingering bitterness."

Several felt the decision was racial. "It just became the fact that we were going to have this white quarterback," said Sam George, a quarterback prospect who was academically ineligible that year. "It wasn't about ability no more." Teammates picked at Jacoby's weaknesses—he didn't have "fast feet" and rarely scrambled—and joked that he was the typical bland white athlete, which angered Coach Richardson. "A lot of minorities, they want the flash," the coach said. "We felt we needed a system in order to be successful and a quarterback to operate within the confines of that system."

Except for the coaches, he was isolated. In the locker room, Jacoby recalled, "I would walk around the corner and people would just stop talking." Even in the huddles there was dissension. Scott Cloman, a Southern receiver, recalled: "The minute Marcus was like, 'Everybody calm down, just shut up,' they were like: 'Who are you talking to? You're not talking to me.' You know, stuff like that. If it was a black person it wouldn't be a problem. They all felt that 'I'm not going to let a white person talk to me like that.'"

His entire time at Southern, Jacoby kept his feelings about all this inside, "sucking it up," repeatedly telling the inquiring reporters what a great experience it was being exposed to a new culture. "As soon as I signed and walked onto the campus," he told one interviewer, "I felt like part of the family. I definitely feel at home here."

On September 7, 1996, Southern opened at Northwestern State, with Marcus Jacoby at quarterback. Of the 25,000 spectators, half had made the three-hour trip from Southern, not unusual for this football-crazy place. "Fans plan their lives around games," Coach Richardson said. "They fight to get schedules, to see where we're going to play so they can take holidays and go to games."

Southern University families like the Morgans will take more than twenty people to an away game, filling several hotel rooms. Mo Morgan, a supervisor at the local Exxon plant who attended Southern in the 1960s, went so far as to buy a motor home just for Southern football, which made him the object of good-natured ribbing. Friends insisted that "black people don't drive Winnebagos." His wife, Wanda, and about twenty-five of their relatives are Southern graduates, and his youngest son, Jabari, a freshman drummer and cymbals player, was on the field for that same opening game.

For the youngest Morgan, the band was only partly about music. More famous than Southern's football team—having performed at five Super Bowls and three presidential inaugurations—

it had real power and importance on campus. The 180-piece Southern band thrived on intimidating lesser rivals on the black college circuit. With its hard-brass sound and its assertive style, the group had a militant edge that old-timers on campus attributed to the influence of the civil rights era, when the band's show was honed.

Robert Gray, who played cymbals with Morgan, said: "When people think about Southern band, they think about a bunch of big, tough-looking, tight-looking dudes with psychotic looks on their faces, ready to go to war. I just think—Southern band—black, all male, just rowdy, loud."

Families like the Morgans were fiercely proud of their school and its role in helping generations of blacks into the middle and professional classes—even if the state had long treated it as second-rate. In the early 1900s, legislators planning to create a new campus for Southern considered several locations around Louisiana. But in city after city, white residents rose in protest, and finally the state settled on a site that no one else then coveted. In the 1950s, blacks like Audrey Nabor-Jackson, Wanda Morgan's aunt, were prohibited from attending the big white public campus across town, Louisiana State University. Southern was their only alternative.

Even as late as the 1970s, Louisiana's public higher education system was capable of inflicting deep racial wounds. Wanda Morgan was required to take several courses at LSU as part of a master's program at Southern. In one class she was one of four blacks, and for every exam, she said, the four were removed by the professor and put in an empty classroom across the hall, one in each corner, while the white students took the exam in their regular seats. The message was missed by no one: black students would cheat.

By the mid-1990s, change was brewing. The year before Jacoby arrived, Southern and LSU settled a twenty-year-old federal desegregation lawsuit. Both institutions pledged sharp minority increases on their campuses, with 10 percent of enrollment set aside for other races—more whites to Southern, more blacks to LSU. Alumni like the Morgans were worried. Would Southern soon become just another satellite campus of LSU? Was the white quarterback the beginning of the end?

Mo Morgan and Audrey Nabor-Jackson agreed with an editorial in Southern's student paper saying that a white quarterback did not belong. "There are plenty of young black athletes," it said, "who could benefit from Jacoby's scholarship." Mo Morgan said, "I didn't like the fact that he was there." About the only Morgan not upset was Jabari. Mo Morgan worried that his eighteen-year-old son was not race-conscious enough. "I came through the movement, I was confronted with things," said the father. "That's one of the things that concerns me—that he hasn't." But it didn't concern Jabari Morgan—he was consumed with the band. Long before starting college, he had begun assembling on his bedroom wall what he called his shrine, a montage about the Southern band that included a picture of the first white band member, in the early 1990s.

Now, in his freshman year, his long-nurtured fantasy was coming true. Standing there that day with cymbals weighing nine pounds each, ready to march into Northwestern State's stadium, he was at the front of the band. The director, Dr. Isaac Greggs, always positioned his tallest and most imposing players—his "towers of terror"—at the front, and Jabari Morgan, at six foot one, was one of them. Football, he said, was about the last thing on this mind.

"It was like winning the lottery." He wouldn't have cared if Marcus Jacoby were purple, as long as Southern won and people stayed in their seats for the halftime show.

Southern lost its first two games. The team was young—ten of eleven offensive starters were new—but what people remembered was the 11–1 record the year before. For fans, the quarterback, more than any other player, is the team—hero or goat. During the second loss, Jacoby recalled, "I heard the entire stadium booing me."

Jean Harrison, the mother of the quarterback prospect Sam George, remembered, "One lady had a megaphone and she was screaming, 'Get that white honky out of there!' It made you sick."

Chris Williams, an offensive lineman, believed that the other team hit Jacoby harder because he was white: "Teams took cheap shots at him. I really believe that. I mean they hit him sometimes blatantly late after the whistle." Scott Cloman recalled that after one Southern loss, opposing players said, "That's what you all get for bringing white boys on the field."

Jacoby was hit so hard and so often during the first game that he was hospitalized with a concussion. Glen Jacoby, Marcus's father, was sure the blockers were sandbagging their white quarterback, but in interviews at the time, the young man denied it. He still says he believes that it was just the mistakes of an inexperienced line.

After Southern's second loss, an angry fan threatened Jacoby. A coach had to jump between them. For the rest of his career, Jacoby would have a police escort at games. There was a disturbance outside the stadium at another game. Gunshots were fired. Jacoby recalls thinking the shots were aimed at him. They were not.

The Tuesday after the second loss, Jacoby rose at 5 A.M., worked out in the weight room, then walked to the cafeteria for the team breakfast. No one was there. He checked his watch. Shortly after he sat down, Coach Orlando came in, took him by the arm, and led him through a nearby door. As Jacoby remembered it, the entire team and coaching staff sat squeezed into a small room. All chairs were taken, so he stood alone against a wall. No one looked at him. Coach Richardson stood. "I think Marcus should know what's going on," he said, adding, "Who wants to say something?"

Virgil Smothers, the senior defensive end, rose. The night before, he had talked about staging a strike. Now he mentioned some minor gripes, then added: "We're losing and we feel changes ought to be made. Some guys aren't getting a fair chance."

Someone else said, "Guys are playing who shouldn't."

Coach Orlando walked to the front. As offensive coordinator he naturally worked closely with the quarterback. But several players felt he favored Jacoby because they were both white. "Let's get this in the open," Orlando said, adding, "This is mostly about Jacoby, isn't it?" Insisting that the quarterback had been chosen fairly, he said: "You have to accept Marcus, he's one of us. We're 0 and 2, but we have to put this behind us."

Lionel Hayes, who had lost the quarterback job to Jacoby, interrupted Coach Orlando. "You're just saying that," Mr. Hayes said, "because you're Jacoby's Dad." It got a laugh, though his tone was angry. Jacoby said later: "There was a lot of hate in that room. I felt like I was falling into a hole, and I couldn't grab the sides."

Coach Richardson spoke again: "We win as a team, we lose as a team. Jacoby's doing what he's supposed to be doing, and he'll get better. We all will." He said practice would be at three. "If anyone doesn't want to be on the team with Jacoby as the starting quarterback, don't come."

Richardson remembered: "What I saw was a frustration by some players—mostly seniors—who weren't playing. They weren't playing because they didn't deserve to. And so they needed a scapegoat."

Jacoby remembers feeling like the invisible man. "It was almost as though I weren't there, and they were talking about me," he said. "I wasn't sure where to turn. I felt they didn't want me there—not me personally, but any white quarterback—that I was just another problem."

Three or four players didn't show up for practice, and Coach Richardson cut them. Not long afterward, Virgil Smothers and one of the coaches argued, and Smothers was told, "Clear out your locker."

When the players gathered the next day at practice, before the coaches arrived, Jacoby said, he stood to talk. A few tried to shout him down, but John Williams, a star senior cornerback and devout

Christian who would go on to play for the Baltimore Ravens, rose and said, "Man, let the man talk."

"I don't care if you like me or hate me," Jacoby recalled saying. "All I ask is that we can go out and play football together. This is not a popularity contest. I'm trying to win. I'm just trying to be your quarterback."

Things improved dramatically. Southern won six of its next seven games, beating the two top-ranked black colleges, and was invited to the Heritage Bowl in Atlanta, the black college championship. "I wasn't getting booed nearly as much," Jacoby said. Some teammates began warming to him. More than anything, they were impressed by his work ethic. During a practice break, players drank from a garden hose. "Sorry, Marcus," one teased, "this is the black water fountain." They called him "Tyrone," and "Rasheed."

"I appreciated it," he recalled. "Things had changed to the extent that some of the players were calling me 'the man.'"

Before games, he and John Williams prayed together. One Sunday the two went to the black church where Williams was a minister. Occasionally strangers would wish Jacoby well. One day the band's legendary director, Dr. Greggs, greeted him warmly and urged him to persevere.

He felt he was developing real friendships with teammates and Southern students. When Scott Cloman needed a place to stay for a month, Jacoby had him to his parents' home and the two grew close. "Marcus was the first white person I ever really got to know," Cloman said. "I always felt a lot of tension around whites. I'd go into a store and I could just feel the tension. Sometimes you just feel like, 'I can't stand white people.' I didn't understand them. I really didn't want to be near them."

"His parents treated me like a son," added Cloman. Some players now joked when they saw him, "Where's your brother?"

"And some," he said, "called me 'white lover.' Didn't bother me. I had come to understand the Jacobys. A lot of times people fear what they can't understand. Because of being around the Ja-cobys, my attitude toward whites in general changed."

At the Heritage Bowl that first year, on national television, Southern took a 24–10 halftime lead against Howard University, then fell behind, 27–24. In the closing minute, Southern drove to Howard's fifteen-yard line. On third down, with forty-two seconds left, Marcus Jacoby dropped back and, under pressure, threw off the wrong foot, floating a pass into the end zone.

"I heard the crowd gasp," he said. "I couldn't believe this was happening." He'd been intercepted. "Their fans must have cheered, but I remember everything being silent." A camera captured Coach Richardson on his knees, hands over his head.

"I dragged myself off the field and sat on a bench and buried my head in my arms," Jacoby said. "A few people, like John Williams, came by and patted me on the back, to be encouraging. But I heard, 'You screwed up real bad this time, Whitey,' and, 'You're as dumb as they come.' It was the lowest point of my life."

After the game, Coach Orlando received an anonymous call: "If Jacoby ever plays for Southern again, we'll kill him—and you." The coach said he averaged a threat a week that season. Later, as Coach Orlando and Jacoby headed to their cars, the coach pointed to several trees. In the light of the street lamps, Jacoby could see a yellow rope hung from each tree. The ropes were tied in nooses.

On campus, Jacoby struggled with all the daily irritations that go with being in the minority. As a white who grew up among whites, he was used to being inconspicuous. Here he always felt on display. "I hated that," he said, "because it was like I had become just a novelty act."

He found that things he had done unconsciously all his life were suddenly brought to his attention and analyzed. One was the way he dressed. He liked to wear a T-shirt, shorts, and flip-flops to class; most students at Southern dressed up for class in slacks. Another was that the way he spoke, his slang, was different from

the black majority's. "Many times I would say something at Southern and they would repeat it and I wouldn't get my point across,"
he said. "It would get lost in the mocking of how I said it instead
of what I said. I might walk into a room and I'd say, 'Hey, how y'all
doin'?'" Instead of answering, someone would do an imitation of a
white person talking, enunciating slowly. "They'd say 'Hi, guy, how
are you doing?' So I just learned to say, 'Hey.'" He believed the
classmates were only needling him, but being constantly reminded was exhausting.

"People's eyes were on him," said Chris Williams, a teammate,
"He just didn't blend in. I mean, like me, I just blended in wherever I went."

A white with a different personality might have fared better.
There was one other white on the seventy-man squad, Matt
Bushart. And though as a punter he was at the periphery of the
team and little noticed by fans, Bushart had the personality and
experience possibly to cope better as a minority. While Marcus
had seemed protected and naive even to the middle-class white
students at Catholic High, Matt's years at a local public high
school where most of his football teammates were black had
taught him how to live comfortably among them. While Marcus
was more introspective, a little too sensitive for some of his
coaches' tastes, Matt was noisy, funny, sometimes crude—so out-
going, his girlfriend said, that he could talk to a wall.

When Bushart's teammates made fun of the country music he
liked, he gave it right back to them about their rap, and kept listening to his music. "I get kidded about it," he said, "but there's
been a song that's been playing and one of the black guys will
come by and say, 'Play that again, that's actually not too bad.'"

Jacoby loved music too; playing guitar was an important outlet
for relieving the pressure, but he would not play on campus. As he
put it: "At times the rap just blared from the dorms; I longed for
something that was my own. I couldn't play it on campus because
for most of the time I was apologizing for who I was. I didn't want

to cause any more turmoil than there was. I didn't want to make myself look like I was any more separate than I was."

Interracial dating is complicated at Southern. Ryan Lewis, Jacoby's roommate, says most black men would not openly date a white woman on campus. "They would keep it low so nobody knew about it but them," Lewis said. "I've never seen it."

As quarterback, Jacoby often had female students flirting with him. He felt uneasy, caught between the white and black sides of town. Among whites, he said, "everybody just assumed the worst, that I was dating a black girl now because I was at Southern." But even though there were some "gorgeous light-skinned black girls over there," he said, and a couple of women from his classes became good friends, he wasn't attracted. He thinks it was "a cultural thing."

Though college students are confronted with new ideas—sometimes only partially understood—and encouraged to speak out about them, Jacoby felt that when he did, he was criticized. At first, in his African-American literature class, when they discussed slavery, he said he tried to be conciliatory in an oral report. "I would say something like, 'I can't imagine how terrible it must have been, that people could do those kinds of things to other people.' And others in the class made some kind of jokes, but it was like bitter jokes: 'What are you talking about, Marcus? You're one of those whites.' It was like they were saying to me, 'Quit Uncle Tomming.'"

Then he worried he wasn't being true to his white roots. "I felt that I had lost my pride and the respect of friends that I had grown up with," he said. For his next oral report, he decided to speak his mind and said that it was unhealthy for blacks to dwell too much on past racial violence. "There have been tragedies like slavery throughout time," he said. "I don't think one is more important than any other." When he finished, he recalled, "there was an eerie silence and I saw at least three or four people glaring at me."

Increasingly, being in the minority alienated him, made him feel alone. "I learned early on that I was a pioneer in all this and no one else had gone through it, and often the best advice I could get was from myself. Because I was the only one who knew the whole situation."

It didn't help that his preoccupied parents were going through a divorce. At one point when he was upset about not fitting in, his mother gave him a copy of *Black Like Me,* the story of a white man in the 1960s who dyes his skin and travels the South to experience being black during segregation. At the time, Jacoby said, "I resented my mother giving me the book. She was just trying to help me understand the other side, but I felt she was almost taking the other side."

Blacks, of course, are much better at being in the minority, since they have far more practice and, usually, no choice. When Jabari Morgan was considering colleges, his father told him he was free to pick Southern or a "white" college, but if he picked white, he had better be prepared. Then he gave him the talk about being in the minority that so many black American men give their sons. "You are going to face being called a nigger," Mo Morgan told Jabari. "Now, are you ready to deal with it? If you're not ready to deal with it, don't go."

The Morgans have a family council of elders that meets regularly to guide their young, and one message emphasized is this: "A black person in America has to be smarter and sharper and work harder to achieve the same things as a white person of the same abilities." Mo Morgan says, as a minority, he understands that "the majority is white, and you have control and you want to keep control."

But Jabari Morgan did not think like his father. He had always dreamed of attending Southern, but for him its great appeal was not as a racial sanctuary. He considered race simply part of the rough and tumble of life, the cost of doing business in a mostly white world. Southern was the place where he might be able to play in the best marching band in America, as his father had before him. He determined very early that the best high school marching bands, like the best college bands, were black, and so he fudged his address in order to attend a nearly all-black Baton Rouge school where the band rocked. He figured that that would give him an edge when he tried out at Southern.

As a marketing major who graduated in May, Morgan fully expects that he will one day work for a big white-controlled corporation. But as a marching band member at Southern for four years, he was in many ways the ultimate insider in the self-contained black-majority culture of the Yard, as Southern's campus is known. All the things that Marcus Jacoby found so foreign, and sometimes irritating, were second nature to Jabari Morgan—the music, the dress, the vernacular of put-downs and nicknames that is the campus currency. He loved African-American literature class because the poetry and stories reinforced what his family had taught him about black history.

Like all new band members, Morgan went through hazing. But as part of the majority, he never worried that it was about race. Jacoby, on the other hand, felt so unsettled as part of the minority that he often had trouble sleeping.

Morgan eventually joined a fraternity—a support in its own way as strong as the band's. And, where Marcus Jacoby the minority had no steady girlfriend during his years at Southern, Jabari Morgan the majority began, in his second semester, dating Monique Molizone, an economics major from New Orleans. She had also come to Southern partly for the band—to join the Dancing Dolls, who perform at the band's side.

As much as anything, what got Jacoby through his second year at Southern was a determination to avenge that Heritage Bowl interception, to show everyone—including himself—he could be a champion. He moved through the 1997 season with a passion, working so hard in the weight room that he could now bench-press 350 pounds; running endless drills to improve his foot speed; and doing so much extra throwing that by day's end it took an hour to ice and treat his arm.

Again he was first string, but he had competition. Sam George had returned from academic probation. George was a popular figure on campus, known not only for his hard-partying ways but for his small-man grit on the playing field. Though he was only five foot seven, he had a strong arm and terrific speed. His teammates, responding to his take-charge style in huddles, nicknamed him the Little General. "And," Scott Cloman said, "he was black."

Although Jacoby started, Coach Richardson liked bringing in George when the team seemed flat. Both quarterbacks saw race as the true reason behind the coach's substitutions. Jacoby was convinced that Richardson was giving the black quarterback playing time to pander to the black fans; George was convinced that Coach Richardson—influenced by Coach Orlando—was starting the white quarterback because of favoritism.

George wound up playing in five of twelve games. By Southern's third game, against Arkansas–Pine Bluff, both quarterbacks were bitter. After winning its first two games, Southern was losing to Pine Bluff 7–6 at the half. Coach Richardson decided to replace the white quarterback with the black. Jacoby was devastated; he felt he had proved effective and should not be yanked for one bad half.

Given his chance, George threw a last-ditch thirty-seven-yard pass that tied the game, and threw another touchdown in triple overtime for a 36–33 Southern win. And yet, come Monday practice, Jacoby was the starter again. Now George was frustrated.

Southern had a 9–1 record going into its two final games. A victory in the next game—the Bayou Classic, against Grambling, its archrival—would assure a return to the Heritage Bowl and a chance for Jacoby to redeem himself. His parents and teammates had never seen him so obsessed. He had trouble sleeping and little appetite. His father called Coach Orlando, worried that Marcus's weight was down.

In a journal account of that period, Marcus Jacoby wrote: "I sat down and wrote out a detailed plan of how I was going to get through these last two games, including my political and motivational moves. My survival as a person depended on these last two games. Nobody, including Coach Orlando, knew the amount of outside forces that were pressing on these last two games. I was at a point where I felt that I was crawling on my knees."

He added, "I dreamed of a time when I could just say that I had accomplished something, instead of fighting for respect, fighting in a classroom full of people who disagreed with everything I stood for, and could have a day of true rest."

Before the big game against Grambling, he pleaded with Coach Orlando. "If you don't pull me," Jacoby said, "I guarantee we'll win our next two games."

"You can't guarantee that," the coach said.

"I just did," Jacoby said. Coach Orlando suggested that if Marcus Jacoby played a little more like Sam George, sometimes scrambling out of the pocket, he might be more productive. Jacoby felt that he was being told to become something he was not, but he was so desperate, so nervous about being yanked, that he followed the advice. He scrambled, and it worked. In a 30–7 win against Grambling, Jacoby threw three touchdown passes and played the entire game. He was named the Bayou Classic's most valuable player.

A month later he achieved his redemption, throwing the winning pass in a 34–28 Heritage Bowl victory over South Carolina State, capping an 11–1 season that earned Southern the black national championship. "I was happier than I had ever been at Southern," he recalled. On the bus trip back from that game he slept soundly for the first time in months.

The more you achieve, the more is expected. After that 11–1 season, the talk on campus was that Southern would go undefeated in 1998. But in the opener, with the team trailing 7–0 at the half, Jacoby was pulled for George. Southern lost anyway, 28–7.

In practice on Tuesday, Jacoby overthrew a pass to one of his ends, John Forman, who yelled at him in front of everybody. Forman would say later that it was just the frustration of having lost the opener, but to Jacoby it was so much more—the final straw.

He was sure that Forman was trying to subvert his control of the team to help George, his roommate. "If you have a choice, you choose black first," Jacoby would later say. "I felt that I was all alone again, on an island by myself. It was like I was right back where I had started two years before, with a lot of the same attitudes against me."

He quit football and Southern.

Coach Richardson was surprised and asked Jacoby to stay. But more recently he said he understood the decision. Because of "the type person he is," the coach said, "it was the best thing for Marcus because it would have killed him." The coach meant that Marcus Jacoby was not emotionally equipped to continue being the solitary white.

When Branch Rickey of the Brooklyn Dodgers wanted to break major league baseball's color line in 1947, he chose Jackie Robinson, not simply because he was a great black ballplayer—there were greater black stars—but because he had experience inside white institutions. Jackie Robinson was twenty-eight that first year in the majors, a mature man who had attended UCLA and served in the army. He knew what it was like to be in the minority.

When Coach Richardson went after Jacoby, he was just looking for a quarterback.

Reporters hounded Jacoby to find why he had left, but he never spoke openly about it. He never mentioned race. In brief interviews he told them he was burned out, and in a sense this was true. He had burned out on being in the minority. And as a white, he didn't have to be. In those last months at Southern, he often thought about returning to a white life. "You kind of look over your shoulder and see your old life and you say, 'I could go back.'"

There had been such anguish over the Jacoby-George quarterback battle, and all its racial nuances, but at least on the field, in the end, it didn't seem to make much difference. That year Southern, with Sam George at the helm, finished 9–3, once again winning the Heritage Bowl.

A white quarterback at Southern did make people think. Mo

Morgan had been against it, but not after watching Jacoby at practices. "I looked at the three quarterbacks that were there, and he was the best at the time. I'm just telling you straight out. It wasn't his ability, and I'm not saying he was brighter than the other kids. He just put in the work."

Morgan's son Jabari said he, too, was sorry to see Jacoby go; he liked the idea of a white guy being open to attending a black college. This past year, as a senior, Jabari Morgan reached out to a white freshman tuba player, Grant Milliken, who tried out for the band. He helped him through the hazing. One of Morgan's friends said he had done it because Milliken was white, but Morgan said no, he had done it because Milliken was really good on tuba.

Morgan even helped Milliken create a dance solo full of shakes and shivers and fancy steps, which was performed at half-times to wild applause. What the crowd loved, said Morgan, was not just that a white guy could dance. "The whole point of letting the white guy dance is that we were saying to the world, 'Hey, you can learn our culture just like we can learn yours.'"

Morgan's father continues to be both fearful of his son's more relaxed attitude about race and a little in awe of it. "He doesn't think it's something he can't overcome," said Mo Morgan, "and you know, I think he's right. You can get caught up in this, and it will screw up your thinking."

One weekend last fall, at the request of a reporter, Jacoby went to a Southern game for the first time since quitting. This was Homecoming Day, and from his seat in the stands he watched Southern seniors and their families being introduced to the crowd at midfield. It could have been his moment. Ryan Lewis, his old roommate, was there, and so was Matt Bushart, the white punter. Bushart's name was called, to applause. Jacoby had read in the newspaper Bushart's saying how much he had enjoyed Southern.

The team had won seven straight games at that point, and so Jacoby was surprised during the first quarter when Southern's starting quarterback was replaced after throwing an interception. Jacoby had always been so sure he'd been replaced with Sam

George to pander to fans; now Coach Richardson was using the same strategy with two black quarterbacks. In the paper the next day, Richardson said he had just been trying to light a spark under the offense.

After the game, outside the stadium, a large black man spotted Jacoby and, extending his hand, said, "Hi, Marcus, how ya doin'?"

"Okay, Virgil," Jacoby said. "How you doin'?" The two chatted for a moment outside the stadium—the man said he had left school and was working as an account executive for a drug company—then they went their separate ways.

"That was Virgil Smothers," Jacoby said afterward. It was Smothers who had led the aborted strike against Jacoby. "I guess he figures it's all in the past."

It was not all in the past for Jacoby. Though he had moved on—he was now majoring in finance at LSU—his Southern experience still unsettled him. "Just last night I had a dream about it," he said. "Weird dreams. Like some of these people are coming back to haunt me in some way. By these people I mean some of those who I considered friends and who I felt kind of turned on me."

At times he talks about being lucky to have experienced another culture; at others he describes it as "a personal hell." His sister Dana says, "There are some scars that haven't gone away, from the bad things."

After leaving Southern, Jacoby took a while to realize how much pressure he had felt. "I remember one time a few months after I quit—and this was part of the healing process—I said something about country music, that I liked it. And I remember standing around with four white people and thinking, 'Oh, my God, I can't believe I just said that.' And then I caught myself right before I got through that whole thing in my mind and I looked at the people's faces and they were agreeing with me. I went 'Whoa,' I didn't have to apologize for that anymore."

These days he appreciates walking around anonymously on the mostly white LSU campus. "I got burned out as far as being somebody," he said. "At LSU I've just enjoyed being a part of the crowd."

[2000]

Sections of this story about the Morgan family were reported by Kirk Johnson.

A Life Without Blockers

♥ HE IS still asked on the street, "Hey, Riggo, how's Sandy baby?" And John Riggins must answer in all candor: "Don't know. Haven't seen her lately." And he still hasn't heard from her, either, even after sending a dozen roses as an apology to her at her Supreme Court office.

The apology came after the last time—the only time—he saw her, almost seven years ago, in January 1985, when Riggins, then a star running back for the Washington Redskins and the hero of their 1983 Super Bowl victory, was seated across the table from Justice Sandra Day O'Connor and her husband, John, at the black-tie National Press Club dinner in Washington. Riggins, trying to make conversation while inebriated, called out: "C'mon, Sandy, baby. Loosen up. You're too tight."

Then he got up to talk to her husband, but never quite made it around the table. He collapsed and fell asleep under a chair, in his tuxedo and cowboy boots, pinning the wife of Senator John Glenn into her seat—"I must have been like an eighteen-wheeler lying there," he recalled. He stayed there, snoring, for about an hour, though the justice was gone by the time he was awakened and escorted from the premises by the security guards. (He also sent a dozen roses to Mrs. Glenn and the three or four other women at the table that night.)

Riggins spoke about his life and times earlier this week in the quiet of a Manhattan restaurant. Upon arrival, the 6-foot-3-inch Riggins, following the maître d'hôtel as he once followed blockers, made his way between tables, busboys, and waiters as easily as he shed tacklers on the football field. He weighs 240 pounds, just 5 pounds more than in his playing days, and it appeared that all he needed was to remove his turquoise bolo tie and black corduroy sports jacket and don helmet and pads to take his place in the Redskins backfield for their game this afternoon against the Giants in Robert F. Kennedy Stadium in Washington.

"In those days," said Riggins, "I thought people in Washington didn't allow themselves to enjoy a party. They were stiff. That wasn't my idea of a real hoedown good time. I liked to have people swinging from the chandeliers. I'd like to think I've grown up a little since then."

The speaker when Riggins was motivated to take his snooze under the table happened to be the vice president of the United States, George Bush. "He wrote me afterward," said Riggins, "and said something like, 'Well, John, we all have our bad days.'"

Riggins, now forty-two years old and retired from football for six seasons, told this story with a bit of a sheepish grin on his face, a broad, intelligent face with eyes that look as though they still, on occasion, might covet a chandelier.

Much has happened for Riggins since his last game in pro football in December 1985: a recent divorce, difficulties accepting separation from his four children, living for a reclusive year and a half in a trailer on the Potomac River, and perhaps some problems with alcohol. He has begun a career in radio (he does commentary on football on a radio talk show in Washington). And now he hopes to begin one in acting, too. He plans to move back to New York from his home in northern Virginia. Meanwhile, he still keeps an eye on football.

He wondered about the motivation of the Redskins for the Giants game today, one that is meaningless in the standings. "I know I'd be bored to tears right now if I was on the team." Somehow one got the feeling that he would, as he usually did, find something to relieve the boredom, as he usually did. He has been called variously "independent," "boorish," "witty," and, to be sure, "bibulous." At one time he sported an Afro, later a Mohawk, and sometimes he shaved his head bald.

He held out for all of one season, 1980, because the contract the Redskins offered wasn't to his liking. "And something else. It was a kind of revenge against the owners. There's a seamy side to football. There's the thing about when you're hurt and they stick a needle in your arm and say, 'Okay, go back out there.' And there's the way they treat the players, like some of my friends, who were dropped when they weren't of any more use. I had just gotten fed up with some of that stuff."

Riggins was a country boy from Kansas, from the small town of Centralia (population: five hundred), but had learned that he didn't have to do things in a small-town way or the way others wanted him to. And that if he could carry a football, eventually people would come around to him. And it happened. The season after Riggins sat out, the Redskins paid him close to what he asked for, and he would repay them by becoming one of their finest runners. He led them to Super Bowl XVII in January 1983, in which he made a spectacular 43-yard run against Miami that broke open the game in the fourth quarter and helped the Redskins win, 27–17. He ran for a total of 166 yards, then a Super Bowl record.

"Not many athletes have a big game in the biggest game there is," said Riggins, "and it changed my life in a number of ways. One of them was that it made Washington kind of a small town for me, Centralia all over again. I'd walk down the street and people would be calling, 'Riggo.' You have to remember, Washington only has two things that most of the people there care about, government and the Redskins. And a lot of the time they don't care for the government."

Sometimes Riggins's way of relieving his boredom was not always in his best interests. He admits he likes to drink, although he insists that he is not an alcoholic. He is able to stop for long periods of time and then return to moderate drinking. "I've heard that an alcoholic is someone whose life and work is affected by drinking," he said. "I don't think my work was. I mean, I played fourteen years in the NFL, and I was the oldest running back, at thirty-six, to gain more than a thousand yards. Me and the woolly mammoth."

He still holds records for most touchdowns scored in a season, 24, in 1982, and his 104 career rushing touchdowns are third behind Walter Payton's 110 and Jim Brown's 106.

He drank regularly after practice. "To celebrate," he said. "I was always looking for a reason to celebrate. And the Redskins understood that I did what they wanted me to do on the field, so they put up with my off-the-field stuff."

But his drinking did get him into a problem with the law. In one publicized case, in 1985, he was arrested as an intoxicated passenger in a car in Reston, Virginia. "At least I had the good sense not to drive in my condition," he said, "but the police stopped the car because they felt my friend was too drunk to be driving. And when they were going to arrest him, I said, 'Hoo, I'm not going to let him take the rap.' So I got into trouble too."

He said he didn't think his problems with his divorce had anything to do with drinking. "My ex-wife may disagree with me," he said, "but I think she might disagree with me on a lot of issues."

When they separated in January 1989, Riggins bought a twenty-one-foot trailer and went to live in it on a piece of property that he owns along the Potomac River in Virginia. "When I moved out of the house, I couldn't see myself renting an apartment," he said. "I wanted to try living alone, isolated, like that." But he said he also lived in the trailer "for pecuniary reasons." "I had money from football," he said, "but I was never sure how far it would go."

He retired from football after the 1985 season and had not thought much of his future. He had a lot of time to think about this in his trailer, as he hauled water to drink. And he wondered about all this on freezing mornings in his sleeping bag when all the heat was off and the frost was on the window. "And I thought,

'Well, what do I do now?' The one thing I knew I didn't want to do was get out of that sleeping bag."

He seemed, to an outsider, the classic case of the man-child ex-athlete who can't grow up and who was lost in the so-called real world. "I don't know about whether I had lost my way," said Riggins. "It was more like I never knew my way." His whole life, he said, was playing football. "And playing football for as long as I did can give you a distorted view of life. I mean, I was fast and big and had good balance. I was a better animal than most. And I didn't even have to practice hard. But when you retire at thirty-six, and everyone else is more or less just getting their legs in other endeavors, you wonder about yourself. I've often thought that a pro career should never go more than four years, like in college. Then you're forced to get on with your life in something else."

He had no real skills other than being an entertainer. "That's what a football player is, isn't he?" asked Riggins.

In the summer of 1990, Riggins moved out of the trailer and into an apartment. He came up to New York, a place that had awed him and attracted him ever since he played for the Jets from 1971 to 1975. Riggins found a place to live in Chinatown and stayed there for about six months. He then moved back to Virginia. He was searching for something, and wasn't sure what.

He soon came to another realization. He wanted to be closer to his children. He sees them now once a week and sometimes on weekends. "Sometimes it's disruptive for them," he said, "and you see them going on with their lives, and you're not always a part of it. And I feel maybe I'm letting them down. It can make you melancholy."

Riggins has four children: two girls ages five and twelve, two boys, seventeen and eight. The oldest, Bobby, is a high school senior and a wide receiver on his high school football team in Virginia.

"Now that I'm out of the game," said Riggins, "I realize more than ever how dangerous it is and how lucky I was to get out of it with relatively few injuries. I thought about this when Mike Utley of the Lions became paralyzed for life while blocking a few weeks ago. I'm not sure I want Bobby to play in college. But that's up to him."

Riggins has decided that he will try to be an actor. He has signed on with a theatrical agent, J. Michael Bloom of Manhattan, and plans to take acting lessons. He dreams of becoming an actor like Robert Duvall. "I want to play real people," he said, "not those larger-than-life guys that Schwarzenegger and Stallone play."

Riggins said that he often thought he played football to please his father, Gene Riggins, a depot agent, who was an avid sports fan. "I know he dreamed of me or either of my two brothers becoming a pro," said Riggins. His brothers, Frank and Billy, were, like John, running backs for the University of Kansas. "And I think I wanted to make my dad's dream come true. But acting I feel is for me, and me alone." And if that doesn't work out? "Maybe I'll go back to Kansas and buy a farm, or a ranch. But I want to give this acting a real shot."

With dinner over, and most of the restaurant cleared of patrons, Riggins rose to leave. "You know," he said, "I wonder about Justice O'Connor sometimes. I did make a fool of myself that night, but I wonder if, on the flip side, she's a little more festive at a party. All I know is, she gave me a little smile when I suggested she loosen up. It was one of those Rodney Dangerfield looks that says, 'Cute kid. Now I know why tigers eat their young.'"

He laughed, and, in turquoise bolo tie and black jacket and black kangaroo cowboy boots, walked out into the cool New York night, the old football player but still a young man, in search of a cab, and maybe of himself, too.

[1991]

The "No-show" Man

 TIMM ROSENBACH remembers clearly the beginning of the end because everything was pitch black. He woke up in a dark room with his head strapped to a table, still wearing his Phoenix Cardinals uniform and shoulder pads and hip pads and cleats. He was frightened and alone, not sure if he was alive or dead. He couldn't move, didn't want to move. He knew he had been hurt but didn't know how badly. He thought about his friend and former college teammate, Mike Utley of the Lions, who the year before had taken a tumble in a game and been left paralyzed for life from the chest down.

Then Rosenbach remembered the hit he had taken earlier that day. Was it minutes ago? Was it hours? Rosenbach, a 6-foot quarterback, was dropping back to pass in the third quarter of the season opener when he was blindsided by Santana Dodson, the Tampa Bay Buccaneers' 6–5, 270-pound defensive end, in one of the brutal encounters that is commonplace in a National Football League game. Rosenbach remembered only the resounding impact, as if being leveled by a tank, and then nothing. Until that moment in the room. And then, just as suddenly, he blacked out again.

This was Sunday, September 6, 1992, in an x-ray room at St. Joseph's Hospital in Phoenix. Rosenbach was not aware that he had been taken, unmoving, from the field at Sun Devils Stadium on a stretcher and rushed to the emergency room. He was not aware

114

that he had suffered only a severe concussion when his head slammed into the turf. He would walk and talk normally again, even report back for work two days later, but the grim experience would not leave him. In the following game he returned to the lineup only to be blindsided again, this time by Clyde Simmons, Philadelphia's 6–6, 280-pound defensive end, on the Cardinals' second series of the game.

"I made sure that the next time I get hit, I don't go head first," Rosenbach recalled, "and I didn't. I went shoulder first." And he suffered a separated shoulder. He was out of action for a month.

After the last game of the season, December 27, 1992, Rosenbach, at age twenty-six, did what some thought was unthinkable: he walked away from professional football and $1.05 million, the salary for the fifth and last year of his $5.3 million contract. He left the field and the money because he had developed fears that he might be crippled if he continued to play and because he began to "despise," as he said, the dehumanizing aspects of football that "can turn you into an animal."

It wasn't always that way. Two years earlier, in 1990, in his second year in the NFL, he took every snap for the Cardinals, all 1,001 of them, throwing for 3,098 yards to rank third in the National Football Conference. He ranked second in the NFL in rushing yardage for a quarterback, behind Randall Cunningham. He threw sixteen touchdown passes. He was admired, as one Phoenix sports reporter wrote, because "He was feisty. Gutsy. Combative. Ornery." His coach, Joe Bugel, called him "a throwback," a "gun-slingin', beer-drinkin' tough" in the mold of the late and colorful Bobby Layne.

Last summer, when it became apparent that Rosenbach had made his decision to quit football and return to Washington State University—where he had starred in football and where he was thirty-eight hours short of a bachelor's degree in general studies with an emphasis in psychology—he didn't call the team. His agent, Gary Wichard, did. Rosenbach changed his unlisted phone number so that no one from the Cardinals organization could call to try to talk him out of retiring and no reporter could call and ask why.

Football generally had been fun for Rosenbach in school, and even into the pros—he once relished the contact, proudly looking in the mirror at his bruises as an affirmation of manhood. But he was not prepared, as a twenty-two-year-old right out of college, for the hard-edged business of professional football, nor for the debilitating injuries that had sidelined him. And while his associations with a number of his teammates remained close, his view of this odd occupation became deeper, and darker.

There was speculation that Rosenbach had decided to become a professional rodeo rider, since he had participated as a team roper in a half-dozen events. When he married Carrie Serrano in June 1992, at his new ten-acre ranch in Gilbert, Arizona, the ceremony was held outdoors under a sagebrush arch with groom and groomsmen bedecked in black cowboy hats, tuxedo tops, black jeans, and black cowboy boots.

"It's all a mystery to me," said Bugel. "I'd like for him to tell me right to my face what the problem is."

"I've seen young guys retire, un-retire, but certainly not a player of Timm's stature," said Larry Wilson, the Cardinals' general manager. "This is kind of strange."

But there was more to it than just the bruises of the business. "I thought I was turning into some kind of animal," Rosenbach said in a recent interview. "You go through a week getting yourself up for a game by hating the other team, the other players. You're so mean and hateful, you want to kill somebody. Football's so aggressive. Things get done by force. And then you come home, you're supposed to turn it off? 'Oh, here's your lovin' daddy.' It's not that easy. It was like I was an idiot. I felt programmed. I had become a machine. I became sick of it."

He remembered those "barbaric yawps," as he called them, when breaking from a huddle and the players began screaming like maniacs. "It lightened things up," said Rosenbach, "but it's still a part of the craziness of football. Like screaming at the other team at the top of your lungs all kinds of threats and obscenities."

He remembers his center, Bill Lewis, telling an opposing lineman, "You touch my quarterback and I'll end your career." He remembers players like Refrigerator Perry snarling with his huge face scrunched up inside his tight helmet. And then there was Reggie White: "He is very religious, and he'd hit you a murderous shot and then say, 'God bless you,' as he pulled you off the ground."

Rosenbach also felt the pressures that go with winning, or losing. "I began to despise the whole business of the NFL," he said. When he was injured, he felt that the coaches, particularly head coaches, hardly recognized him. Since he was of no value to them, he was a virtual nonentity. When he was hurt, he wasn't even asked to travel with the team. "They asked, 'How're you feelin'?' But with no feeling," he said. "Their answer to injury is to give you painkiller pills. And the whole concept of medicine is to get you ready to perform—what happens to you down the road is not of any interest to them.

"Team doctors often lose touch with humanity, too. They are working for the team and love the association. So you hear players on the plane after a game saying, 'Hey, Doc, give me some Percodin or Percoset or Codeine Tylenol or something else.' When did players become pharmacists?

"And coaches are so absorbed in the X's and O's that they lose any feeling of being a human being. I guess the pressure is so great on them. I feel they viewed me—us—as robots. A mechanism. And if you don't fit the slot, you're nothing to them."

One trick of being a professional athlete, he understood, was not to think too much. He had been a kind of daredevil quarterback, enjoying the contact, loving that glazed feeling when you hardly know where you are, even baiting some of the huge opponents like Perry during the heat of a game—"It takes a long time to get all that into motion, doesn't it?"—but when he returned to the lineup in the latter part of last season, things were different.

He couldn't move the way he used to because his knee was wrapped in a brace, and for the first time he felt fear on a football field, the fear of ending up a cripple. He had already missed the entire 1991 season because of a severed ligament incurred in a pre-season practice a week before the opener. The injury required re-constructive surgery and rehabilitation and made him question his existence as a pro football player.

The challenge of going against ferocious linemen like Lawrence Taylor and White and Simmons and Perry, which had whetted his competitive appetite, had taken a different turn. "I got scared looking at the linemen before the snap," he said. "I remember I could feel the earth pounding when they chased me. When I went back to pass now, I was more concerned with where those guys were and less about where my receivers were going."

He said there was a lot of fear in the NFL. "Guys don't talk about it," he said, "but they feel it. And when you really know the game, you can spot them. But a lot aren't making the kind of money I did. And when a guy's making, say, $65,000 a year, and this is the only place he can make that kind of money, he's not about to get out."

After the injuries, his confidence, as well as his enthusiasm, ebbed noticeably. He was booed. He remembers the discomfort of meeting people and feeling he had to apologize for his performance or the team's losses. "Timm would come home in these moods," said his wife, Carrie, "and we were newlyweds. I didn't know what the problem was. He'd sit in a dark corner. I thought it was me. I thought, 'Why can't I make him happy?' But then I began to understand all the pressures he was under. And of course the pain. After some games, Timm was so bruised and battered it would take him a half-hour to get out of bed. And sometimes it would take him a half-hour to get off the couch and into bed."

The other side of life in the NFL for Rosenbach was that of "royalty," as he describes it. In those earlier, more relaxed days, he felt pampered, and that it was his due. "I had a lot of money— more than I ever dreamed—a great apartment, several cars, and wanted for nothing," he said. "I had become pretty arrogant. My neighbors hated me. I lived in an exclusive condominium in my first few years and played my music loud and didn't throw my garbage in the dumpster but left it on the porch."

"I almost never washed my clothes," he said. "When they got dirty, I threw them into the closet and went down to the mall and bought some more. I was young and rich and a professional athlete and I had no sense of reality. Just like most of the rest of the guys I played with."

Rosenbach's late father, Lynn, was a high school football coach and later the assistant athletic director at Washington State. His mother, Rosie, is an interior decorator. His brother, Todd, teaches special education, and his sister, Dana, is a high school teacher. "When I went back and saw their lives," he said, "saw how they were all doing well on salaries that weren't a million dollars a year, and happy with their lives, I felt embarrassed for myself."

He spoke with Carrie about quitting and giving up that $1 million as well as the millions that he might earn in football in the coming years. "I didn't know how he could just give up all that money," said Carrie. "But after a while I understood. He said that if he had to pump gas, he'd do it rather than play football. And it was true."

In Phoenix he was being called a "no-show," and a "mystery man." But his agent, Gary Wichard, said: "Timm's an intelligent, sensitive guy, and he has made a decision that he's had it with football. He could have come in for a year and held for extra points and field goals, but that's just not Timm."

"I'm proud of Rosey," said Jim Wahler, a defensive lineman for the Redskins and a former Cardinal teammate of Rosenbach's. "I'm glad he did it. There are not many people in that position to do that. That's a standup thing to walk out on your own terms and not somebody else's. Most guys would like that opportunity."

He still has his ranch in Gilbert but now lives with Carrie and seven dogs in a small house in an isolated area about eight miles outside of Pullman, Washington. She is a graduate of Arizona State and is in school at Washington State going for a master's degree in agricultural economy. Rosenbach has returned to general studies with a psychology emphasis.

Is he happier? "Yes," he said. "I was getting no enjoyment out of football anymore. It's funny, but when I was in school here before, I sat in the back of the class and never said a word. Now I'm involved in the classes, and I'm always raising my hand. I'm sure some of the students are saying, 'Why doesn't that old guy just shut up?'"

Rosenbach hardly looks ancient in his sweatshirt and jeans. He still has that broad, boyish look and a cowlick in his short blond hair. And he also hasn't totally given up on football. He says a college game is still one of the exciting spectacles for him. And he still watches pro games on television, remembering the pleasure of the camaraderie of teammates, though he sees the action differently than he once did. And he still has his memories of playing the game, every morning. His knees, his back, his shoulders still ache when he wakes up and slowly gets out of bed. When he drives for any distance in his truck, or walks distances when he is out hunting birds, his body hurts.

"And I'm still an alumnus of the NFL, it is still something I'm proud of," he said. "And I guess one day I'll be invited to some of those alumni golf tournaments, and wear an NFL cap and play, if I can stand up."

[1993]

The Ghost Was
Not a Ghost

❦ A HARD grey rain whipped at the fourteen-year-old high school freshman in the yellow hooded slicker. Amy Lemieux and her search party of about one hundred volunteers and state law enforcement officials made their organized way through a wooded area in Lewiston, Maine, in what seemed more and more a vain attempt to find her schoolmate.

Scott Croteau, seventeen, was a senior and perhaps the most popular student at Lewiston High, a pride of the heavily French-Canadian community, co-captain of the football team and a straight-A student who had a stack of more than fifty recruiting letters on his desk at home from colleges like Harvard and Princeton and Holy Cross. By that rainy Sunday afternoon, September 17, 1995, as the search group in the woods parted and smelled the wet grass and the leaves that were beginning to turn fall colors, Croteau had been missing for ten days. It seemed everyone in this old mill town of 65,000, best known for being the site of Muhammad Ali's controversial first-round knockout of Sonny Liston in 1965, was at a loss to explain the mysterious disappearance.

At about 3:40 P.M., Amy Lemieux took a step through some brush and as she passed beside a rain-blackened cherry tree her head almost hit someone's knee. She stopped in her tracks. Croteau's deteriorating body in dark, blood-stained T-shirt, blue jeans, and sneakers, and nearly hidden by leaves, was hanging by a

121

rope from a thick limb of the tree. The girl froze, unable to scream, unable to breathe. Then she ran to one of the patrolling Maine game wardens, looking, said a nearby searcher, "like she had seen a ghost."

What the freshman volunteer had not noticed in her fright was the .22-caliber Ruger revolver lying beside the tree and the bullet hole through Croteau's right temple. The state medical examiner would determine that the "manner of death was by self-inflicted gunshot wound and hanging." It was deemed "a double suicide."

Many Lewiston students and townspeople, including Croteau's father, couldn't and wouldn't believe that Scott had committed suicide. Their disbelief underscores a problem: Suicide has become one of the major causes of death among American teenagers, following automobile accidents and homicides. From 1952 to 1992, according to the Centers for Disease Control and Prevention, the incidence of suicide among teenagers and young adults nearly tripled. In 1992, the most recent year for which figures are available, 1,847 teens killed themselves, which is 10.8 for every 100,000.

"Suicide, especially among teenagers, is a virtually unrecognized national public health problem," said Dr. Lloyd Potter of the Centers for Disease Control. Making the situation more difficult is that some teenage victims are high achievers and seemingly well-balanced individuals. "It's basically a problem that isn't being addressed on national, state, or local levels," Potter said.

Two elements in the Croteau case fit profiles that medical authorities said can frequently be associated with teenage suicide: the presence of disturbing family issues and the possibility that longtime hidden feelings of depression can become suddenly and terribly distorted.

Unlike many suicides, or those who attempt suicide, Croteau did not threaten it or talk about it. He appeared the most well adjusted of teenagers. "But beneath the serene waters," said the Reverend Christopher J. LaRoche in his funeral sermon for Croteau in Holy Family Church, on Sabattus Avenue, just a few blocks from the Croteau residence and from the cherry tree in the woods, "there were turbulent depths."

Scott Croteau had simply vanished from his home, a single-story brick house on Goulet Street, some five hundred yards from where his body was found. He lived with his father—his parents having divorced twelve years ago—and his kitten, named Tyson. He went to bed on Thursday night, September 7, after dinner with his father and his father's longtime girlfriend, Mary-Jane Bishop. The next morning his father, Ron Croteau, with white hair and white mustache at age forty-seven, having finished his regular 6 A.M. walk, looked in his son's room to rouse him for school and found only an empty, rumpled bed and the bedroom light on. Scott's wallet and his glasses were on a dresser.

There was no note, and no clues. Later that morning, Ron Croteau called the police. Was Scott Croteau a runaway? Was he abducted? Had he been murdered? Was he a suicide? And, to be sure, if it had been suicide, the question was why?

Croteau, the starting fullback and middle linebacker, was winner of the previous season's Ironman Award for the football player who showed greatest dedication to weight training and conditioning. And in the first game this season, against Lawrence High School in Fairfield, he rushed for sixty yards in eight carries, scored one touchdown, and made several hard-hitting tackles on defense. He was a champion weight lifter, a state track qualifier in the shot put, and a member of the National Honor Society. He was nice-looking, with short dark hair, a gentle smile, and, said a onetime schoolmate, Jen Mynahan, who admitted to once having had a crush on him, "he had these pretty, pretty blue eyes."

Croteau was modest almost to a fault, said his friends, and appeared to have no enemies. "He was always nice to everyone," said a football teammate, center Steve Beauparlant, who had started in kindergarten with Scott and gone all the way through school with him. "You didn't have to be in the 'in' crowd for Scott to be nice to you. He knew no other way."

"No one's perfect," said Scott's older brother, Brian, "but Scott was as close to it as anyone in the world. He was really the all-American boy."

Russ Barlo, Scott's weight-lifting coach for the last six years and a family friend, considered the manner of death and thought: "It's sad to say, but it sounds like Scott, to be so methodical. He was always so thorough. If he was to kill himself, he was going to make sure he accomplished his goal."

There were no scratches on the body to indicate a struggle, and the sneakers Scott Croteau wore when his body was discovered had mud and grass stains that had apparently come from the broad field that separated his house from the woods, and where he had apparently walked in an early morning hour after quietly leaving home, rope and revolver in hand, and passing under the lights on Farwell Street. The law enforcement officers involved in the case, from the Lewiston police chief, Michael Kelly, to the state police Lieutenant Michael Harriman and Sergeant Steve Holt to Dr. Kristin Sweeney, the deputy state medical examiner, firmly believe, after investigation and analysis, that it was a clear case of suicide.

Scott Maurice Croteau was born January 21, 1978, to Doris and Ron Croteau, she an office secretary, he an automobile salesman who, at the time of his son's death, was the sales manager for Viking Motors in nearby Norway. The Croteaus had deep marital discord and divorced in 1983, when Scott was six years old. Earlier, however, in 1982, Doris Croteau twice sought protection-from-abuse orders against her husband. And in the divorce judgment, the judge ordered psychological counseling for Scott, his brother, and their mother.

In 1986, Ron Croteau purchased a .22-caliber revolver to protect himself, he said, from threats made by his ex-wife and her boyfriend. He said he never used the gun and put it away and forgot about it until the gun was found near his son's body nine years later.

Scott's mother married again and divorced. In recent years,

Doris Croteau-Robinson had been arrested several times on charges of petty theft. She now lives in a public housing unit in Lewiston. Ron Croteau married again in 1988 and was divorced again within nine months.

Meanwhile, Scott was succeeding in grade school and high school, in the classroom, in sports, and in his social life. For whatever reasons, he appeared nearly compulsive in being the perfect kid. By the time he reached high school he carried with him 3-by-5 note cards with uplifting sayings, like "Some people dream of worthy accomplishments while others stay awake and do them."

"He was a neat kid," said his father. "He was goal-oriented and he loved what he did."

He was polite. When, for example, a study-hall teacher assigned him a seat, he said, "Thank you."

He was humble. "He was very proud of his body, and he had these muscles," said Jamie Menneahy, a classmate. "We'd say, 'Scott, flex for us.' And he'd say, embarrassed, 'Aw, c'mon.' He always said, 'Aw, c'mon.' But he wound up flexing for us, anyway."

He was straight arrow. "He was not street smart," said his father. "He was really kind of naive. He was nonconfrontational. As far as I know, he never got into a fight in his life. But he could play football hard because the rules were there, and they were clear. The other stuff wasn't so clear."

And he was competitive. "I was five years older than Scott and, of course, as older brothers do, they kind of harass the younger brother," Brian Croteau said. "I remember that I called him a wimp when he was about twelve, and we wrestled and he screamed at me, and then he went out and began taking weight-lifting classes. And pretty soon I wasn't about to call him a wimp any more."

He was popular with girls as well as boys, and dated regularly. He had broken up a month before his death with a girl he had been seeing for some time, Tracy Gendron. "But we remained friends," she said. "And the day before he died, on that Thursday, he called my house twice to make sure that my mom went to his football game on Friday. He gave me no signs that anything was wrong."

Those close to him, like Jason Auger, a football teammate who picked him up in his car every morning for school, or Mike Good, a classmate, said he showed no signs of being anything but the easygoing guy they had always known. "He talked excitedly about the team's home opener on Friday," said Good. "I just don't understand."

That afternoon he had posed twice for his senior-year portrait, the first time saying he was unhappy with the photo. Then he led a highly charged football practice. "We ate dinner that Thursday night," said his father, "and he watched 'Seinfeld' on television. I went over and sat down next to him, and asked him about the football game the next night." It was the team's home opener against a major rival, Gardiner. "He said, 'No problem, Dad, we'll do very well.' He was really looking forward to it. We said good night. There were no arguments, no nothing else. And that's the last time I saw him. No one can imagine the terrible, empty, empty feeling I have."

In the last month, Scott had noticed his mother watching him in football practice from a distance, but he made no effort to speak to her. "He looked sad to me," she said. Other classmates, in retrospect, thought Scott had seemed depressed. Still, he took no drugs or alcohol—he even persuaded his father to stop smoking—and the police have ruled out anything that might have been considered a problem with his sexuality. There seemed no new, or exploding, problem at home or at school, no loss of appetite or diminishment of activities.

"It's not rare, though, to find a developing depression among teenagers," said Dr. Thomas Jensen, head of the adolescent psychiatric unit of St. Mary's Hospital in Lewiston. "With the chemical changes that occur after puberty, many mental illnesses develop in the teen years and may not be obvious to others."

While Jensen did not know or evaluate Scott Croteau, some

Lewiston High School students who had expressed thoughts of their own feelings of suicide to Jensen later told him their observations of Croteau. "They told me that it seemed no one really knew what Scott's feelings were, that he seemed to hide them behind his striving for perfection," said Jensen. "He always seemed too good to be true to them—that he was so driven, so focused on his goals.

"And when you are depressed, you could have a million things going right for you, but if one thing is wrong, the depressed person completely loses perspective. And he focuses on that one negative thing, and he convinces himself that suicide is the only option. In psychiatric terms, it is called cognitive distortion. And we treat it effectively with medication and psychotherapy.

"It was very poignant after it was learned about Scott's suicide. A number of kids I treat came to me and said that they thought they once identified with Scott." And, Jensen said, one student told him: "My God, I was so distorted. It was scary. I look back now and think, 'How could I have even thought of killing myself? But I thought it was the only option. I know better now.'"

Others wondered if Scott's striving for perfection made him feel it was impossible to continue and live up to. "It seemed he was always trying to live up to other people's expectations of him," said Jen Mynahan. "That could be a lot of pressure. And he never seemed to get upset. Maybe that's what the problem was. He kept everything inside him."

But even if Scott Croteau was simply an overachiever with intense family problems, he fits the profile of about one in ten suicides, according to the Center for Suicide Research and Prevention in Chicago. There have been a number of reported cases like Croteau's, in which an exemplary high school student and athlete commits suicide. Rod David, a popular, eighteen-year-old high school senior from Tucumari, New Mexico, who was an all-state football, basketball and track athlete and honor student, shot himself to death in April 1984. "It was unbelievable; there were no signs at all of any deep problems," said his oldest brother, Stan

David, a former linebacker for the Buffalo Bills and Denver Broncos. "He was very good at covering up. After his death, we saw a diary he was keeping, and at one point he wrote, 'I think there is something wrong with me.' There were no other details."

On Thursday night, September 21, at the funeral parlor in Auburn, across the dark Androscoggin River from Lewiston, more than a thousand people quietly filed in to pay respects to Scott Croteau and his family. Outside, teammates of Scott's wore their football jerseys, and students and teachers hugged each other and cried. Ron and Brian Croteau were at the end of the receiving line, painfully accepting condolences. Across the room sat Scott's mother, also stricken but having no contact with her Brian or her ex-husband.

The funeral service the next day at the Holy Family Church drew an emotional crowd of about two thousand, many of whom stood in front of the stained-glass windows and in the rear. When the red mahogany coffin was wheeled to the altar, the sobbing of mourners filled the church. Afterward, in a steady drizzle, a long line of cars followed the hearse to St. Peter's Cemetery, where Croteau was buried, his sky-blue football jersey, with the white number 42, having been placed on top of the lowering coffin.

"Parents are looking at their kids more and asking more questions, which is good," said Dave Bernier, a schoolmate of Croteau. "In the long run I guess it will get easier. Right now it's real hard."

Lewiston High School has set up special counseling areas for students who continue to have a particularly difficult time with the tragedy. "We're very concerned about cluster suicides," said the principal, Richard Sykes. "Kids have to know that there are solutions available beyond the one Scott chose. They have to know that suicide solves nothing."

And many students still go to the tree in the woods where Scott died. They have made a shrine, strewing flowers and placing small candles in glasses under the tree, and pinning to the trunk balloons and notes to Scott. "Scott—Our big mistake was not letting you know how much we loved you—until it was too late!" one wrote. Another person, still refusing to accept the harsh and disturbing reality, wrote: "One day someone will slip up and tell the truth. You as a model citizen could not ever commit suicide."

The day after the funeral, which was front-page news in the local papers, the sun shone brightly as an airplane began its ascent to depart from Lewiston. Teddy Atlas, a fight manager in town for a weekend match, looked out the window at the wondrous panoply of fall leaves, glistening reds and oranges and browns. "Look at all those pretty trees down there," he said, shaking his head. "And to think that that kid was hanging from one of them."

[1995]

The Heisman Trophy
and Obscurity

W SEATED at dinner in a restaurant in Miami one evening last week, a young man in short-cropped blond hair and wire-rim glasses, which lent an academic look to him, was approached by one of his fellow patrons. "May I get your autograph?" the second man asked. "My son would be thrilled."

"Sure," said the young man. "What's his name?"

When the other man left with his request satisfied, the young man turned to his dinner companion. "This doesn't happen too often," he said, as though trying to allay any wrong impressions.

It doesn't happen often anymore, anyway. Not to Gino Torretta, who, though scholarly appearing from the chin up, has the thick neck, and, as was obvious beneath his blue shirt, the broad, sloping shoulders and the considerable chest of a professional football quarterback. Five years ago this month, Gino Torretta, quarterback for the University of Miami's defending national champions, was named the winner of the Heisman Trophy, emblematic of the best college football player in the nation. He was at the top of the heap, just as Peyton Manning or Ryan Leaf or Charles Woodson might be when the 1997 Heisman winner is announced on Saturday.

Now, after having been released or waived by five National Football League teams in five years—the last was the Indianapolis Colts last month—and having completed just five passes in the

NFL, Torretta is an unemployed quarterback who has been depicted as the ultimate journeyman. And, at age twenty-seven, the prospects of his realizing his dreams and expectations of a great pro career—of an even commonplace pro career, for that matter—seem to be growing ever more distant.

He has played in just two regular-season games. In one of those games, for the Vikings in his rookie year, he got in for the last play of the last game of the 1993 season. "I handed off," he said, with a wan smile. "But I was thrilled to get into the game. I knew that next season would be a season when I could shine."

It was not to be. The Vikings released him the following August. This came as a surprise to Torretta, even though he was drafted by the Vikings in the seventh round, the 192nd pick in 1993, after quarterbacks Drew Bledsoe and Rick Mirer were the first and second picks in the draft, and two other quarterbacks were also chosen ahead of Torretta. His arm and his mobility were suspect.

"I couldn't believe the draft when it happened," said Torretta. "I had a 26–2 record in college and was on two national championship teams. But it didn't matter. I had confidence in myself." The Vikings offered Torretta a three-year contract not substantially above the minimum, which was $100,000 a year. "I believed I could do better than that once I proved myself in about a year, and so my agent negotiated for a one-year contract" at the minimum salary.

"This was just a start," he said. "I saw myself playing something like ten years and eventually making enough money to set me up for the rest of my life."

Two months after Minnesota released him, the Lions, needing a fill-in for an injured quarterback, signed him. Torretta suited up for Detroit but did not play. The next summer he played for the Rhein Fire in Düsseldorf, Germany, Detroit's team in the World Football League. He returned to the Lions, who released him that September.

"That was my lowest point," Torretta said. "When you get released for the second time . . ." The thought trailed off. Now the bloom was off the rose, as it were. He called Bill Walsh, who was then at Stanford, and whom Torretta admired growing up near Oakland. Torretta asked if he could work out for him. Walsh agreed.

"I want you to tell me if I can play in the NFL," Torretta recalled saying. "If you don't think I can, then I can take it. I have a life after football. I can do other things. But I respect your opinion. I know you'll be honest with me." Torretta worked out for a week, and then came Walsh's assessment: "Gino, I believe you can play in this league."

Two months later Torretta was signed by San Francisco, as insurance when Steve Young was hurt, in early November. Two weeks later Young returned, and Torretta was gone. He was re-signed and released three more times by the 49ers, under similar circumstances. The last time was on November 19, 1996.

Two days later Seattle, whose coach, Dennis Erickson, was Torretta's college coach, signed him. Mirer, the first-string quarterback, was hurt and unable to play; John Friesz, next in line, broke a bone in his leg and was out. And so against the Raiders, in the last game of the season, the Seahawks' started quarterback number three, Stan Gelbaugh. But he tore a groin muscle on the second series of downs. There was no one else. Erickson signaled for Torretta to enter the game. Torretta played the entire game and Seattle won, 28–21. He threw one touchdown pass, had one pass intercepted, and completed five of sixteen passes for forty-one yards.

"I didn't think I played well," Torretta said, "but I played well enough to win. That's how I think of myself. Someone who can go in and win a game."

Erickson said: "I thought he was excellent under difficult circumstances. He'd been with us only a few weeks—he hardly even knew the plays. I was sending in plays in the language of what we did at Miami." Nonetheless, Torretta was released shortly after the season ended. He was signed by Seattle again early this year, and was released again.

"It was one of the hardest things I've ever had to do," said Erickson. "If you know Gino, you have to like him. He's smart—like he picked up on the plays so quickly—and he's a hard worker and all his teammates like him. But there's just a numbers game that he has fallen prey to time and time again. In this instance we thought that Jon Kitna, who was our third quarterback, was going to be the quarterback of our future.

"But I know Gino can play in this league, maybe not as a star, but surely as an insurance quarterback. It's just a matter of time that he finds the right situation—if he has the will to hang in there."

The release by Seattle on October 28 was followed by Torretta's swift stay with the Colts. In all, Torretta has been signed and released eight times by NFL teams. But he can, after five frustrating seasons, look at a cup that is half full rather than half empty.

"I've been vested," he said. "The average career in the NFL is what—less than three years."

But the disappointment clearly takes up the rest of that half-empty cup. "I see guys who never had anywhere near the success I had in college get opportunities that I've never had," said Torretta, who at 6 feet 2 inches and 220 pounds is about 10 pounds lighter than his college playing days. "But I'm not giving up. I believe one day I'll get my chance. And I'm going to be ready. I work out almost every day—I jog, I do wind sprints, I do my weight training—and then I check the Internet, or I watch 'SportsCenter' on ESPN to see if there've been any changes in quarterback situations on any of the NFL teams."

That primarily means, injury. If a quarterback goes down, a slot opens up, even temporarily.

Last week Torretta learned that Washington Redskins quarterback Gus Frerotte was out for the season after suffering a broken hip in the November 30 game against the St. Louis Rams. Torretta's agent, Leigh Steinberg, contacted the Redskins. The Redskins were interested. "Then I heard that they had signed Jamie Martin," said Torretta. "Sure, it's disappointing. But what can you do? You go on."

This is the world of the backup quarterback, or the backup to the backup, and more fact-of-life than vulturous. When the three top quarterbacks for Indianapolis all suffered injury, a call on November 11 was put through by the Colts to Torretta: "Hurry." Torretta was, as now, home in Miami. With his suitcase still not unpacked from his last football foray, Toretta jumped on a plane for Indianapolis.

"Why change clothes?" he said, with a smile. "There's no dress code in the NFL locker room, and as long as I have clean underwear, no one cares."

When one of the Colts' other quarterbacks was given medical clearance to play, Torretta did not suit up for the game. He was released the following day, six days after joining the team. So he returned to the city of his greatest triumphs, where a friend allows him to live in the penthouse he owns in an oceanside apartment building. It is a week-to-week arrangement, or until Torretta finds another football team.

Torretta doesn't spend all his time on the Internet. He and his fiancée, Bernadette Carney, plan to marry next summer. He is a licensed stockbroker, driving most mornings from Miami to the office of Slavic Mutual Funds Management Corporation in Boca Raton.

In college Torretta not only made first-team All-American but was also named to the All-Academic football team. He received his undergraduate degree in three and a half years and is six classes short of a master's degree in business. "After all the pro football disappointments," said his friend, Marty Margulies, whose penthouse Torretta occupies, "the exceptional thing about Gino is how he's kept his perspective. I'm amazed at how he maintains this even keel."

In Pinole, California, where Torretta grew up, there is another side. It is where Torretta's family owns a bar. "And sometimes you get a smart aleck in the place who makes a remark about Gino," said Torretta's eldest brother, Gary. The remark is sometimes about Gino being "a bum."

"I tell them, 'How many guys you know personally who ever played in the NFL?'" said Gary. "He says none. And I say that I know Gino will get his chance, that he deserves it. But I still have to hold back from getting physical."

Why hasn't Torretta made it?

"He's gotten so close on several occasions," said Steinberg, Torretta's agent. "He just hasn't had good luck. It seems he just gets beaten out by a hair every time." Torretta, though, has carried a double-edged reputation since his junior year in college. One NFL team scout, who asked not to be identified, gave this appraisal of Torretta:

"The positive is that he's very smart, and so he's able to pick up a team's system faster than most, and he's durable and has proved in college that he can lead a winning team. The negatives are that he does not have even average NFL arm strength and he lacks mobility. You can get away with some things in college that you can't in the pros."

Torretta is, of course, aware of these criticisms. "I can throw as well as most quarterbacks in the league," he said. "I don't have the cannon that a Jeff George or Brett Favre or Dan Marino have, but not many do. I know that my accuracy was once questioned, too. And early on when I was trying too hard to prove myself, I'd jam passes that I shouldn't have. I don't do that any more."

Erickson agreed. "I think Gino has an above-average NFL arm. And it has improved considerably in the last five years. As for his mobility, he's not going to establish any running records, but he is agile enough to avoid tacklers, like most quarterbacks."

Torretta is also aware of the history of Heisman Trophy winners. Some have been pro busts, to be sure, but not all. "There are seven or eight of them in the Pro Football Hall of Fame, out of about sixty-one," said Torretta. "That's a pretty decent record." However, he is aware of Heisman-winning quarterbacks, like Gary Beban and Pat Sullivan and Terry Baker, who did not make it in the NFL.

"But they went on to successful business careers," said Torretta. "And I don't think they put in the effort of years that I'm putting in. But guys like Roger Staubach and Jim Plunkett were very successful in the pros. And I take heart in guys who've been around for some time before they get a chance, like Plunkett, even like Steve Young."

One recent morning Torretta was driving in his black Lexus from Miami to his brokerage office in Boca Raton. He was speaking on the car phone when there were repeated technical snags. In some ways this seemed a metaphor for Torretta's pro football career: not quite completed. Frustratingly interrupted. Yet not quite dead, for Torretta finished the conversation at his office. But his last words on the car phone were: "Sometimes like this, driving along the road, I've imagined that one day I come back and lead a team to the Super Bowl. Wouldn't that be—." Crackle, crackle, crackle.

[1997]

Jason Watts
Had It All

🐾 THE LAST TIME some sixty thousand people saw Jason Watts, most of them cheered lustily for him and his University of Kentucky football team in Commonwealth Stadium in Lexington. It was last November 14, a beautiful fall afternoon in bluegrass country. Fans waved their blue-and-white banners, and the Wildcats walloped Vanderbilt and were joyously headed for a bowl game, their first in several years.

Watts was the starting center, snapping the ball to Tim Couch, the All-America quarterback and eventual number one pick in the National Football League draft. Watts, a senior, was playing his last game before the home crowd, in front of his proud family and friends. There was a lot to celebrate, and that night, Watts and two of his closest friends did.

That was five months ago. On Tuesday afternoon, the day after his twenty-second birthday, Watts shuffled into the small, grey courtroom in the Pulaski County Courthouse on Main Street in Somerset, a quiet south-central Kentucky town. His walk was impeded because his ankles were chained. He also wore handcuffs with a chain that wound around his back and glinted under the fluorescent lighting when he took his seat. Three weeks before, on March 31, Watts had pleaded guilty to two counts of reckless homicide and asked to begin his jail term immediately. His celebration with his friends that November night had turned tragic.

Drunk, and on a whimsical pre-dawn hunting excursion, the young men were involved in a horrific crash that sent all three flying out of Watts's black pickup truck. Only Watts survived.

So this week Watts was back in court for sentencing, facing a maximum of ten years in prison, reduced in plea bargaining from twenty years. Even with head bowed and wearing navy blue jail garb, Jason Watts, at 6 feet 3 inches, 270 pounds, still appeared imposing. His dark hair was cut short, and his features clean and fresh-faced. Genial and seemingly big enough to lift the front end of a bus, he sat at a table with his lawyer, James Lowry, and faced the bespectacled judge, Daniel Venters.

The cheering of a football crowd was not even an echo now. The only sounds were the scraping of chairs and an occasional low sob from the nearby visitors' bench, where Watts's mother, Debbie, and older sister, Laura, sat holding crumpled tissues in their fists. Alongside them was Watts's father, Jim. They had driven twelve hours from their home in Oviedo, Florida, to attend the sentencing.

Absent were the parents of Christopher Scott Brock and Artie Steinmetz, the two friends who were killed in the crash on Highway 27 in the grey, early morning some twelve hours after the 55–17 victory over Vanderbilt. Watts was behind the wheel. None of them wore seat belts. Blood tests showed that all three of them were drunk at the time of the crash, with Watts having a blood-alcohol content of 0.15 percent, well above the legal limit of 0.10.

Lowry made an appeal to the judge for leniency because Watts had shown profound contrition, accepted responsibility from the beginning, and agreed to speak to high school students in alcohol- and drug-prevention programs. The prosecutor, Ed Montgomery, acknowledged all this. "Nonetheless, two people were killed in an accident he caused," Montgomery said. "We have to make clear the severity of the offense, and a lesser sentence would depreciate the seriousness of it."

The judge asked Watts if he had anything to say. "I just want to say," he said, eyes lowered, words coming slowly, "that—that I'm sorry again for all the people I let down." The judge acknowledged the various positions, said he was somewhat skeptical about Watts's talking to students—implying that obtaining a lighter sentence might have been an ulterior motive—but said that if it had done some good, then it was, ultimately, good. "Ten years," he decreed.

Jason Watts's mother let out a low moan, and his sister sobbed and buried her head in her mother's shoulder. His father had reached over and was holding their hands, tears welling behind his glasses, as Watts was led out of the courtroom and back to the Pulaski County Detention Center.

"It began," said Watts, hands self-consciously in his pockets, "on what was the greatest day of my life. I could never have imagined that twelve hours later it turned into the worst day of my life." This was in mid-April, and Watts was in the Russell Springs High School gymnasium, talking to twelve hundred students as part of a state Drive Smart campaign. He noted the victory over Vanderbilt. "After the game we were screaming and yelling and we were all on cloud nine," he continued. "Nothing could bring us down. After I showered and changed clothes, I went outside and there was a big crowd of people waiting for the players."

One of those waiting at the gate was Brock, twenty-one, whom everyone called Scott, a high school teammate of Tim Couch's who attended Eastern Kentucky but who still visited Couch and Watts a lot. They went back to Watts's apartment and were eventually joined by Artie Steinmetz.

Steinmetz, nineteen, a lineman, practiced with the team but as a transfer had to sit out a year. "Artie and I became good friends because we played against each other in practice every day," Watts told the students. "We'd insult each other, but it was all in fun."

The three of them, along with a few others in the house on Linden Walk, broke out some beers, and they laughed and talked and went out for dinner and returned and drank some more in what became a long night of partying. "Old Scott had them laughing, as he always did," Watts told the students. "Everyone loved

Scott. And Artie was like Scott in that nothing you could do could make them mad.

"Scott kidded me that I couldn't hit a deer if my life depended on it, and I argued about that. And we kept talking and laughing and we decided to go hunting. Right then."

Watts was a thrill seeker. He would race motorbikes and take his truck mudding near his home in central Florida. On the football field he was quick and mobile, and he enjoyed the hitting. He had started every game for Kentucky for three years.

He was an agriculture major but did not have quite enough credits to graduate this spring, and he planned to return to Florida after school. He said that perhaps he would work with his father, who harvests lotus pods in an airboat in the swamps for the floral industry. And, he said, he would try "to just relax with whatever life brings me."

In the months since the accident, he says, he has come to believe that one reason he may have been spared was so that he could talk to young people about the dangers of drinking. Yet alcohol had been a dangerous part of Watts's life previously; sixteen months before the accident, he paid a fine after shooting a teammate, Omar Smith, in the buttocks as they handled a rifle together. He had been drinking then, as well.

Watts missed no playing time because of the incident but was made to undergo alcohol tests at random twice a week for nine months. He was also given a curfew and a strict schedule of classroom and practice time. "Jason's a good, bright young man," said Kentucky's athletic director, C. M. Newton, "but he is very much a risk taker who is an alcoholic." Newton persuaded Watts to attend Alcoholics Anonymous meetings but said he was not sure how many Watts had gone to.

The shooting incident did not prevent the drinking and subsequent recklessness that caused Watts to get behind the wheel of his truck last November. It was already four or five in the morning when the young men headed out to go hunting. Alcohol was on their breaths. The three pals drove southeast from Lexington on a two-lane highway. There were few other vehicles on the road as they sped past Junction 70. One car, though, was just ahead of them. Watts tried to pass it and slid off the road into a rut.

"I was trying to hold on to the steering wheel, and I threw my arm up to shield me from smashing into the window, thinking, 'This is going to hurt.'" The last thing he remembered was feeling a terrible thump on his head. "I guess," he said, "that's when I went through the windshield, and when they went through the windshield."

The Russell Springs students, some with graduation and prom night just around the corner, were quiet and still as Watts talked to them.

When he opened his eyes, he said, he found himself in a ditch. He saw the truck, crushed, toppled over some twenty-five yards away. He was covered in blood. The pain in his ribs and lungs was excruciating. "And then I saw Scott lying on the ground, a bad cut in his head," Watts said. "I ran over to him. 'Come on, Scott. Come on, buddy. Please don't let this happen. I'm begging you.' He didn't answer me. Then I saw blood draining from the side of his lips. I looked around for Artie. I saw him lying not far away. I ran over to him. 'Come on Artie, man, you're all right.' He breathed, a kind of whoosh, and then that was it. I started screaming: 'Help! Help!' Some people had stopped their cars and come over. The sheriff was there. He said, 'Your friends are gone.'"

Watts was carried into an ambulance and taken to a nearby hospital. "On the way," he said, "I kept thinking, 'I was the one driving; I should've been the one to go.' And I tried holding my breath, hoping I would die."

Lying in University Hospital in Lexington, Watts wondered how he could ever face the families of Brock and Steinmetz. "I had ruined my life and killed two of my best buddies," he said, "and all because of doing something so stupid, something that could have been so easily avoided."

Then, several days later, he was told, "Mr. and Mrs. Brock are here to see you."

"It was like a bolt of lightning," he recalled. "It gave me cold chills. I said: 'I can't speak to Mr. and Mrs. Brock. Their son is dead because of me.'" But they came in, with Scott's brother, Jeff. Watts went on to describe the scene:

"How're you doing?" he was asked, and they hugged him.

"How can you be like this?" he asked.

"We just wanted to let you know, this can happen to anybody," came the reply.

Watts paused in the telling. "I was crying. I didn't know what to say. Except how sorry I was."

Today Scott Brock's mother, Wilma, says, "We went to visit Jason because, well—I don't know hardly how to say this—but because he was Scott's friend." As to whether they hold Watts responsible for their son's death, she said: "My emotions—and my husband's—are so mixed up we don't know exactly how to feel. But we do believe in forgiveness."

The ambivalence among those involved—the Watts, Steinmetz, and Brock families—is profound. Two young men are dead, and the survivor, their close friend, seems full of remorse. He had been reckless, fatally so, but he is not viewed as a monster.

Watts's parents called the Brocks and asked permission to come to their son's funeral. Therlo Brock, Scott's father, a retired vocational teacher, and Wilma Brock, a retired kindergarten teacher, said yes. They spoke to Watts's parents after the services. "We just wanted to show that we cared deeply about their loss," Jim Watts told the Brocks, according to Wilma Brock. "I just could never fathom what it would be like to lose a child."

"God has to have a reason for all this," Wilma Brock told them. "Some good has to come out of it because my son was such a good boy."

Watts said that after his nine-day stay in the hospital, which included three operations on his arm, he decided to visit the Steinmetz family, who live in northern Kentucky. "I was scared to death to do it," he said. "But it was something I just felt I had to do."

142

Steve and Theresa Steinmetz were not condemning. "The Steinmetzes said, 'God spared you for a reason, and it's up to you to figure out what that reason was for,'" Watts recalled. But recently Steve Steinmetz, who owns a trucking company near Cincinnati, said, "I don't care to comment on Jason Watts." And when asked if he had said that about God's sparing Watts, he replied, "I didn't say anything like that."

A study on drinking on college campuses published last September by the Harvard School of Public Health stated that 42 percent of American college students have engaged in binge drinking, which it defined as a man's consuming five or more drinks in a row or a woman's consuming four or more. Athletes were found to be the greatest abusers of any group.

Lisa Palumbo, a former bartender at Haney's, a Lexington bar, testified at Watts's trial that one night she saw him drink eleven cans of beer in forty minutes.

Dr. Ruth Staten, a substance-abuse counselor at the University of Kentucky Health Service, said alcohol abuse was all too common among American college students. "Getting drunk, vomiting in dorms, urinating in elevators, seems just to be an accepted societal norm on campuses by too many students," she said. "It's considered just part of Friday night."

The tragedy of Watts, Brock, and Steinmetz caused people in Lexington and beyond to look at the problem of drinking in various ways. One week after the accident, Newton, the athletic director, issued new guidelines for punishing abusers of drugs or alcohol. They stipulate that any Kentucky athlete convicted of driving under the influence will be immediately dismissed from the team and lose his or her scholarship.

Watts could get out of prison in two years, or a little more. But his true punishment, he told the Russell Springs students, was having to ask himself, "How can I live with this?"

"I dream about Scott and Artie, and I don't see them in happy times," he said. "I picture them the last time I saw them, at the scene. I picture them bloody and broken up. I picture my two buddies dying in my arms. I know their families can't sleep. Mine can't either. You make a terrible mistake and you pay the consequences.

"Every morning I wake up and look in the mirror, I see the scar on my arm from my wrist to my elbow. I'm reminded about what happened, and while I'm brushing my teeth I see the scar on my shoulder, and there's one on my back, and these physical scars will be with me the rest of my life, like the memory."

In the Pulaski County Courthouse on Tuesday, Judge Venters's last words to Jason Watts were: "Remanded to the custody of the jailer." Watts shuffled out in handcuffs and leg irons. Just before the rear door closed behind him, he turned with difficulty to catch a glimpse of his family over his shoulder, and moved his lips. "I love you," he said silently.

[1999]

The Miracle of Young Tyler Hostetler

 ONE YEAR AGO, Tyler David Hostetler, age eight, died. Last week he played in a Little League game. This is the story:

The soft, spring rain had stopped and the evening sun angled through the clouds as Jeff Hostetler walked the family's six-month-old buff-and-white cocker spaniel, Rookie, down a path from his spacious house in Morgantown. It was about 7 P.M. last June 14 when they headed to Cheat Lake, which sparkled alongside his property. Hostetler moved with Rookie down a hill—this is West Virginia, after all, "almost heaven" as the locals often refer to it—and the hills and mountains are indelible to the majesty of the terrain.

At age thirty-eight, Hostetler, the former Giants quarterback who helped his team win two Super Bowls, had fashioned, surely, an idyllic life. He had married his college sweetheart, Vicki, and the Hostetlers had three boys: Jason, age fourteen at the time, Justin, eleven, and Tyler.

Tyler, the youngest and perhaps the most willful, was spending the night at a friend's house. He was tall and strong for his age and had recently been chosen for his Little League's all-star team. Like his brothers, he was an honor roll student as well as a good athlete.

Hostetler, still sporting the mustache familiar to Giants fans, saw Rookie trot onto the tennis court. As Jeff was about to chase

145

him off, he suddenly heard anguished screams from Vicki, up at the house.

"Jeff! Jeff! Hurry! Something terrible has happened! Tyler's hurt! Hurry!"

He ran toward the house.

"Beth Ann called," cried Vicki, in the doorway. "She could hardly talk. She said: 'Come immediately. Tyler had an accident.'"

Jeff and Vicki jumped into his white Suburban and flew down Eastlake Drive, up Sunset Beach, and around to Snake Hill Road to the France farm, about six miles away, where Tyler had gone to stay with nine-year-old Charles France.

Charles and Tyler had hopped onto the Gator, a six-wheel all-terrain vehicle used for hauling lumber and other farm objects. Charles drove it a short distance, then jumped off and told Tyler to get on and follow him as he chased locusts. Tyler had never driven one before, but that would hardly have bothered him.

Tyler lost control and hit a fence post, and the vehicle flipped over on its side, pinning Tyler. A bar from the thousand-pound vehicle wedged into Tyler's neck. Charles screamed for help and began running the seven hundred or so yards over a hill to the farmhouse.

Dr. John France, a local trauma injury and spinal-cord surgeon who is Charles's father, does not usually leave the hospital until much later in the night. But by a quirk of fate this night he had come home early. He was speaking with a contractor building his barn when he heard his son's shouts. "I didn't know what he was screaming about," John France recalled, "but it sounded terrible. I took off running in the direction of Charles." The contractor was at his heels.

"I found Tyler lying under the Gator. He wasn't breathing. It looked like his neck had been broken. His face had turned a purplish white, indicating cardiac arrest.

"I thought he might have either a spinal-cord injury or brain injury. I don't remember how this other fella and I got the vehicle off Tyler, but we did. I gave Tyler CPR. He began to breathe again, and he had a thready, barely palpable pulse. I've seen a lot of cases of accidents where someone's neck is broken, and I wondered if I was saving a little boy who would be a quadriplegic the rest of his life, who might be ventilator-dependent the rest of his life, and was I doing the right thing?

"But I kept giving him breaths, and breaths, and breaths. And he opened his eyes. I stopped the CPR. Then his eyes shut and he stopped breathing again, began to discolor again. I applied CPR again. By this time my wife had called an ambulance, and within about ten minutes it came. I had kept Tyler perfectly still to keep him stabilized, to keep from having further damage to his neck."

It had begun to drizzle again, and someone brought out a poncho to place over Tyler to keep the sandy-haired boy dry and warm. Tyler was now alert, and John France assumed correctly that he had got to Tyler within three to five minutes of the accident, otherwise the lack of oxygen to his brain would have been disastrous.

Tyler was carefully placed in the ambulance, and the vehicle began to pull up the winding, mountainside roads from the farm when the Hostetlers drove up. "We just knew that Tyler was in the ambulance, and we followed it," Jeff Hostetler said. "All the while we saw from the back window the medics working on Tyler. We still didn't know what had happened."

"I can't begin to describe what our feelings were, to see our little boy like this," Vicki Hostetler recalled.

When the ambulance arrived at Ruby Hospital and Tyler was carried out in a stretcher, Jeff would remember the absolute fear in his son's eyes when they looked at each other.

"Daddy, Daddy," Tyler said.

"It's all right, Tyler," he said. "Everything's going to be all right."

John France emerged from the ambulance and told Jeff and Vicki what had happened.

"How bad is he, John?" Jeff asked.

"He was dead, Jeff," France said. "He's alive now, but he's

badly injured. There's some paralysis. We just don't know yet how bad it's going to be."

"Does he have a chance to recover, to have a normal life?"

"Yes, he's young, he's moved each extremity; the field's wide open for recovery."

Jeff and Vicki understood, of course, that there was also the distinct possibility of little or no recovery.

In bed now, with tubes in his arms and wearing a halo, Tyler asked his parents if he would get better. "Will I be able to play with the all-star team next week?" he asked.

"We'll have to see what happens, Tyler," Vicki said. "We're all praying for the best."

That night Tyler took a turn for the worse. He stopped being able to move his arms, his legs, his fingers, his toes. He was completely paralyzed from the neck down. Doctors told the Hostetlers that they could help by continuing to massage Tyler's feet, to keep the muscles limber, to give healing a chance.

For six weeks, either Vicki or Jeff or both were with Tyler every minute, day and night. They took turns sleeping overnight in his room, talking to him, trying to encourage him, and kneading his feet to try to maintain muscle tone. Everything was devoted to Tyler.

Jeff, a free agent, had offers from the Tennessee Titans and the St. Louis Rams. "It would have been impossible for me to leave my son," he said. "There was simply no question about it." Dr. Russell Biundo, medical director of the Healthsouth Mountain View Regional Rehabilitation Hospital in Morgantown, where Tyler was eventually sent, called the Hostetlers "two of the most devoted parents I have ever seen."

For six days after the accident, Tyler lay in the intensive-care unit, his left side paralyzed totally and only the slightest bit of motion in his right hand and right leg. His nerve endings were so sensitive that a breeze could cause him pain. He yelped in agony when his mother's hair brushed against his bare arm.

"I hate my life," he said. "I want to die."

148

"You can't say that, Tyler," Jeff said. "You're tougher than that." Jeff reminded Tyler about his own struggles in football, how he didn't give up. He talked about his injuries and the rehabilitation he had to go through, and his time as a second-string quarterback, just waiting for his opportunity.

"Quit has never been in my vocabulary, and it's not going to be in yours," he told Tyler.

Jeff recalled, "All of the lessons I learned in football—discipline, motivation, drive—all came into play in how I tried to deal with Tyler."

After eight days in Ruby Hospital, Tyler was transferred to Healthsouth for rehab. A little more movement appeared in his right side. In the third week there was some motion in his left leg. One day Tyler's aunt Janie came to visit and asked if she could kiss him. "Okay," he said, not altogether thrilled. When she did, it appeared that he had moved the forefinger on his left hand, the hand that had remained paralyzed.

"Did you see that?" Jeff asked. They had.

"Tyler," Vicki said, "can you do that again?" And he did. It was the first movement of an extremity in a week. "There was such joy, just for this little moment," Vicki recalled. "I turned away. I didn't want Tyler to see me crying."

After that, Hostetler said, "Tyler really took off." In the fifth week he started to try to walk again. "He had to relearn everything, every step," Hostetler said.

Tyler had the advantage of youth, but rehab was arduous, exhausting, and painful. He wanted to quit. "You can do it, Tyler," Jeff said, with a decisive tone. "You will do it!" He helped him to take one more step than Tyler thought he could take. And then another. This went on day after day.

Several things helped Tyler's improvement, besides the various medications and, as Hostetler said, "incredibly wonderful care by the doctors." Visitors were important for Tyler, from his Little League teammates to his family—his brothers, uncles, aunts, grandparents—to family friends and even his beloved Rookie.

Calls came from a host of friends, and beyond. There were phone calls from people like a longtime family friend Jon Miller, senior vice president of NBC Sports; as well as Barry Larkin, the Cincinnati Reds' shortstop and a hero of Tyler's; and Michael Jordan. (All the tongue-tied Tyler could say to Jordan was: "Uh-huh. . . . Uh-huh. . . . Uh-huh. . . . Okay.")

There were the stories Tyler enjoyed hearing, such as how his parents met, when Jeff was quarterbacking the West Virginia Mountaineers in the Gator Bowl in December 1982. He saw the pretty daughter of his coach, Don Nehlen, in a convertible. "Can you give me a ride?" Jeff asked her, and she said yes.

"And what about when you kissed her, Daddy?" he asked. Indeed, on that first day, there was a kiss. It seemed comforting to Tyler to hear of the romance of his parents, since he was feeling so apart from everyday things.

And he asked his father to tell him the football stories that he had heard on many other occasions. The story, perhaps, that he liked best was framed on the wall of Jeff's business here, Hostetler's Cafe, which specializes in bagels, a taste that he acquired not on the Pennsylvania farm where he grew up but in Hillside, New Jersey, where he lived during football seasons with the Giants. On the wall is an article from the *Tampa Tribune,* written the day after Super Bowl XXV, on January 27, 1991, after the Giants' 20–19 victory over Buffalo. The headline read, HOSTETLER'S 7-YEAR WAIT WORTH IT NOW.

Jeff, who had been a career backup, passed for 222 yards, one touchdown, and no interceptions in the Super Bowl, filling in for the injured Phil Simms. "The greatest thing about Jeff," George Young, the Giants' general manager, said in the article, "is that no matter how frustrated, he hung in there and waited several years for his great opportunity, and he had it now."

Jeff indeed knew frustrations. He had had a scholarship to Penn State, but after starting a few games and doing well, he was still second string to Todd Blackledge. The 6-foot-3-inch, 220-pound quarterback transferred to West Virginia; he starred on the football field as well as in the classroom, where he was a dean's list student.

In the pros, where Jeff also played for the Redskins and the Raiders in a fine fifteen-year career, he suffered a wide range of injuries, including a torn rotator cuff, a broken back, and several concussions. He also had three knee operations and ankle surgery.

Tyler was strong and tough like his dad, even to the point of being the lone third grader at Cheat Lake elementary school to pass the Presidential Physical Fitness test with, among other tests, push-ups, pull-ups, and a mile run. "And something else helped, I want to believe," Jeff said. "And that is prayer. We're a religious Christian family. Every night, Vicki and I and the two boys knelt and said prayers for Tyler. Every night."

Six weeks after the accident, Tyler went home. The environment proved to be therapeutic. In a week he was able to brush his teeth by himself. Two weeks later Tyler was able to move about without help. Shortly after, he started school with the rest of his classmates. Dr. Gary Marano, a radiologist who is a neighbor of the Hostetlers, read the x-rays after the accident and observed the boy recently. "Tyler," he said, "is a little miracle."

But Tyler's head still did not sit properly on his neck. It listed ever so much. Last December, Jeff took Tyler to Miami so Dr. Barth Green of the Miami Project could operate on Tyler's neck, to straighten it out. The operation was a success, and Tyler, Green said, "was walking around the next day like a champ."

Things have resumed a relatively regular pace in the Hostetler home. When Tyler was in the hospital, his two older brothers were eager to please, were even a bit deferential to him. No more. "He's buggin' me again," Jason said, stating an older brother's time-honored position.

Bugging you about what? he was asked.

"Everything," he said.

Just a few weeks ago, Jeff turned down an offer to quarterback the Minnesota Vikings. "My football days are over," he said. "Tyler's injury and recovery have been the most significant period of my life. And I realized that my time is much more valuable here, with my family, watching my kids grow up, being a part of it. I understand the frailties of life better than I ever have. How precious each day is."

What does Tyler think of his dad giving up football?

"I think he's crazy," said Tyler, not one to mince words. "We watched the Super Bowl between the Titans and Rams, and I thought it would be great if Dad was in the game. I'd play."

Not football, not for Tyler, or hockey. The regular pounding in those sports could cause a recurrence of problems for him. Basketball, baseball, golf, and tennis are permitted.

Tyler is back in the Cheat Lake Little League, playing first base and wearing number 5 for the black-jerseyed BlaineTurner Advertising team. He is still not 100 percent back, the doctors say. He still has some problems with mobility in his left hand, for example, but he is almost there.

On a close play at first base in the first inning on a sun-splashed early afternoon recently, the runner stopped before he might have run into Tyler. "I hold my breath on plays like that," said Jeff, sitting in the bleachers along the first-base line. "You're always on pins and needles," Vicki said, "but the doctors said that Tyler could take a hit like that and still be okay."

Now Tyler came to bat, a left-handed hitter. In his age group, a pitching machine serves up balls to the batters. In his first three games of the season, Tyler had nine hits in ten at-bats. He gets respect.

"Get back, Joey," the coach of the opposing team called to his center fielder. The words had hardly escaped from him when Tyler cracked a line drive over Joey's head. In the stands, Vicki and Jeff jumped up and clapped. The ball hit the wooden fence and bounced back, and Tyler David Hostetler, age nine, pulled up at second base with a double, standing there, under his black batting helmet, as if nothing much had happened.

[2000]

PIVOTAL

PLAYS

Draft Day
in the Ghetto

✌ IT WAS Draft Day in the ghetto. That's what everyone there called it. On a few days each year, chieftains of the notorious Vice Lords street gang appeared at certain homes on the West Side of Chicago to take recruits. On this summer night in 1966, twenty-five Vice Lord chiefs stopped in front of the home of Mary Thomas. She had nine children, seven of them boys, ranging from Lord Henry, fifteen years old, to Isiah, five. The Thomases lived on the first floor of a two-story red brick building on Congress Street, facing the Eisenhower Expressway.

One of the Lords rang the bell. Mary Thomas, wearing glasses, answered the door. She saw behind him the rest of his gang, all wearing gold tams and black capes, and some had guns in their waist bands that glinted under the street lamps.

"We want your boys," the gang leader told her. "They can't walk around here and not be in no gang." She looked him in the eye. "There's only one gang around here, and that's the Thomas gang," she said, "and I lead that." "If you don't bring those boys out, we'll get 'em in the streets," he said. She shut the door. The gang members waited. She walked through the living room where the rest of the family sat. Isiah, frightened, watched her go into the bedroom and return with a sawed-off shotgun. She opened the front door.

She pointed the gun at the caped figure before her. "Get off my porch," she said, "or I'll blow you 'cross the Expressway." He stepped back, and slowly he and his gang disappeared into the night.

Isiah Thomas never joined a gang, and was protected from the ravages of street life—the dope, the drinking, the stealing, the killings—by his mother and his brothers, even those who eventually succumbed to the streets. Two of his brothers became heroin addicts, one was a pimp, a couple would be jailed, and one became a Vice Lords chief.

Isiah, though, was the baby of the family, and its hope. He became an honor student in grade school and high school, an All-America basketball player in high school and college, and, as a six-foot-one-inch point guard, led Indiana University to the National Collegiate Athletic Association championship last month. After only a few weeks out of high school, he was a standout on the United States team that won the gold medal in the 1979 Pan-American Games, and was a starter on the 1980 United States Olympic team.

The pros liked what they saw. "He's a terrific talent," said Rod Thorn, general manager of the Chicago Bulls. "Not only physically—and he seems adept at every phase of the game—but he has a charisma, an ability to inspire confidence in his teammates that only a few players have, like Larry Bird and Magic Johnson and Julius Erving."

Last weekend Isiah Thomas, a nineteen-year-old sophomore and B student majoring in forensics, with an eye toward law school, made an important decision. He passed up his last two years of college basketball to declare his eligibility for the National Basketball Association's draft on June 5. Thomas said that three teams—New Jersey, Detroit, and Chicago—had been told he could expect an offer of at least $1 million to sign.

Thomas had wrestled with his decision all season. "Don't do it," said Bobby Knight, the Indiana basketball coach. "You can still improve in basketball. You could be worth more." "Stay in school," said Quinn Buckner, a former Indiana player and now with the

Milwaukee Bucks. "The college experience at your age is valuable and can't ever be repeated."

"What's left for you to prove in college?" asked his brother, Gregory. "Go only if the price is right," said his former high school coach, Gene Pingatore. "Don't sell yourself short." "Son," said Mary Thomas, "do what makes you happy."

The idea of turning pro had been with Isiah for as long as he can remember, instilled by his brothers who had their own basketball dreams squashed.

"There was a lot to consider," said Thomas. He sat on the arm of a couch in his small apartment in the Fountain Park complex on the Indiana campus in Bloomington. He wore a red baseball cap, a blue USA Olympic jacket, jeans, and yellow sneakers. He speaks softly, thoughtfully, with careful articulation. Sometimes he'll flash that warm, dimpled smile that has become familiar from newspaper photos and national magazine covers. Behind that smile is also a toughness and intensity—twice last season he was involved in fights in games.

"I know I'm a role model for a lot of people back in the ghetto," said Thomas. "Not too many of us get the chance to get out, to go to college. If I quit school, what effect would that have on them?

"And I had said I wanted to be a lawyer, and one day return there and help the people. They need it. I've seen kids who stole a pair of pants and they get a five-year prison sentence. Literally. Because there was no adequate legal help for them. I know that I'll get my law degree. I know you can only play basketball for so many years. Then you've got the rest of your life ahead of you.

"And I have to think of my family. My mother worked hard all her life and for not much money. My father left when I was three years old, and my mom kept us together by herself. She worked in the community center, she worked in the church, she did whatever she could. She's got a job with the housing authority in Chicago now, and she shouldn't be working. Her eyes are bad, and her heart's not good. I'd like her to quit."

He feels that with the connections he makes in basketball he can help his brothers. He has already opened a few doors. Larry has a job with city housing, and Mark is with the police department.

"I can always go back to school," Isiah said. "But I can't always make a million dollars. I won't always have a chance to provide stability for my family. And I'm doing it at basketball, a game I love."

He was a prodigy in basketball the way Mozart was in music. At age three, Amadeus was composing on a harpsichord; at three, Isiah could dribble and shoot baskets. He was the halftime entertainment at the neighborhood Catholic Youth Organization games. "We gave Isiah an old jersey that fell like a dress on him, and he wore black oxfords and tossed up shots with a high arc," said Ted Kalinowski, who was called Brother Alexis before he left the order. "Isiah was amazing."

By the time Thomas was in the fourth grade, he was a standout on the eighth-grade team at Our Lady of Sorrows. His mother and brothers watched him closely. Mary Thomas made sure that he went straight home from school and did not dawdle in the streets. "If I did," he said, "my brothers would kick my butt."

From the time he was in grade school, his brothers lectured him. The seven of them sat in a bedroom and closed the door so that their mother and two sisters would not hear the horror stories of the street. They would take him for a walking tour and point out dangers. "They told me about the mistakes they had made so that I wouldn't have to make them," said Thomas.

Lord Henry, for one, had been an all-city basketball player at St. Philip's; people in the neighborhood contend that he was the best basketball player in the family. He still holds the Catholic League single-season scoring record. But he had problems with discipline and grades and was thrown out of school. He went into the streets and became a junkie. Isiah could see the tortures his brother went through and the suffering it caused his mother.

As an eighth-grader, Isiah sought a scholarship to attend

Weber High School, a Catholic League basketball power. The coach turned him down, too short. He was five feet six inches. "Look, I'm six-four," Larry Thomas argued to the coach. "My brother will grow just as tall."

Gene Pingatore, coach at St. Joseph's in Westchester, a Chicago suburb, was convinced. "He was a winner," said Pingatore. "He had that special aura."

At Westchester, a predominantly white school in a white middle-class neighborhood, Thomas endeavored to learn textbook English. At one point his brother, Gregory, was confused. Isiah recalls his brother saying: "'You done forgot to talk like a nigger. Better not come around here like no sissy white boy.'"

"Hey," Isiah said, laughing, "pull up on that jive." But the brothers, like Isiah, understood the importance of language and how it could help them escape the ghetto, a dream they shared.

"What I was doing," said Isiah, "was becoming fluent in two languages." Isiah would rise at 5:30 in the morning to begin the one-and-a-half-hour journey by elevated train and bus to Westchester. "Sometimes I'd look out of the window and see Isiah going to school in the dark and I'd cry," said Mary Thomas. "I'd give him grits with honey and butter for breakfast. And felt bad that I couldn't afford eggs and bacon for him, too. He sure did like to eat."

Although he excelled in basketball, Isiah neglected his studies and nearly flunked out of high school after his freshman year. "You're a screwed-up kid," said Larry. "You can go one of two ways from here. I had a choice like this once. I chose hustlin'. It's a disgustin' kind of life. You got the chance of a lifetime."

Pingatore emphasized that without a C average he could not get a college scholarship under the NCAA rules. "From that point on," recalls Isiah's sister, Ruby, "he was a changed kid." He made the St. Joseph's honor roll in each of his next three years.

He also led his team to second place in the Illinois state high school tournament and was chosen All-American. He had his pick of hundreds of college scholarships. He chose Indiana because it was close and because Bobby Knight played it straight. "He didn't try to bribe me," said Mary Thomas. "Other schools offered hundreds of thousands of dollars. One coach promised to buy me a beautiful house. Another one said that there'd be a Lear jet so I could go to all Isiah's games. All Bobby Knight promised was he'd try to get Isiah a good education and give him a good opportunity to get better in basketball. He said that I might not even be able to get a ticket for a basketball game. I liked that." She also got tickets, and went to all of Isiah's games, sometimes traveling to Bloomington by bus.

He made All-Big Ten as a freshman. Last season he was a consensus All-American. Despite this, he and Coach Knight had conflicts. Thomas appreciated Knight's basketball mind and knew that the coach relied on his ability as a floor leader, but Thomas had trouble swallowing what he considered Knight's sometimes insulting and dehumanizing behavior. He used vile language to his players in private and in public. He physically abused them (in the Pan-Am Games, Knight, coach of the United States team, had grabbed Thomas by the jersey and shaken him).

Once, Thomas, who had been appointed team captain, decided to talk with Knight about the team's poor morale. Thomas believed that Indiana—going badly at the beginning of the season—had some of the best players in the country and could win the championship if they could pull together and not fight the coach. "There's a problem here, coach," said Isiah.

"There's no problem here," replied Knight.

Indiana, however, did improve and made it to the final of the NCAA tournament against North Carolina at the Spectrum in Philadelphia on the night of March 30. Amid the blaring of the school bands and the waving of pom-poms and the screams from the crowd—the Indiana rooters were sectioned on one side of the court in red and white, the school colors, and the North Carolina fans on the other side wearing blue and white—the game was tightly played. North Carolina led by 26–25 as Isiah Thomas took the ball from under the Tar Heels' basket and dribbled slowly upcourt. There were only twelve seconds to go in the half, and tense Indiana fans wondered if the Hoosiers would get another shot off, especially with Thomas's casualness.

"I didn't want the team to press, I wanted them to relax, and if they saw I wasn't rushing I hoped they wouldn't either," Thomas said later. With two seconds to go he hit Randy Wittman with a pass in the corner, and Wittman connected, giving Indiana its first lead of the game and a terrific lift as it went to the locker room.

Starting the second half, Thomas stole two straight passes from North Carolina and scored on each. Indiana went ahead by 31–26 and went on to a 63–50 victory. "Those two steals," said Dean Smith, the North Carolina coach, "were the turning point in the game." Thomas scored a game-high twenty-three points and had five assists and four steals. He was named the outstanding player in the championship tournament.

As soon as the game ended, Indiana fans rushed onto the court. One of them, Thomas saw, was a black woman in a red suit jacket with a button on her lapel. The button read, "Isiah Thomas's Mom. Mrs. Mary Thomas." Near the center of the court they embraced. She was crying, and it looked as if Isiah was holding back tears.

"Thanks, Mom, thanks for everything you've gone through for me. I hope I can do something for you." "You done enough, honey," she said. Reporters and camera men were all around them. And Isiah whispered in his mother's ear. "Well, you can do one more thing for me," he said.

"What's that, baby?"

"I heard you in the first half when I threw a bad pass. You hollered, 'What the hell are you doin'?' Don't cuss at me on the court. I was fixin' to get it together."

Then Isiah was scooted off to receive the winner's trophy. And the woman who wore the button proudly saying she was Isiah Thomas's mom, took out a handkerchief and wiped her eyes.

[1981]

The Senator with a Jump Shot

◈ IN Senator Bill Bradley's large new white office on Capitol Hill, with high ceilings and high windows, there is an echo. "Listen," he says. And the sound of the word is faintly reheard. The Democratic United States senator from New Jersey is standing near the center of the room, a yellow pencil behind his ear, a blue lightweight suit casually worn, his vaulted left eyebrow raised, and he laughs in his throaty manner at the sound. That, too, reverberates lightly. There are other echoes in the room, these silent. They depict what the senator, with characteristic irony, refers to as "my past life."

A desk plaque, a kind of inside joke, reads "Senator Bill Bradley," then right below it "Former New York Knick." And on the floor against the wall—he has been in this office in the Hart Building for only a month, so papers and photographs are piled around the room awaiting shelves and carpenters—can be seen, amid pictures of sober civilian scenes, two enlarged black-and-white photos of him in a Knicks jersey and shorts. One picture shows him racing across the basketball court, arms pumping in triumph, just after the Knicks had beaten Los Angeles to win the 1970 National Basketball Association championship. In the other photo he has leaped into the broad arms of Willis Reed, the former Knick center. Bradley, his legs wrapped around Reed's waist, is facing the camera and his mouth is open with a yelp of glee. The Knicks had just won the 1973 NBA title.

Senator Bradley walks behind his desk and eases his six-foot-five-inch body into a plain, hardback chair. "A back injury from my playing days—I couldn't take sitting in a big leather chair for long," he explains. He smiles. "That's the way it is with us old jocks."

Senator Bradley was named recently to the Naismith Memorial Basketball Hall of Fame. The senator, along with Dave DeBusschere, the other starting forward on the Knicks' two championship teams, his former roommate, and still a close friend, will be among six men inducted tomorrow into the hall at Springfield, Massachusetts. "I think I'm a senator today as much because I had the experience of playing professional basketball for ten years on the road in America as for any other college experience or for anything I studied," he said.

Senator Bradley, by his own estimation, had grown up relatively sheltered in Crystal City, Missouri, a suburb of St. Louis. The only child of Warren Bradley, a well-to-do banker, and Susan Crowe Bradley, a former junior high school teacher, Bill Bradley enrolled at Princeton, became an All-America basketball player, was a starter on the United States Olympic championship team in 1964, then a Rhodes Scholar at Oxford in England, played for the Knicks from 1967 to 1977, and, at age thirty-five, won election to the Senate in 1978. Now thirty-nine—he will be forty on July 28—he is one of the youngest senators and, by most accounts, one of the most capable on Capitol Hill.

"I played with a team—the Knicks—at a time when the people on it were not only great basketball players but good people," he said, "so the experience for me was remarkable, living and traveling with them a hundred days of the year and getting to know them." Blacks and whites, men from all over the country, from a variety of backgrounds. DeBusschere from a working-class family in Detroit; Reed a black from the rural South; Walt Frazier a black

163

from Atlanta. Earl Monroe was a black from Philadelphia, and Phil Jackson a white man from Montana.

"I remember one night when I had been in the Senate for only about four or five months," said Senator Bradley. "It was about eleven o'clock, and the Senate was still in session. I was sitting around the Democratic cloakroom, which is just off the Senate floor, and a lot of senators were there.

"I looked around and saw one guy joking, another guy was quiet, another one was talking. And it occurred to me that this wasn't a lot different from the Knicks' locker room, in that it really was a matter of people getting along together in a small space, each of whom has his own individual agenda but who must subsume it in a broader, more general context—if he's actually going to get anything accomplished.

"That process still fascinates me—how to get people with different backgrounds, different experiences, different personal agendas to agree on a shared goal and work toward it."

As a professional, he had a career average of 12.4 points per game and made one mid-season all-star team, but he was the ultimate role player. Never the most gifted athlete—most of the NBA players could run faster and jump higher—he understood that he needed constant motion to frustrate his defender. He developed an uncanny ability to get open for a shot off a screen, and he was deadly with a jump shot. If need be, he might hold another player's jersey or step on his toe when the referee's vision was blocked.

It was suggested that he was the least talented, grabbiest, and smartest player in the NBA, and that each of those explained the other. "None of that's true," Senator Bradley said with a laugh. "A reporter called me after I had been named to the Hall of Fame and asked me what I thought had been my contributions to the game," he said. "I had never prior to that question ever thought that I had made a contribution to the game, not like somebody who breaks the DNA code or makes a contribution to medicine. I think my whole orientation was to view myself only as part of a larger whole, which was the team. And while you always looked at individual stats, you didn't really pay that much attention to them.

"But of course I was flattered and pleased that an honor like this would happen to me. And I'm especially glad to go in with De-Busschere. I figured that for six years I walked behind him and carried his bag, so I might as well walk behind him and carry his bag into the Hall of Fame."

But playing well wasn't the only thing. Winning was essential. "Certainly winning is important," the senator said. "If you didn't win, you wouldn't have proved anything by the way you played. It was winning by playing the way you did that was the key. In amateur sports you could take a lot of satisfaction from your efforts. You could tell a grade school or high school student—as I tell my daughter, Theresa Anne, who's six—'Go out and play and do something just as well as you possibly can, as well as your ability will allow, and then be satisfied with your performance, regardless of whether you won or lost.'

"But not in professional sports, because the nature of it, the reason you're playing, is to win. Now, there were other levels of the game for me, obviously, in addition to winning—such as playing in a certain manner." He meant the humanness of the experience—not only knowing where your teammate was going to move to be open for a pass, but being congenial to the point of discussing personal problems with him off the court.

"But winning justifies your success," he said. "Some people justify their success if they don't win by their individual achievements. I didn't."

But is there not an overemphasis on winning in America? "Some of that has been exaggerated," he said. "There is a flip side to winning, of course, and that's losing. And part of personal growth is being able to deal with that. Losing has a flavor, a taste all its own. And in some sense it is as much responsible for the personal-growth component in sport as is winning. Simply because you emphasize winning doesn't mean you don't have a healthy respect for the personal-growth potential in losing, and coping with that."

Bradley, too, "lost." With Princeton in 1965 he went to the semifinals of the National Collegiate Athletic Association and lost to Michigan. He struggled in his rookie year with the Knicks—the highest-paid player in the game at the time—and made bad plays at the end of several games that contributed to Knick losses. And he was disappointed in not winning four straight championships with the Knicks. He thought they might have.

"I still think that sports are overwhelmingly positive," he said. "I think that elements such as commercialism and overemphasis in certain segments of sports have become like many of the areas of our life. And the problems associated with those areas are part of sports as well. But I still think that the dominant motive for playing and the dominant experience of the game is positive. The motive is to excel, and the experience provides a range from discipline to dedication to community to what else that sports has always had when you are with the right group of people at the right time.

"And I always said that I think sports as a model for other things—as a metaphor—is limited. That's why I have to be pushed by a writer even to draw a parallel to my own experiences. But the parallel I've chosen to draw is a very personal one. Not what sports means for America, but what sports meant for me, and how that related to what I do now. The practice really did establish habits for me that carry over into what I do now. I work very hard." He often puts in sixteen to eighteen hours of work a day. "And I work because I want to be the best senator I can be. In a way it's like when I started practicing basketball four or five hours a day when I was thirteen. I wanted to be the very best basketball player I could be."

The senator no longer plays basketball. "I just don't have the time," he said. He also has said that much of the fun would be gone for him if he wanted to make a move he once made, and now could not. "I haven't really shot since 1977, when I walked off the court in Detroit in Cobo Arena. An odd thing is, the last shot I took was a jump shot which I hit from the left base line. It was a kind of symmetry because that was the first jump shot—against the same team—the first shot I took as a pro in 1967. So ten years later, the same team, the same shot.

"The only time I touch a ball now is when I'm visiting a high school and someone throws me a ball and says, 'Shoot.' Sometimes I'll be campaigning for a Democratic candidate and we'll have a meeting in the high school. We may be discussing the military budget or the health of the economy, and it never makes the local news. But if a free-throw shooting contest is arranged, that's always covered. So the candidates want me to do that, and so I do. That's the extent to which I do any playing at all."

Bradley has recently lost about 30 pounds. He now weighs 212, about 3 pounds fewer than when he played with the Knicks. "Basically, I lost the weight by not eating," he said. He was once an aficionado of junk foods. "I try to jog a few times a week for about thirty minutes a time. Or I'll ride an exercise bicycle. My athletic experience now is no different from that of about eighty million other Americans who are in sports to try to flatten their stomachs and widen their arteries."

His interest in pro basketball remains, but on a sedentary level. "I watch the playoffs when they get down to the end," he said. "It's then that you really see the psychology of the game. You see what the teams that have gotten to know each other will do in a period of stress. And more times than not, the team that loses has really not been through the pressure cooker."

It was mentioned that Larry Bird of the Celtics plays in a manner reminiscent of Bradley. "The most distinguishing characteristics of Bird," he said, "are that he always moves and the ball doesn't stay in his hands very long. And obviously those are the two things I can identify with as a player."

For the most part, Bradley has downplayed his participation in sports, though he says he remains very proud of it. "But I wanted to prove myself in a different field—in the Senate—and I had to prove myself by the standards of the institution." So he refused to rely on his basketball celebrity status as a crutch. "But I am still often referred to in newspaper stories as 'Senator Bill Bradley, the former New York Knick.' I laugh about that, but I have the feeling it will be with me the rest of my life."

Senator Bradley, like some intensely hardworking people, uses humor as a release—at times, a zany sense of humor. Once, when he was with the Knicks, he went to a party dressed in a priest's frock and supposedly heard confessions. He was also known for his unconcerned sartorial style of dress. Walt Frazier remembers Bradley's raincoat, for example. When it wasn't raining, he would roll it into a ball and carry it under his arm.

He was also known as "Dollar Bill," because of his frugality. Rumor had it that he had kept the first dollar he ever made. He seemed to enjoy the ribbing and attention of the other players in regard to his unusual habits. It made the boy from the suburbs feel a part of the team.

It was mentioned to him that when he played on the all-star team, he had told Pistol Pete Maravich "to do something crazy when you get in the game."

"Did I say 'crazy'?" asked Bradley. "Maybe I did. Or maybe I said, 'Do something different.' You can't take yourself too seriously. Not only did I feel that as a player, I feel that in this job. You have to have a sense of humor about who you are and what you do. You maintain a personal stability that way. It relieves tension to recognize that you can't always do everything and that you do the best you can for as long as you can. And recognizing that you alone are not responsible for things happening on the court, or in the Senate. Ultimately you recognize that the institution goes on. When you see yourself that way, it's hard to take yourself too seriously—though you can take what you're doing seriously."

Looking at the photo of him jumping into Reed's arms, he was asked if he has had such a moment of elation since. "That's a feeling that's never been duplicated," he said. "It's a clear-cut victory,

something that rarely happens in life. We had established our-
selves as the best in the world. It's like anything—it lasts about
twenty-four hours. But the moment is intense."

What's the closest he has come to it since? "Haven't." He
thought for a moment. "Afterward you experience a whole range
of satisfactions and achievements and series of accomplishments," he said. "The point is, the moment depicted in that photo
was a peak in that narrow category of experience—basketball.
Then life goes on."

[1983]

At Ninety-five, He Could Still Ripple the Net

W SUDDENLY in the last few weeks the name Nat Holman has been in the news again on a daily basis, on the front page of newspapers, in the lead stories on television newscasts. It had been forty years since people had heard and read the name so often, when the man and not just the name was in the news. The reason for the reemergence was because the Nat Holman Gymnasium on the campus of the City College of New York was where the recent stampede of a crowd attending a basketball game of rap music celebrities resulted in nine deaths.

"It destroyed me, made me very unhappy," said a ninety-five-year-old man sitting in his room, holding his cane, in the Hebrew Home for the Aged in the Riverdale section of the Bronx. "All these things are shockers. I'm sorry for those involved."

The man is Nat Holman, who, some fourteen years earlier, in November 1977, attended the dedication of the gymnasium in his honor, after having coached basketball at City College for forty-two years, from 1917 to 1959, and whose good and bad days included having been the coach of the only team to win both the National Invitation Tournament and the National Collegiate Athletic Association in the same year, 1950, as well as coach of some players who were convicted of point-shaving in the famous college basketball scandals that broke in 1951. Holman has since been honored in numerous ways for his contributions to basketball, including inclusion in the Basketball Hall of Fame in Springfield, Massachusetts, and the New York City Basketball Hall of Fame.

"You know that old expression, 'God, give us memories so we can have roses in December?'" Holman said at the time of the dedication. "Naming the gym after me was like the college giving me a bunch of roses in the month of December."

Holman's name, or at least his influence, lives on in another way, one more congenial to memories in December, and to memories of what he calls his "first love," basketball. His legacy is evident at the highest levels of the game today, with the reigning National Basketball Association champions, the Chicago Bulls. The coach of the Bulls is Phil Jackson, who credits his coach with the championship New York Knicks of the early 1970s, Red Holzman, as a primary influence in his coaching concepts. Red Holzman, in tandem, credits his college basketball coach, Nat Holman, as a significant influence in his coaching philosophy.

"Nat Holman was always preaching to us to hit the open man, to be unselfish, throw more fakes, pick, screen, to be in constant movement," recalled Holzman, who was an All-American guard for the City College teams in the early 1940s. "Some of us on the team—including me—were a little hardheaded, and we couldn't believe a lot of things he was saying could be done. Now, at this time, Coach Holman was about forty-five years old and always in good shape. He was one of the top-ranked squash players in the country then. And of course he had been one of the best basketball players with the Original Celtics in the 1920s.

"Well, this one time, he put himself on the second team in a practice session, and the guys on the first team decided we'd show him. It turned out, he showed us. He was fantastic and made us all look bad. He was a great teacher. He was tough, but a great teacher and a great coach."

Although Holman, once known as Mr. Basketball, still watches some basketball on television in his room, he was not familiar with the Bulls or their style of play. And while he recalls Larry Bird with admiration among today's players ("He impressed me a lot— a good ball handler, he does things while on the move, he's clever, excitable, and a joy to watch"), he did not know Michael Jordan. "Michael Jordan, the name rings a bell," he said, "but I can't place him, though I may know him by sight."

"My memory," added Holman, "is not as keen as it should be. After all, I'm a ninety-five-year-old youngster." He smiled. "Ninety-five. I can't believe I'm saying that."

His physical health remains good. He suffers from arthritis in the shoulders and legs but otherwise appears fit, if not quite as robust as in days gone by. Those days are reflected both in photographs and in the colorful, vibrant paintings that he has been doing for the last seven years, since he has been at this home. The photographs and paintings adorn the walls of his small room, a room with a large window that lets in the morning light.

One photograph shows him with dark wavy hair posing in his Original Celtic uniform, wearing knee guards and holding a basketball—there is a self-portrait on the wall that was taken from that photograph—and there is another photo, taken at a war bond rally at the Waldorf-Astoria in 1944, in which some of the famous sports names of the day are seen together: golfer Gene Sarazen, football player Sid Luckman, fight champions Jack Dempsey and Barney Ross, Earl Sande in his jockey silks, Alice Marble in her tennis outfit, Eleanor Holm in her swimsuit, Babe Ruth, looking wan, in a Yankee uniform and slippers, and also Nat Holman, at forty-eight, in basketball togs and black sneakers.

Now, at ninety-five, Holman, retaining an elegant air of old, wore a well-tailored brown pinstriped suit with vest and a tan handkerchief carefully tucked into his breast pocket. His brown shoes were shined, his brown tie was straight, and his hair was still rather thick and wavy, but white as linen. He uses his cane, he said, "in case there is a misstep."

"He's still vain, and proud about his appearance," said one of the officials at the home. "So he tries not to rely much on the cane. He can still walk fairly well without it."

The name Nat Holman was also in the news forty years ago when the basketball scandals broke. Returning from a game in Philadelphia, three of his City College players were arrested on charges of shaving points and taken from the train. Before they left, Holman called them aside individually and said: "I don't know what the story is, but if your conscience is clear, have no fears. Tell the truth and don't back up from anyone." The players were convicted, along with twenty-nine other players from six other schools.

Holman, who insisted that he was totally unaware of what his players had been doing, was suspended by the school for conduct unbecoming a teacher and neglect of duty, but two years later, after a vigorous fight, he was reinstated by a trial committee of the Board of Higher Education. All charges against him were dismissed. "I thought the biggest thrill of my life was winning the double championship," he said at the time. "But it isn't anymore. Today's vindication is my greatest victory."

He remembers those players as "good boys" but says, "You do whatever you can for the boys, and if the boys don't do the right thing, then they must suffer the consequences. They have to be straightened out."

Nat Holman was born on the Lower East Side of New York on October 19, 1896, in Grover Cleveland's second term as president, and about five years after the invention of basketball. As a young man he turned down a chance to sign as a pitcher with the Cincinnati Reds in order to play basketball. He remembered playing when there were nets, or chicken-wire cages, hoisted up around the basketball court so that roistering fans couldn't get at the players and the referees.

"Listen, this is the story, and I can recall it as vividly as I see you before me," he said. "The net was hung up on hooks, and the ball was in bounds if it hit the net. The trick was to tie up a man with the ball in a corner, sometimes get him in the net. It was a very enjoyable game, and very tough."

As a player, Holman described himself as "fast and a good passer and a team player, and I never gave a damn if I got my name in the paper as long as we won the game, or played well, the way the game should be played."

"Teamwork" is the essence of the game, and, as a coach, he can still recite the old litanies with relish, that "making sacrifices on the court, and fitting in, applies off the court as well." The game today, he said, is faster, but he thinks there is not as much of a premium put on defense as in his day, and the players "aren't as selfless." "But there's more movement today, where we had more fixed positions," he said.

He grew up shooting the two-hander and told his players when the one-hander was first seen, in the late 1930s, that it was "showboating" and that he'd "break their arm if they tried that." But he gradually adjusted to the one-hander and the jump shot. "You'd be a fool not to," he said.

At times in recent years, Holman has suffered from depression, sometimes associated with his frailty. "But even in his deepest doldrums," said an official at the home, "whenever he talks about basketball he perks up."

The last time he held a basketball was last fall, he remembered. Several people from the Hebrew Home had asked him to demonstrate some basketball techniques at a basket nearby. He rose from his chair in his room now, placed his cane on the bed in front of him, and demonstrated the passing he had showed them. "You can zip it like this, across your body, or you can duck and throw it over your head, or bounce it behind your back to a receiver," he said.

Did he shoot a basket? he was asked.

"Yes," he said.

One-handed or two?

"Two-handed."

Did he make it?

He looked at his companion seated nearby, raised an eyebrow, and smiled. The look said, "Are you kidding?"

Then Nat Holman took his cane from the bed and sat back down on the chair. "You know what I'd like?" he said. "A corned beef sandwich for lunch."

[1992]

The Referee Was
Bribed

🐾 SUSAN RUDOLPH remembers that it happened around 1973, shortly after she and Mendy were married. Mendy Rudolph, the dark-haired and fastidious National Basketball Association referee, the most respected and one of the best, if not the best, to have blown a whistle on a court, seemed deeply troubled.

"It scared me," she said. "Mendy was never like that. He was usually so upbeat, and when he wasn't, he was still able to disguise his feelings. But not now." She would ask what was wrong, and he would say, "Nothing." But after a couple of days, Rudolph said to his wife one night, "Let's take a walk."

"And then he told me about a phone call he got," she said recently, sitting in the same midtown Manhattan apartment that she shared with her late husband. "The call was from a gambler in Las Vegas. He offered Mendy a lot of money to shave points in games."

"It would be the answer to all our problems," Rudolph said to his wife.

"Are you crazy?" she replied.

"He made it sound so easy," Rudolph said. "All I would have to do is look away maybe one time during a game. Maybe twice."

At this time Mendy Rudolph, a chronic gambler, someone who loved "the fast lane and bright lights," said Susan Rudolph, was feeling "crushed."

In the past, Rudolph would disappear for a weekend at the craps and roulette tables in Las Vegas, or, because he bet large sums at the ticket window, would wear a Groucho Marx disguise at the race track so no one would recognize the widely known official. He had owed a great deal to casinos and to friends and family and business associates he had borrowed from to pay gambling debts and income tax, as well as alimony and child support. He had cashed in his $60,000 from the referees' pension fund and all of that went to pay his debts. He received $10,000 from workmen's compensation for an injury, and that went to pay his debts. He was still perhaps $100,000 in arrears.

With two jobs, one as a referee and the other as a national sales manager for WGN television in New York, he was earning close to $100,000 a year, but it was not nearly enough to cover his expenses and his continued high life.

"You can't do it," Susan Rudolph said to her husband that night when they had that talk. She recalled that he nodded, and replied: "It goes against all my principles. I love the game too much, respect it too much. I couldn't do it to you. I couldn't do it in the memory of my father, and I can't do it to myself. If I have to go into bankruptcy, something I'd hate to do, I'd do it."

Rudolph, born and raised in Wilkes-Barre, Pennsylvania, and the son of Harry Rudolph, a celebrated sports official in the area, died in 1979 of a pulmonary embolism at age fifty-two. He never declared bankruptcy, and until he retired as a referee in 1975 on doctor's orders because of a heart condition, he retained his reputation as one of the best officials ever, and one with the highest integrity.

Over eighteen years Rudolph officiated in a record 2,113 games. Acute observers—ranging from Red Auerbach to John Nucatola, a Hall of Fame referee and Rudolph's boss as director of NBA officials during Rudolph's last seven years in the league—agreed that his high standards and control of the game were unsurpassed.

The little-known story of Marvin (Mendy) Rudolph off the

court was recalled recently because the NBA playoffs are heading into the final series, and this used to be Mendy's time: he refereed more big games than anyone in history. It was recalled because the man many consider the finest referee in history is not in the Basketball Hall of Fame, which earlier this month held its ceremonies for the most recent crop of inductees.

And the story of Mendy Rudolph was also recalled because the influence of gambling in the games the nation watches and loves remains a fearsome specter. The story emphasizes once again how fragile the integrity of these games could be, and that even the best and strongest people involved in them may undergo potentially destructive temptation.

Pete Rose and Chet Forte, the former All-America basketball player and sports television director, were convicted of fraud and tax evasion stemming from their compulsion for gambling. There have been reports of sports gambling rings on college campuses and the questionable gambling associations of Len Dykstra and Michael Jordan. All attest to the vigilance that is necessary to keep the games clean.

Rarely, however, are officials involved, though one was under suspicion in 1951 during the college basketball scandals, and in 1961 another was banned from college games in the Midwest. In baseball, one umpire at the turn of the century was convicted of conspiring with gamblers to throw games.

Today the NBA office has a security department of three plus a security representative in each of the league cities, a setup similar to that of the other major professional leagues and college sports organizations. NBA representatives are in close contact with local police authorities. In regard to its officials, the league regularly makes security checks as well as credit checks—the healthier the officials' finances are, the league figures, the less vulnerable they will be to temptation.

"Sure, you get approached on occasion," said Earl Strom, the former NBA referee who was a contemporary and friend of Rudolph's. "Gamblers are always looking for an edge. I remember once getting a phone call in a hotel room just before I was to work a game. The caller said, 'Remember, we had a drink together last year?' And then he asked me what the condition of Wilt was. I hung up immediately."

Mendy Rudolph said he welcomed scrutiny. When he was asked about a federal investigation of point-shaving into pro basketball, which included its officials, in the early 1970s, he told Robert Vare of the *Village Voice*: "I think it's good that they scrutinize the game. They should patrol it. I think that's a healthy sign." But there were pleas from the NBA commissioner at the time, Walter Kennedy, for Rudolph to cool his gambling.

"I remember Walter Kennedy calling me with great concern," said Strom. "He wanted me to speak to Mendy about his gambling. He had been observed at the $50 and $100 ticket windows at the track and buying packs of tickets. I did talk to Mendy. And I think he did try to cool it. But my wife, who handled our finances, used to say to me when I got my paycheck in the mail, 'How much should I put aside for Mendy?' He was always borrowing from us. But he usually paid us back."

At that time, referees were allowed by the NBA to go to the race track. They no longer are.

"I really never knew the depth of Mendy's gambling," said Susan. "I saw the high he got at the gambling tables and the exhilaration he felt betting at the track, but I was eighteen years younger than he was. And he was an accomplished man, a celebrity. I thought, 'I'm sure he knows what he's doing.'"

And she also liked the life-style and the bon vivant flair of Mendy Rudolph. They met in 1961 when she was a receptionist at the WGN office in New York. He was thirty-five, she was seventeen—she had lied to him about her age and said she was twenty. "I think I got a crush on him the minute I first saw him," she said.

Rudolph was then married to his childhood sweetheart and had three children. There were problems in the marriage, however, and one day Rudolph asked Susan out for a drink. Over time, their romance blossomed.

But they had, she said, "a roller coaster affair." And gambling was often at the center of their travels, from race tracks to the casinos in Las Vegas and Puerto Rico. And some of their numerous breakups were over his dependence on gambling and his lost weekends. "Once I called the Dunes Hotel in Vegas and had him paged," she said. "I was angry and hadn't heard from him and only guessed he might be there. He picked up the page. 'You're sick, do you know that?' I said. 'You're sick!'"

While he refused to seek professional help, Rudolph did begin to cut back on his gambling. And despite their problems, Susan and Mendy remained in love and were married in 1973. Two years later a daughter, Jennifer, was born to them. That same year, 1975, Rudolph suffered a blood clot in a game in Washington—it was to be his last game—and had to be carried off the court.

John Nucatola said that no referee he has seen could handle a game with the grace and power of Mendy Rudolph. "He had an instinct for being in the right place at the right time, and knowing how to let the players play," said Nucatola. "I've written to the Basketball Hall of Fame that Mendy should be in it. There are eleven referees in the Hall of Fame. Sometimes you just never can understand how and why the voters vote the way they do."

"Mendy Rudolph was simply the greatest referee of all time," said Earl Strom.

"You knew that when Mendy was refereeing a game, it would be squarely officiated," said Tom Heinsohn, the former Boston Celtics player and coach. "I can still see Mendy on the court during a timeout. He'd pull out his handkerchief with a flourish, flick sweat off his eyebrow with his thumb, then neatly fold his handkerchief and carefully slip it back in his pocket. Then he'd call to us, 'Let's play ball.'"

Rudolph was employed as a sportscaster when, on July 4, 1979, while going to a movie theater on Third Avenue, he collapsed on the street in front of the entrance. Susan Rudolph was at his side and desperately gave her husband mouth-to-mouth resuscitation until an ambulance came. He was taken to a hospital, where he died about an hour later.

There is still pain in Susan Rudolph's eyes and voice when she speaks of that time. "Mendy was so full of life that it's hard to believe he's dead," she said. "But I believe he died of anguish, of trying to pay back all his gambling debts and the money he owed the IRS. He was gambling relatively little at the end of his life, though he still loved to go to the OTB. He'd take Jennifer there and tell her they were 'going to the bank.' But he still owed a lot and was too proud to declare bankruptcy. He was also too proud and honest to get money by devious means. He might have thought about it, yes, but in the end he said, 'No,' and hung up the phone."

[1992]

The Call of a Lifetime

✎ THE PHONE CALL, he knew, could change his life. And it scared him. He had been told to expect the call at three o'clock last Friday afternoon.

The call was coming from the basketball coach at American University in Washington, and Ronnell Williams, age eighteen, did not want to miss it. He was the lean, six-foot-six-inch leading scorer for Cincinnati's Taft High School at twenty-nine points a game and an honorable mention on the McDonald's All-America basketball team. He was also an honor student who had succeeded in advanced placement courses like calculus and Latin and had been a student council vice president and had graduated recently in the top 10 percent of his class and who, at about the same time, was convicted of drug dealing. His basketball scholarship hung in the balance, hung on that phone call.

Friends and teachers and support people in the community waited to hear. Some of them remembered three years ago when President Bush came to speak at the school and ten of the best and brightest students were chosen to meet privately with him, and Ronnell Williams was one of those students.

They had all been shocked at Williams's arrest and conviction. He had received a two-year suspended prison sentence by the judge in Hamilton County Common Pleas court on June 14 because, Judge Donald Schott told him, "I believe you can make a worthwhile contribution to society" and because it would enable Williams to go to college. The judge believed Williams when he said that he wasn't "a real criminal" and that he was attempting to sell the three grams of crack cocaine in a small plastic bag—the equivalent of three packs of Sweet-n-Low—so that he could pay for abortions for both of the young women who were pregnant by him.

"I felt I was too young for the responsibility of being a father," Williams told the court.

It was apparent to the arresting officer that cold February night that Williams, in Starter jacket, sweatshirt, jeans, and baseball cap and under a neon sign, was a relative novice at drug sales, since all others in the group ran when the officer appeared. "This kid just didn't know what to do," said the officer, Bob Randolph.

"The policeman hollered 'Freeze!'" Williams would recall. "I wasn't about to get shot."

"Even though he's lived a life on the streets, Ronnell is not slick," said his lawyer, John Burlew. "He's no different from most kids his age."

In a way, though, he is. From a deeply troubled young life, he took good advice when he was fourteen years old in the ninth grade and changed from a bad student into what his basketball coach, David Lumpkin, called a "model student." He went from poor attendance, chronic lateness, and failing grades, to regular attendance, no lateness, and soaring grades.

Despite the arrest, Williams had been offered a full basketball scholarship worth $23,000 a year by American, but now there was some question about the school's fulfilling its end of the agreement. "I talked to Coach Knoche last night," said Williams, referring to Chris Knoche, American's head basketball coach, who had recruited him, "and he said the admissions department and others in the school might be getting cold feet. There was going to be a meeting, and he's calling me right after it."

He was hoping that the same thing wasn't going to happen that happened in February when Ohio University backed off. He had signed a letter of intent that bound the two of them—school and student athlete—but then came the drug arrest on February 9, exactly one day after Williams had been named player of the week by the *Cincinnati Post*. And sometime after that he received another call from another coach, at Ohio University. Williams said he was told, "We don't think that you and the university can meet as one." "I said fine, okay," recalled Williams. "I would never go somewhere I'm not wanted."

Williams was saying this about 2:30 Friday afternoon, a sunny, hot day, as he turned from Derrick Turnbow Street into the courtyard of the Laurel Housing Projects on Cincinnati's West Side where he lives part of the week in a small fourth-floor walk-up apartment with his sister and her stepmother. He goes to live with his mother for the other day or two of the week in another part of town.

Williams's eyes are youthful and direct, and, growing up in the "ghetto," as he calls it, he can fairly well disguise his emotions in them. But not always. He has gone through a lot of emotions that many others can hardly conceive. His father was shot by his mother's boyfriend when Ronnell was three years old. "I think my life would've been different had my father lived," he said. "I would have lived with him. I think he would have come to my games and been there for me. But," and his eyes shifted to look away, "I try not to think about it."

He had problems with his mother, Patricia Williams, as he was growing up. He was the only child in the household, but social workers found that he wasn't getting the care at home that he should have. He got into fights regularly, and he became a frequent runaway who was sometimes caught stealing to feed himself. He was then placed in a reform school in a juvenile jail sentence and was allowed home on weekends. As his high school coach, David Lumpkin, told the judge in the sentencing procedure, "He was away from Mom because Mom was trying to get herself together at the time also."

Williams was asked what that meant and he hesitated, as

184

though unwilling to give up a confidence, especially when it came to drugs. "I guess Mom was usin'," he said finally, quietly.

"Hey, Ronnell," someone called from across the street, "What's up, man? You got it?"

"Don't know," called back Williams. "They're checking me out. Gonna get rung up in a few minutes."

At American University there was a meeting between members of the athletic department and the academic side. Knoche argued that Williams was a kid "who was a product of his environment. He came from nothing in regard to material benefits, and he had nothing." He had been told by the Taft High School principal, Orlando Henderson, that "this is a great, great kid who needs very much to get out of Cincinnati."

Williams had been recommended to Knoche by a former associate, Larry Henderson, now assistant basketball coach at Cincinnati. Henderson said Cincinnati would have liked him but it had run out of scholarships. "I think we can make a little bit of a difference," Knoche said. "I know a lot of people seriously questioned this. And I'm not a bleeding heart. But it doesn't take an especially compassionate person to really feel for this kid and his circumstances. He made a mistake, and he admits it. And if we're not in the business of giving second chances and opportunities, then what good are we?"

While Ann Ferren, the interim provost, was unable to attend the meeting, her thoughts were relayed. "We know that he can make it academically, by his school record," she said. "And as a university, we do take risks with incoming students. For all our students, it's not where they start, it's where they end up."

But concerns remained, just as they had at Ohio University. Was Ronnell Williams worth the risk if he didn't make it, and embarrassed the school, and the school came off looking as if it cared more for basketball than for books? This debate, or its undecided result, continued to haunt Williams as he walked through his courtyard where, in the middle, a garden had been planted by one of the neighbors. Williams looked at the small red and yellow and blue flowers. "They're trying," he said, with a smile. It was too easy, thought a companion, to make a metaphor out of this.

Williams entered his sister's apartment and climbed the steel staircase. He entered the two-bedroom apartment where his half-sister, Joanna Hill, also eighteen, and a friend and the grandmother, Margaret Coleman, sat on stuffed black couches watching a soap opera. The apartment, in contrast to the stairwells, was tidy and clean. A few dresses were hanging on a door ledge.

"Anyone call yet?" asked Williams.

"Not yet," he was told.

It was 2:45. Fifteen minutes to go.

Williams sat down at one end of a couch. The air-conditioner hummed nearby. Some tribulation was occurring on television.

Williams says that what he did in attempting to traffic in crack was wrong, that it was "stupid," that he wasn't thinking. "I felt I was desperate, that I needed $700, and since the neighborhood is filled with people selling this stuff, I was able to get some," he said. "Sometimes when you're in a situation like that, you're not thinking too clear."

He said he was embarrassed to tell anyone—his coach; his mother, whom he said he didn't want to add pressure to; Karen Oldham, the truant officer who had become close to Williams; as well as his mentor, David Poignard, who had become close to Williams through the Excel Mentor program in Cincinnati that matches a person of substance in the community (Poignard is the owner of an insurance company).

It was Poignard who met Williams as a ninth-grader, saw his potential—although he was a D student—and told him that if he took school seriously he could parlay basketball into exceptional things. The next quarter Williams made the honor roll, and made it every quarter after that. He now was hoping to study at American to be a dentist ("I've never had any cavities, and I'd like to find out why," he said) or be involved in computer science.

At the sentencing, lawyer Burlew said: "I told Ronnell that we're looking for zero tolerance in terms of drug usage in the community. I looked him in the eye and told him that he had done some wonderful things in his life but that he's a menace and will be a menace as long as he's involved in this behavior. But despite all this, I think Ronnell is in a position where he can be saved."

When Schott addressed Williams for sentencing, he said: "I know that it's a traumatic experience to come in here and stand in the position you're standing in front of somebody who basically holds your life in their hands. Because I do right now. I can send you to prison and you're finished. I mean you're not going to go to college because when you get out of jail nobody is going to want you, right?"

Williams said, "Yes, sir."

"You've got the ability to go and contribute to society," Schott said. "If I put you in prison I've destroyed that, haven't I?

"I'm not going to stop you from going to college because ultimately you may be able to contribute something to society that's good. And the only way you're going to do that, in my opinion, is to take advantage of your grant."

Judge Schott said he would suspend the two-year sentence and the $5,000 fine as long as Williams demonstrated good behavior in the coming few years. Next summer he would be required to stay at home and wear a bracelet that allows authorities to know his whereabouts, unless he gets a job helping in the community, which he said he wanted to do.

At 2:50 the phone rang. He jumped for it. "Hello?" It was for his sister. He looked at her as if to say, be brief. She was.

At 2:57 the phone rang again, again Williams answered it. This time he held the receiver. His face took on a very serious aspect. "Uh, uh," he said. "Okay." Silence. "I'm gonna call you back tonight." The voices on the soap opera on television continued to speak, although no one now paid attention. "Okay," said Williams again, and hung up. A broad smile creased his face.

"Hey, Jo!" he shouted to his sister, his eyes alive. "It was Coach Knoche. I leave for school on *Monday!*" He slapped her a high five. He hugged Mrs. Coleman.

"What did he say?" asked Joanne.

"He said, 'Make sure you do good.'"

Tomorrow Williams is scheduled to take the bus to Washington to start the program at the university that helps acquaint freshman with the school and the city.

Williams now took his basketball, an indoor leather ball that had been rubbed smooth from outdoor play, and bounded down the stairs and out to the playground.

"Any news, Ronnell?" called a woman leaning on a windowsill.

"Everything's cool," he said. "Leaving Monday."

"Well," said the woman, "at least you could get a haircut."

Williams smiled. In the sunlight he headed down the sidewalk, dribbling the ball sweetly between his long legs.

[1993]

When Basketball Is
a Matter of Faith

FIFTY OR SO basketball players—college players or college bound—were shooting in the gymnasium at the State University of New York at Stony Brook last Sunday. Amid the thump of balls, the snap of nets, and the morning sunlight streaking in from windows, one would hardly have picked out the skinny, redheaded kid as unusual. Among the players trying out for the American team to the Maccabiah Games in Israel next summer, he was not as physically impressive as others. He was, however, the only player wearing a yarmulke, a small, round, light-blue skullcap pinned in place.

There was little definition to his arms and legs, and at 6 feet 3 inches and 170 pounds, he seemed even smaller and slighter, this despite a rigorous weight-training schedule in which he has gained 35 pounds in the last two years. At eighteen years old—and having graduated from high school in June—his face retains the youthful quality of someone even younger. He seemed almost out of place in this gym of athletes, perhaps over his head. But could looks be deceiving?

This was Tamir Goodman, and, under closer observation, one could discern a certain grace, an unmistakable intensity, the palpable confidence of an athlete in his moves, in the way he handled the ball, even his light banter with other players.

In the past two years, Goodman has had a great deal of attention thrust on him. It began when he played for Talmudical Academy in his hometown, Baltimore—the academy is a yeshiva, or Orthodox Jewish parochial school—and averaged thirty-seven points a game. He played point guard, shooting guard, small forward, and anything else that was needed, with a repertory that included effortless no-look passes and spectacular dunks. He was being hailed as the Jewish Jordan, a hunk of pressure capable of sinking the greatest of young talents, even emerging pros, let alone a kid from a school that emphasized Torah study over the pick and roll.

The yeshiva's gym held barely one hundred spectators. When it was announced that Goodman was headed to the University of Maryland, the ensuing publicity and growing interest forced home games to be moved to the Loyola College Arena, which was filled to capacity with three thousand spectators and hundreds turned away. Some yeshiva officials frowned upon the attention. Basketball, they believed, was something too much of the material world, and detracted from study of Torah, considered broadly as the body of Jewish religious literature that includes the Scripture and the Talmud.

In his senior year, seeking better competition, Goodman transferred to Takoma Academy in nearby Takoma Park, Maryland, a Seventh-day Adventist school that observed the Sabbath on the same days he did. Goodman did well enough at Takoma that an assistant coach for Towson University, Julius Allen, who scouted Goodman, said, "I'm a New York guy, and it's obvious that Tamir could go into Harlem or anywhere and play well and be comfortable doing it."

At Takoma, Goodman averaged twenty-five points a game but "shared the sugar," hoops jargon for providing assists, with an average of nine a game. This generous attitude surely contributed to "T," as he was called there, being popular with his teammates.

While the high school leagues Goodman played in were of less than the highest caliber, the Maryland basketball coach, Gary Williams, offered him a scholarship in his junior year. Goodman accepted, saying he could not play games or practice on the Sabbath, from sundown Friday to an hour after sundown Saturday.

He is from a family of nine children. One of his brothers is a rabbi and another is studying to be a rabbi. Observation of Orthodox Jewish rituals and teachings is the center of their lives. "As much as I wanted to play college basketball, I knew that basketball is temporary, but God is forever," Goodman recalled. "I don't want to do anything that might put me in disfavor in the eyes of God." He explained this to Williams.

"It's do-able," Williams said.

A year later, Williams, having watched Goodman scrimmage against some Maryland players, had second thoughts. "In the spring and summer he didn't play well—he may have been hurting with a knee," Williams recalled. In fact, Goodman had sprained a ligament in his knee and was given medical advice not to play.

"I just wanted to play, but I was a bonehead for doing it when I was injured," he said. "I was just a sixteen-year-old kid, and I could hardly move." Goodman shot 4 for 14 in the scrimmages.

Williams said, "We called him in and said we would still honor the scholarship, but would he be happy not playing?"

"The whole story is that if he's a star player, you might make more concessions," Williams added. "But if you're an eighth or ninth man, you take your chances. If you can't play, and the other guy does the job in your absence, he should play. Every once in a while, you make a mistake. We made a mistake."

Goodman did not want to go to a school that was no longer interested in him. But coaches at Towson University, a Division I school in the America East Conference, five miles from Goodman's home, had followed his career and wanted him, seeing great potential primarily as a point guard.

"What we especially like about Tamir is his attitude and floor leadership," Towson Coach Mike Jaskulski said. "He sees the whole court, and he's one of these players who makes his teammates better."

What about the Sabbath restrictions on his playing? "I told

Tamir and his parents that I would do everything I could to work it out," Jaskulski said. Towson went to Chris Monasch, commissioner of the America East Conference. Would the league make some adjustments in the scheduling and allow Towson to play on Thursday and Saturday nights or Sundays whenever possible? The answer was yes.

"In an educational setting," Monasch said, "we're not about to create anything that would be an obstacle to someone's religious beliefs. Within the confines of cost, of building availability and classroom requirements, we try to balance things out. This isn't a first. We have Jewish coaches who we've made similar scheduling accommodations for regarding Jewish holidays in the fall."

Playing Division I basketball at Towson—even though the competition is considered a notch or two below that of Maryland and the Atlantic Coast Conference—is "a dream come true," Goodman said. "My whole life, people have been saying, 'Put down the basketball; it'll never be possible for you to go further than high school ball,'" he said. "And in the yeshiva, basketball was looked down upon by a lot of people. Well, I live my life by the teachings in the Torah. But I can't be sitting around and studying the Torah all day. I need to be running and jumping. Basketball is a great passion for me. It's been that way since I was seven or eight years old. Trying to do what you do best is worthwhile. That's got to be in the Torah somewhere."

He said: "Torah and basketball go hand in hand for me. Torah makes me a better basketball player because it emphasizes good character, integrity, and responsibility. You have to be on time, respect others, and work hard."

Goodman said he had been disappointed by Maryland's decision. "I believe I could play for Maryland," he said. "I respect them, but I don't respect how they went about dealing with me. They aren't enemies. I just move on. And I feel very privileged that Towson did what it did for me."

Adam Ginsburg, an assistant coach at Towson and assistant coach for the United States Maccabiah team, said that Goodman knows he will not be expected to carry the team at Towson, which was 11–17 last season. "He'll play a role," Ginsburg said, "but we have several veterans returning, and the responsibility will be shared."

Goodman's mother, Chava, is happy he is going to Towson. "Coach Jaskulski emphasized academics over basketball, and that showed me proper priorities," she said. Goodman is an honor student who would like one day to work in sports, with children, though before that he would be open to a pro career "someplace."

"We're so proud of Tamir," Chava Goodman said. "He's a young man who always tries to do the right thing. He does the chores required of him, runs errands, throws out the garbage. And he brings me roses every week for shabbos"—the Sabbath.

Goodman had driven from Baltimore to Stony Brook last week, spending Friday night in a rabbi's home and missing the Saturday afternoon and evening workouts. He showed up at the gym at about 9 P.M. Saturday and shot baskets in some drills; he felt he never quite got the stiffness out of his body, and was unhappy with his performance.

Larry Shyatt, the head coach of Clemson University who volunteered to be head coach of the American basketball team for the Maccabiah Games, observed Goodman's workout. "He's a wonderful kid," Shyatt said, "but his shooting, that's his major deficiency." Shyatt described Goodman as a player with "great savvy in the open court, a very diligent worker and very serious about his basketball, and all the hoopla has not ill-affected him."

Goodman was so unhappy with his play on Saturday night that he rose at six the next morning and, though practice was not scheduled until ten, he was in the gym at seven to work on his game. "I'm constantly being tested," he said. "But I believe the saying that God doesn't put on you more than you can handle."

He thought he could handle the competition in the tryouts. After all, this summer he has played in a fast Baltimore summer league, with local products like Sam Cassell of the Milwaukee Bucks. In the Capitol Classic last April, a game that brings together the best high school players in the Washington, D.C., area, Goodman shared the most valuable player award with another.

On defense in a full-court scrimmage at Stony Brook, Goodman allowed his man to go backdoor on the first play. But he continued to hustle as a defender and played effectively from that point. He looked for and hit the open man with passes, though on occasion he forced a pass. He missed his first jump shot, from three-point range. Undeterred, and without hesitation, he shot the next time he was free, and scored from about twenty-five feet.

In quick order, Goodman took another shot from about the same spot and sank that one. Open in the corner, he swished another three-pointer. In between there were a couple of air balls, but also a slashing drive for a hoop, a slashing drive and a good dish-off for a basket, a rebound and a double-pump scoop under the basket for two points, and several more outside jump shots that found the mark.

Afterward, Shyatt said he liked what he saw, especially the shooting that seemed to improve overnight. "He's got deficiencies," Shyatt said, "but they're correctable. He has a good chance to make the team." A second tryout season will be held in April.

Goodman had suffered bruises—the competition was stiff and uncompromising—but he was not displeased with his play on Sunday. He went over to several of the other players, congratulating them on their play, and paid his respects to the coaches. But he did not have time to hang around.

On his return to Baltimore, Goodman wanted to make a side trip to a cemetery in Queens, to visit the grave of Rabbi Menachem Schneerson, the revered leader of the Lubavitch Hasidic movement, who died six years ago. "I want to ask him for a blessing," Goodman said, tugging on his sweats. And as quickly as he would make a move to the basket, the tall redhead with the blue yarmulke, his equipment bag swinging at his side, was out the door and on his way.

[2000]

Soaring Jordan, in Four Parts

1

NO ONE claims to have seen Michael Jordan walk on water, though some basketball fans are convinced he could if he put his mind to it. Many, however, believe they have actually seen Michael Jordan walk on air. Often. In a number of cities in America. With his size 13 sneakers. This they would testify to in a court of law.

There are hardened, longtime basketball experts who are converts to the Jordan phenomenon. "He plays higher than anybody's ever played," said Wayne Embry, the general manager of the Cleveland Cavaliers and a former National Basketball Association player. "He plays so high that even the big guys can't challenge him."

This was after the second Cavaliers–Chicago Bulls playoff game in which the six-foot-six-inch Jordan—who goes by such names as Air Jordan and Rubber-Band Man—scored fifty-five points, following the fifty he had in the first game, the first time in NBA history that any player had back-to-back fifty-point games in the playoffs.

In the following two games last week, Jordan scored thirty-eight points on Tuesday and forty-four on Thursday. The fifth game of the best-of-five series (the Bulls won the first two at home and lost the next two in Cleveland) will be played today in Chicago.

Bob Cousy, who was accused in his time of performing incredible feats on the basketball court, had this view of Jordan: "He goes up, stops for a cup of coffee, looks over the scenery, and then follows through with a tomahawk jam."

To the naked and perhaps ingenuous eye, Jordan, his closely shaved head gleaming in the arena lights, his baggy basketball drawers adding a kind of animated cartoon aspect, appears to do the following:

He drives with the ball into heavy traffic and springs into the air, as that aforementioned traffic springs up too. At this point it is impossible to get a shot off, since some of these basketball vehicles round him have jumped high, and most were taller than him to begin with, and they have long arms too. Then one by one they naturally begin to descend. All, that is, but Air Jordan, all but Rubber-Band Man. He's still up there, bringing the ball down from his ear to his hip, then back up to his left shoulder, then across to his right, and soon he is up in the air all by himself, and flicks the ball through the strings of the hoop.

"I'm not sure myself what I'm going to be doing once I'm up there," said Jordan. "That's when instinct takes over, that's when the mind goes into its creativity."

In Chicago Stadium, the cheers for such stuff reach a decibel level that would rival any rock show, rival any jackhammering of a city street, rival any combined takeoff of a squadron of jets. The joint, in a word, goes bananas.

When he fell hard in the first game of the playoffs against Cleveland and lay in apparent agony for a few moments, the crowd took on a funereal silence. Not to mention the solicitude of the Bulls' management, which is paying him $800,000 a year, going up next season to $2 million a year (and the rooting interest of advertisers, with whom Jordan is said to be making in the neighborhood of $3 million). But Jordan soon rose, seemed unsteady for a moment on those lean, veiny-muscular thoroughbred legs, then gathered strength and remained in the game. The cheers were those of relief and wonderment that there aren't more such scares, and that he hasn't been injured more often seeing that when he drops it's from about four stories high, without a net at landing.

Jordan, at age twenty-five and in his fourth season, has proved durable, playing hard for nearly forty minutes a game in each of his three full seasons. He has sustained one serious injury; two seasons ago he missed sixty-four games because of a stress fracture in his foot.

Some have dismissed Jordan's flight patterns as merely levitation. What's the big deal? they ask. Ghosts and ghouls do it all the time. This smacks of some mean-spirited plot to discredit Jordan, or pure unadultered envy, or hogwash, or all of the above. But how does Jordan do it? Lieutenant Colonel Douglas Kirkpatrick, the acting head of the Department of Astronautics at the Air Force Academy, has observed Jordan on television. "Michael Jordan has overcome the acceleration of gravity by the application of his muscle power in the vertical plane, thus producing a low-altitude earth orbit."

What does all this mean, in layman's terms? "It means he's awesome," said Colonel Kirkpatrick.

Dr. Lincoln Ford, a physiologist in the Department of Medicine at the University of Chicago, observed that Jordan's "center of gravity obeys the usual laws of physics and rises and falls as a parabolic function, like a rubber ball that bounces to a peak and then drops, and the speed with which he's falling increases with the square of time. But he appears to be hanging up there in the air because he brings his body together with the ball, and raises the ball as he's falling. It's a trick that sort of fools his opponents. He can do it because he's so strong, so quick, so coordinated, and has the right mental attitude." That's the answer, doctor? "Possibly," he said. "But one thing I'm sure of: something he does works, and works extremely well."

Phil Jackson, who is neither an astronautical engineer or a

physiologist, has another theory. Jackson is an assistant coach of the Bulls and a former NBA player, too. His theory? "Simple," said Jackson. "Michael Jordan is from another planet."

It's curious that he wasn't always this way. He didn't even jump or run or shoot well enough to make his tenth-grade team in Wilmington, North Carolina. But he practiced every day, and then one day, like in a dream, he went to try to dunk and just "exploded," he said. "I got up so high over the rim it scared me."

He continued scaring people when he played for North Carolina, where he was so fast and traveling violations were whistled so frequently that Coach Dean Smith made slow-motion films of his moves. Smith then assembled referees in a dark room and tried to prove to them in black-and-white that Jordan's steps were, though out of the bounds of the customary, within the bounds of the rule book.

Certainly there have been physical feats in sports that have stunned people. Bob Beamon, in the 1968 Olympics, leaped 29 feet 2-1/2 inches in the long jump to break the record by 2 feet. But he never did it again, and he did it in the rarefied air of Mexico City, which presumably was not a hindrance.

A 5-foot-8-1/4-inch high jumper named Franklin Jacobs held the world best for a while with a leap of 7 feet 7-1/4 inches, 23 inches over his head, an incredible thing. But he did that only once.

And then there was the extraordinary running back of the Chicago Bears, Gale Sayers. Bill Cosby says he swears he saw Sayers split his body like a paramecium. "He would throw the right side of his body on one side of the field and the left side of his body kept going down the left side," Cosby once noted. "And the defensive men didn't know who to catch. They just stood there. Then they looked to the referee for help, because there's got to be a penalty against splitting yourself. But there's not. I looked it up in the rule book and there's no rule against splitting yourself in half."

A similar kind of consternation accrues to Jordan's opponents. There is no legislation in the rule book against walking on air. Not at this writing, anyway. So the opposition devises other ways to bring him down. Primarily the trick is not to let him ascend to begin with.

It doesn't work consistently, since during the regular season he averaged 35 points a game. It was the second straight season in which he was the league's top scorer, having averaged 37.1 the season before.

Some believe that he must be double-teamed as soon as he crosses the half-court line. Another theory is that his running mate at guard should be double-teamed, so that it would be harder to get him the ball.

"What I would have done," said Walt Frazier, the former Knick, who was famous for his defensive prowess, "is start off by giving Michael the outside shot, and hope he doesn't hit it." And if he hit it? "Then," said Frazier, "I was going to be in for a long night."

Cousy also pondered the question of how to guard Jordan. "I would put two guys on him," said Cousy, "and if that didn't work, then three guys or four guys. I'm not kidding. I'd put as many guys on him as I could, until I stopped him, or until I ran out of guys."

What the Cavaliers did, in the words of their guard Craig Ehlo, was "lay some bodies on him."

In Game Three, they played Jordan "physically," as the saying goes, with a little elbow in the rib cage and a little chest in the chest, and it was moderately effective. Jordan scored only thirty-eight points. In Game Four, playing with a strained rib-cage muscle, he scored forty-four.

"I know that people expect fifty points every night from me," he said. "And I know I can't do that. Some nights I'll be better and some nights I'll be worse."

He also doesn't like being typed simply as a scorer. "I was second in the league in steals with three a game, I blocked over one hundred shots, and I made some game-winning defensive plays," he said. "But people just look at the stats, especially the scoring stats, and sometimes that's all overlooked."

He also would like to be considered a team player, and not Team Jordan, as he is sometimes called. "I like to keep things equal, if I can," he said. He had said this after the second game of the playoffs, and the timing was ironic. He was then averaging 52.5 points a game in the playoffs. The rest of the Bulls team was also averaging 52.5 points a game. It was keeping things exactly equal.

Jordan's Bulls have never gone past the first round of the play-offs with him, though the team itself has improved in the regular season, winning thirty-eight games his rookie year, then thirty when Jordan was injured, then forty, and, this past season, fifty games.

Beyond all this, it is Jordan's jumping that remains a matter of deepest interest to the basketball aficionado, the scientist, and those through the ages who have been captivated by people who have laid claim to having jumped tall buildings with a single bound. "Some people tend to forget some of the other great jumpers of the past, especially Elgin Baylor, who could hang in the air for long periods of time," said Lenny Wilkens. "But I have to admit, Jordan is more spectacular in what he does."

"I've heard that Elgin Baylor could do great things," Jordan said. "I've heard about how Connie Hawkins, who had those big hands, could get up in the air. And I remember that Earl the Pearl used to do magnificent things in the air.

"And there was Dr. J, who could soar, but I didn't play against him in his prime, so I didn't see him at his best. But I guess he took it to another level from Elgin, and maybe I've taken it to an-other level after that."

If Jordan has a celestial rival now, it's Dominique Wilkins of the Atlanta Hawks. "The difference between them," said Craig Ehlo, "is that sometimes 'Nique is out of control in the air. Michael is never out of control."

The difference between Jordan and Larry Bird? He laughed a respectful laugh at the thought of that terrestrial star. "Larry kind of plots his moves. Mine are more instinctive. And while I get inspired by a dunk, he'll get inspired by a three-point shot."

And Magic Johnson? "He gets inspired by a good pass."

As he spoke, sitting in the Bulls locker room, Jordan sneezed and reached for a tissue in the box between his feet. What's wrong? "Got a cold," he said. How long have you had it? "About a week."

You mean, you scored all those points with a cold? "Uh, yeah." What are you going to do when you're healthy?

"I don't know," Jordan said, and smiled. There was a faraway look in his eye, a kind of lofty look, a look, in fact, that, as Phil Jackson might have observed, was distinctly otherworldly.

[1988]

2

EVERY MORNING when he wakes up, Michael Jordan was saying, he sees the face of his dead father, James. Every morning, as he did this morning when he rose from bed in his hotel room in Hoover, Alabama, he has a conversation with his father, his greatest supporter, his regular companion, his dearest and most trusted friend.

"I talk to him more in the subconscious than actual words," said Jordan today, in front of his locker in the Birmingham Barons' Class AA clubhouse. "'Keep doing what you're doing,' he'd tell me," said Jordan. "'Keep trying to make it happen. You can't be afraid to fail. Don't give a damn about the media.' Then he'd say something funny—or recall something about when I was a boy, when we'd be in the backyard playing catch together like we did all the time.

"It takes your mind away from what's happening. Lifts the load a little bit."

The memory and the pain of his father's murder are still very much alive in Michael. It has been less than a year since James Jordan was murdered last July, at age fifty-six after having pulled his car to the side of the road one night to take a nap in North Carolina. The police say his killers were two young men who chose at random to rob him.

The days since then have often been wrenching for Jordan, who retired from his exalted state as the world's greatest basketball player and decided to pursue a career as a baseball player. And while he still says his baseball experiment is fun, these days lately for Michael Jordan have not been strictly a fantasy camp. They have been difficult.

"For the last nine years," he said, "I lived in a situation where I had the world at my feet. Now I'm just another minor leaguer in the clubhouse here trying to make it to the major leagues." He is a thirty-one-year-old rookie right fielder for the Barons of the respectable Southern League, considered a "prospects league," and his debut has been less than auspicious.

"It's been embarrassing, it's been frustrating—it can make you mad," he said. "I don't remember the last time I had all those feelings at once. And I've been working too hard at this to make myself look like a fool." In his first two games for the Barons, Air Jordan had hit little more than air, striking out five times in seven tries, along with a popout and groundout.

There has been much speculation about why Michael Jordan would walk away from basketball to subject himself to this new game, one he hasn't played since he was seventeen years old and had played in high school and the Babe Ruth league. "It began as my father's idea," said Jordan, in the season of 1990 when the Bulls were seeking their first National Basketball Association title. "We had seen Bo Jackson and Deion Sanders try two sports, and my father had said that he felt I could have made it in baseball, too. He said, 'You've got the skills.' He thought I had proved everything I could in basketball, and that I might want to give baseball a shot. I told him, "No, I haven't done everything. I haven't won a championship.' Then I won it, and we talked about baseball on occasion, and then we won two more championships. And then he was killed."

On the night last October when Jordan announced to Jerry Reinsdorf, the owner of both the White Sox and Bulls, that he was going to quit basketball, they were sitting in Reinsdorf's box watching the White Sox–Toronto playoff game. Eddie Einhorn, a partner of Reinsdorf on the White Sox, was home recuperating from an illness when he got a phone call from Reinsdorf that night. Reinsdorf told him what had happened and then added, "And guess what he wants to do next. Play baseball!"

In December, Jordan was hitting in the basement batting cage at Comiskey Park. This spring, Reinsdorf allowed him to play with the White Sox in Sarasota, Florida, and then permitted Jordan to try to realize his dream—and "the dream of my father, both our dreams"—by starting in Class AA ball.

"My father used to say that it's never too late to do anything you wanted to do," said Jordan. "And he said, 'You never know what you can accomplish until you try.'" So Jordan is here trying, lifting the weights, shagging the fly balls, coming early to the park for extra batting practice, listening while another outfielder, Kerry Valrie, shows him how to throw from "the top," or over the head, and Jordan then practicing over and over by throwing an imaginary ball.

This morning he sat among players who are as much as twelve years younger than he is. Black-and-silver uniforms hang in his locker with the number 45, which he wore in high school, and not the number 23 he made famous in Chicago. He had several bats stacked there, with the names of Steve Sax, Shawn Abner, and Sammy Sosa on them. He is still looking for a comfortable bat, the Michael Jordan model.

"It's been humbling," he said. And you could see that in his eyes. Gone is that confident sparkle they had at playoff time against Magic's Lakers, or Bird's Celtics, or Ewing's Knicks. "I just lost confidence at the plate yesterday," he said about his three strikeouts on Saturday. "I didn't feel comfortable. I don't remember the last time I felt that way in an athletic situation. You come to realize that you're no better than the next guy in here."

The other day in Chicago, Einhorn offered a theory on Jordan's baseball pursuit. "This is the most amateur form of psychology, but I wonder if Michael in some way is not trying to do penance for the murder of his father," said Einhorn. "I wonder if he's not seeking to suffer—to be with his father in this way."

"Seems to be true, doesn't it?" said Jordan, removing his designer bib overalls and reaching to put on his Barons uniform. "I mean, I have been suffering with the way I've been hitting—or not hitting."

He smiled wanly. "But I don't really want to subject myself to suffering. I can't see putting myself through suffering. I'd like to think I'm a strong enough person to deal with the consequences and the realities. That's not my personality. If I could do that—the suffering—to get my father back, I'd do it. But there's no way."

His eyes grew moist at the thought. "He was always such a positive force in my life," said Jordan. "He used to talk about the time my Little League team was going for the World Series and we were playing in Georgia and there was an offer that if anyone hit a homer they'd get a free steak. I hadn't had a steak in quite a while, and my father said, 'If you hit a homer, I'll buy you another steak.' It was a big ball field, and in the fourth inning I hit that sucker over the center-field fence with two on to tie the game, 3–3. We lost it anyway, 4–3, but I've never experienced anything in sports like hitting one out of the park."

He was reminded about the time his father, bald like Michael, was told that he has the same haircut as his son. "Same barber," said James Jordan. "That," said Michael, "was my father."

The effects of his father's death remain with Jordan in other ways. He has purchased a couple of guns that he keeps in his home in Highland Park, Illinois. He says he always looks out of the rearview mirror of his car and drives down streets he wouldn't normally take. "You never know, someone might be following you. I'm very aware of that. It's second nature now."

And his offer to lease a luxury bus for the Barons' road games had another motive beyond just giving his six-foot-six-inch frame more leg room. "I don't want to have a bus break down at one o'-clock at night in the South," he said. "You don't know who's going to be following you. I don't want to be caught in a predicament like that. I think about what happened to my dad."

The people in the organization see progress. "When I first saw him hitting in the winter," said Mike Lum, Chicago's minor league batting instructor, "it was all upper body. He was dead from the waist down. I think that's been a big change." But Jordan still has not demonstrated power in a game, though in the Cubs–White Sox exhibition game in Wrigley Field last Thursday he hit a sharp double down the third-base line. "He's got to learn to hit before he hits with power," said Lum. "He's got to master the fundamentals."

Jordan has had so much advice that, he said, "I've got a headache." Before today's game he said, "I was thinking too much. It's just got to flow."

He has played adequately in the field, catching all the flies hit to him and playing a carom off the "Western Supermarkets" sign in right field with grace and making a strong throw to second base that held the runner to a single. "My defense has kept me respectable," he said.

The players in the clubhouse, at first in awe of this personage, have come to treat him like a teammate. "And I can learn from his work ethic," said Mike Robertson, a three-year minor league outfielder. "He's good to be around."

One fellow who wasn't so happy was Charles Poe, who was sent down to Class A to make room for Jordan. Poe had said that he resented Jordan's having taken his position. "I talked to Charlie about that," said Jordan. "The coaches told me that he was going to be sent down anyway, that he wasn't ready for Double A. But I said to Charlie, 'Sometimes in life, things don't go your way. You just have to use that as energy to move forward. Never give up.'

"I don't think he really meant to come down on me. But he has to learn that as much as he loves the game—as much as I love the game—it's a business. Charlie's a good kid. He had a tough life, growing up in South Central Los Angeles. "I told him, 'Charlie, you and I are in the same boat. We're hoping to make it to the big leagues. If it's meant to be, we will. I had some bad days in basketball, and things improved. We just got to hang in, no matter what.'"

Jordan said he had planned to play all season, all 142 games, make all the bus rides—some as many as ten and twelve hours long—and then see what happens. As for the NBA, the only reminder is a sticker on his locker that someone had put up. It reads: "Barkley for Gov."

Charles Barkley, an Alabama native, has spoken of his desire to run for governor of the state. "I told Charles," said Jordan, "that if that ever happened, you'd be like Huey Long in the movie *Blaze,* a total dictator. I told him to stick to TV commercials."

Jordan laughed, then grabbed a couple of bats and went out to the batting cage to try again, and again. After that he trotted out to right field, a position his father's baseball hero, Roberto Clemente, played. Perhaps it is only coincidence.

[1994]

3

❦ PEOPLE were scouring the record books to find out when anyone had done in Madison Square Garden what Michael Jordan had done last night against the Knicks. Like most points in a half, or most points in a game, or most points in . . . They were looking in the wrong place.

You don't find what Jordan did in the game in the record books. You check memories, like the time in the Garden that Ol' Blue Eyes had the joint swinging, or the Stones had it rocking, or Gunther Gebel-Williams tamed his lions and mesmerized the crowd, or the first Ali-Frazier fight.

The hype for this game was similar to that for the previous four Jordan had played in since he returned ten days ago from his prodigal stint as a minor league fly chaser in the White Sox organization. That is, Michael Miracle is back. Overall, though, he had been simply a miracle waiting to happen.

Last night, it happened.

The World's Greatest Hoopster scored fifty-five points, including a jump shot to put the Bulls ahead by two with 25 seconds left in the fourth quarter. And then, with the game tied, and with 3.1 seconds left, he went up for the shot that everyone knew he'd take and, with Knicks lunging after him, he passed to Bill Wennington under the basket for the stuff that won it for the Bulls, 113–111.

The game opened about as spectacularly as it ended. Jordan hit a jump shot from the left to start the scoring. The next time down he hit a jump shot from the top of the key. He missed his next shot and then flew down the baseline and laid in the ball. He hit six of his first seven shots before Phil Jackson, the Bulls' coach, removed his shooting star, presumably for a rest. But perhaps he was taking pity on John Starks and Anthony Bonner and Derek Harper and Greg Anthony who, individually and en masse, were taking futile turns trying to guard Jordan.

Jordan returned and wound up with twenty points in the first quarter. At this rate he would score eighty for the game. Inevitably he cooled down. He scored only fifteen in the next period—including one delicious double-pump shot off Patrick Ewing—dropping the pro rata to seventy points for the game. And thus he wound up one of the most preposterous first halves in the history of the Garden. Jordan hit on fourteen of nineteen shots, including your occasional three-pointer.

It was reminiscent of the first Ali-Frazier fight in which

Muhammad Ali, so charismatic, with his red tassel white shoes and his dancing skills, dominated the spectators' attention. In the excitement, however, Joe Frazier was winning the fight. Similarly, at the half, the Bulls were losing, 56–50. But it was everything and more that the capacity crowd of 19,763 could have hoped for.

In Jordan's four previous games since his return to basketball, he had fairly lackluster outings, for him, other than the last one, against Atlanta, in which he hit a jumper at the final buzzer for a 99–98 victory. He seemed not quite his old self, even somewhat nervous, since he hadn't played a National Basketball Association game since June 1993, when the Bulls beat Phoenix for their third straight NBA title.

His opener ten days ago in Indianapolis saw him miss twenty-one of twenty-eight shots. He appeared nervous, as he did last Friday night in his home opener in the new United Center in Chicago. When he was introduced to the crowd of twenty thousand, there followed a crashing, blinding, sound-and-light show that one might have expected for something else, like Moses receiving the Ten Commandments.

Both teams sought to make statements last night, the Knicks that they could whip the Bulls with Jordan, the Bulls that they were monsters once again. And Jordan was eager to return as the great scorer he was when he left the game—he had averaged thirty-two points a game, the highest in history. But if there was a fault to his game last night, it was that he was looking for only one open man—Mr. Miracle. His first assist came with fifty seconds left in the game. He didn't get his second until—well, until it was time to win the game.

"When I was playing baseball, I still felt I could play this game," Jordan said with a smile in the interview room afterward. "I'm starting to get a little hang of it again."

In fact, for fans who came to see something memorable, a performance for the ages, they wound up in the right place. They hardly noticed that he had chilled from his hot start, and finished with only fifty-five points. For those scouring the record book, if they must, it was the most ever scored by an opponent in the new Garden. The previous mark was fifty, by—who else?—Michael Jordan.

[1995]

4

❦ ADAM CARL could never have guessed, one morning several Saturdays ago, that this morning would be like none other he had experienced.

Every Saturday morning the twenty-nine-year-old Carl, often with his Air Jordan shorts tucked into his gym bag, walks the several blocks from his apartment to the Gold Coast Multiplex on North Clark Street in Chicago to play pickup basketball games. Carl, a shade under six feet and a national account executive for an Internet company, is invariably dressed and ready to go when the games start at 9:30. Usually the same fifteen or so players show up. They come in different sizes and different races. Some of the players are quite good, including Carl, who played for the University of Wisconsin and was a teammate of Michael Finley, now with the Dallas Mavericks.

One of the aggressive guys the dark-haired Carl likes to have on his pickup team is an agile, six-foot-five-inch man named Tony. After all, games are competitive, and losers sit. No one likes that. Losers don't get back onto the court for a couple of games.

It was getting close to 9:30, and Carl noticed a man with his back to him working on weights in the room adjoining the court. A huge plexiglass window separates the court from the weight room. Carl banged on the window to alert Tony that it was time to play.

"I didn't understand why he'd be lifting weights just before the games," Carl said. "It's hard to get your muscles loose for basketball after that."

But the man who turned and responded to Carl's call was not Tony. "Oh my God," Carl said. It was Michael Jordan.

Jordan looked quizzically at him through the glass.

"Sorry, sorry, wrong guy," Carl said. "I made a very quick retreat," recalled Carl. "I would never have expected Michael Jordan in a million years."

Carl then ran to a telephone and called a friend, saying, "You won't believe who's here!" The friend jumped out of bed and flew to the gym, calling several other friends and shouting into his cell phone on the way.

The games in the Multiplex had been going on for about an hour when Jordan sauntered out of the weight room and onto the sidelines of the court. He wrote his name on the sheet hanging on the wall for a forthcoming game. "M. J. Plus 4," he wrote. Usually the next five guys on the list play, but no one was going to argue with Jordan about which four guys he wanted on his team.

Carl's team and Jordan's team hooked up. The six–six Jordan was checking a six–four player on Carl's team, even though one of his teammates said that Adam was the best opposing player. Carl hit a fifteen-foot jump shot and a drive. His team went up 2–0, in a game of eleven points, with two points for each shot made from the pro three-point range.

"Stop," Jordan said, and nodded toward Carl. "I got him."

"Must've been a hundred people ringing the court now," Carl said. "Usually nobody watches. It seemed like everything else in the Multiplex suddenly came to a halt.

"I brought the ball down again. Michael was playing loose and I took a shot from three-point range and it went in. On the sidelines they were going, 'Ooohh!' I could see him getting more serious. He hit a three-pointer, and I hit another one! We were up 6–3. I could see he was getting embarrassed. Then I drove to the basket and he slapped my arm. I called 'Foul!' He shouted, 'Foul?!'

"Someone right near us said, 'Dude, you just called a foul on M.J.!'"

Then Michael laughed, and said, "You were right."

Carl continued: "I scored again on a fast break and we won the game. Unbelievable. But now comes the interesting part. Michael didn't leave. He sat on the floor against the wall waiting for next, like everyone else. And we played against each other again. This time he was waiting for me at half-court! In that crouched position I had seen so many times as a Bulls fan.

"'I'm gonna shut you out,' he said to me, and he wasn't smiling. And guess what. He shut me out. His arms were so long, and he was so quick, I couldn't drive around him. He was so strong that after I passed the ball he held me off with his forearm from cutting. And then he started having fun, and doing that trash-talking that he loves. He'd take our big guy into the hole and say, 'Which way do you want your medicine?' And our guy, who was thrilled just to be on the same court, said, 'Any way you want to give it, Michael.'

"His team wiped us out, 11–3, and he left. Imagine, he had just stayed around to win!"

Carl ran into one of Jordan's friends the following Saturday, who told him: "You know what kind of competitor Michael is, to this day? He was calling me all week and saying, 'How did we lose that game to those guys?' I said: 'M.J., it was only the Multiplex. Give it a rest.'"

"I was on the phone all that week with my friends, too. Wow! Michael hasn't been back to the gym. Word got around, and I think he didn't want to deal with all the hassle. And I know he's also busy in Washington with the Wizards.

"What I'll remember most of all about my games with M.J.? That look of surprise in his eyes when I hit my shots from three-point range—and the look in his eyes at half-court when I realized it was all over for me."

[2000]

A KALEIDOSCOPE

OF SPORTS

Age Hasn't Cooled the Fire in Ali

THE SPRAWLING, three-story house was quiet, except for the tinny too-wa, too-wee of birds in a small aviary next to the office room on the first floor. It was early on a recent morning in Los Angles, and the cool, shadowed office was dimly lit by two antique candelabra which had a few of their small bulbs burned out. An antique lamp was also lit and with its slightly crooked shade peered over the large black mahogany desk scattered with letters and an Islamic prayer book. Nearby were several open boxes stuffed with mail.

Behind the desk, three large windows opened onto a backyard, half in sunlight, with cypress trees and pruned bushes and a swimming pool. Along another wall in the office, a pair of black men's shoes stood by themselves in the middle of a brown suede couch. In another corner, a television set, with another on top of it, rested on the oriental rug that covered most of the floor of the room. On the wall facing the desk was a marble fireplace without a fire.

Suddenly a torch appeared in the doorway. The fire, burning at the end of a rolled-up newspaper, was followed by a large man in black-stockinged feet who trotted into the room. "Hoo, hoo," he said, as the flame burned closer to his hand, and he tossed the torch into the fireplace. Quickly the logs in the fireplace crackled with the flame, and Muhammad Ali, the torchbearer, watched them burn. Then he sat down in an armchair in front of his desk and in a moment closed his eyes.

He said something, indistinct, in a gravelly mumble, and the visitor, in a chair facing him, asked Ali if he would repeat it.

"Tired," he said, with a little more effort, his eyes still closed. It was eight o'clock in the morning, and Ali had been up since 5:30 saying his daily prayers.

He stretched his legs. He wore a light blue shirt, unbuttoned at the cuffs, which was not tucked into his dark blue slacks. At forty-three, Ali's face is rounder and his body is thicker than when he first won the world heavyweight championship in February 1964 by knocking out Sonny Liston in Miami. The 6-foot-3-inch Ali weighed 215 then and is now about 240 pounds. In the ensuing years he would weigh as much as 230 in the ring as he lost and re-gained the title two more times—an unprecedented feat in the heavyweight division. Ali, who was stopped by Larry Holmes in a one-sided bout while attempting to win the title yet a fourth time, retired five years ago, but he is hardly forgotten.

A few days before, he had been at ringside at the Hagler-Hearns middleweight title fight in Las Vegas. Numerous ex-champions were introduced before the bout. Ali was saved for last.

He was asked now how he felt about that moment. He said nothing, and it appeared he was sleeping. Then: "A-li, A-li, A-li," he said, opening his eyes and mimicking the chant that arose among the sixteen thousand fans when the ring announcer intro-duced him. "I had to go like this," he said softly, raising his right index finger to his lips, "to calm the people down.

"A lot of fighters, when they quit no one ever hears of them again. But I've gotten bigger since I quit. Look at this," he said, nodding to a box in the corner, "people from all over the world writin' me. Thirty-one boxes full of fan mail in four years."

One was from Bangladesh, sent to "Loos Anjeles," and calling Ali "my unknown Uncle." Another from West Germany asked "Mr. Ali" for his autograph. A third was from Drakefield Road in Lon-don and sent to the New York Presbyterian Hospital, where Ali had gone late last summer for a checkup. He has been diagnosed as having Parkinsonian syndrome, a nerve disorder.

Ali asked the visitor to open the letter and read it aloud. "I am very sorry to know of your temporary problem," wrote the Briton, "and wish you most sincerely a rapid recovery. Many of my friends who are fans of yours are thinking the same, that you will in a very short time be back to your old poetic self and come and see us in dear old London. . . ."

Do you still write poetry? the visitor asked Ali.

"No," he said, "no more. That was in a different time. Eighteen times callin' the round. 'That's no jive, Cooper will fall in five.' 'Moore in four.'"

The visitor recalled a personal favorite, when Ali predicted how his first fight with Liston would go. It turned out that Liston didn't answer the bell for the seventh round. Did Ali remember the poem?

"Mmmmm," he said. The visitor wasn't sure what he meant by that. But he began, his voice still very low:

"Ali comes out to meet Liston, and Liston starts to retreat.

"If he goes back any farther, he'll wind up in a ringside seat."

He paused thoughtfully, then continued.

"And Liston keeps backin', but there's not enough room. It's a matter of time—there! Ali lowers the boom.

"Ali lands with a right—what a beautiful swing! The punch knocks Liston right out of the ring. . . ."

Just then the phone rang. "My phone's ringin'," he said. "Hold on." He reached over to his desk. "Yeah, naw, naw," he said sleepily into the phone. "I wouldn't try that for no $5,000, you crazy?" He nodded. "Check ya later." And hung up. "Where was I?"

He was reminded that he had just knocked Liston out of the ring.

"Who woulda thought," he continued, "when they came to the fight, that they'd witness the launchin' of a hu-man satellite.

"Yes, yes, the crowd did not dream when they laid down their money, that they would see a total eclipse of the Sonny."

Ali's voice was fading again. "I wrote that twenty-two years ago," he said, his words getting lost in his throat. "That was a long time." He is taking voice lessons from Gary Catona, who had come into the room during the recital of the old poem. Catona is a voice and singing teacher who three weeks ago had come to Los Angeles from Austin, Texas, to try to help Ali speak more clearly.

Ali began to speak more slowly and less distinctly over the last several years. There was much speculation about him suffering a variety of illnesses. During his hospital visit in New York last September, doctors determined that he had Parkinsonian syndrome. Catona believes that the only problem with Ali's voice is that his vocal muscles are weak, that they lack resonance.

Ali was asked what was wrong with his voice. "I dunno," he said, "somethin'."

"Muhammad never really had strong vocal muscles," said Catona. "He used to scream out his words. His normal speech was never a normal speech."

Ali and his voice teacher schedule a one-hour lesson every day, but Ali travels a lot and they don't always connect. "But he's good when we do it," said Catona. "It's like building body muscles, you've got to work at it. He sings the sounds of the scales. 'Ah! Ah! Ah! Ah!'" Catona sang, his voice rising at each 'Ah!'

Catona and Ali had already had the session at the piano in the living room, and beyond this Ali was asked what he's been doing with himself lately. "People are interested in you," he was told. "You're one of the most popular figures . . ." "Popular niggers?" he interrupted. "Figures," the visitor repeated. Ali looked at him playfully out of the corner of his eye.

"What am I doin' now, oh, I'm so busy," he said, growing serious now. "I'm busy every day. I've got all this mail to answer—they're startin' fan clubs for me all over the world, in Asia, in Europe, in Ireland, in China, in Paris. But my mission is to establish Islamic evangelists, and to tour the world spreadin' Islam."

He converted from Christianity to the Islamic faith twenty-one years ago, changing his name, as the world knows, from Cassius Clay to Muhammad Ali. On the shelf above the fireplace stood a *Sports Illustrated* cover from May, 5, 1969, laminated on a wooden plaque. The cover showed the young boxer wearing a crown, with the caption, "Ali-Clay—The Once—and Future?—King."

What's the difference between Cassius Clay and Muhammad Ali? he was asked.

"As much difference as night and day," he said. "Cassius Clay was popular in America and Europe. Muhammad Ali has a billion more fans all over the world. Cassius Clay had no knowledge of his self. He thought Clay was his name but found out it was a slave name. Clay means 'dirt, with no ingredients.' Cassius—I don't know what that means. But Ali means 'the most high,' and Muhammad means 'worthy of praise and praiseworthy.'

"Cassius Clay had Caucasian images of God on his wall. Muhammad Ali was taught to believe that there should be no image of God. No color. That's a big difference."

He rose and took a large briefcase from under his desk. He withdrew several religious pamphlets with pictures of Jesus Christ. All but one was white. Then he took out a Bible and opened it to Exodus 20:4, and asked the visitor to read it. "Thou shalt not make unto thee any graven image, or any likeness of any thing that is in heaven above. . . ."

"Ooohh," said Ali. "Powerful, isn't it. But what are all these. Man, you thought boxin' was powerful. Boxin's little. These pictures teach supremacy. The Bible says there should be no pictures of God, no images, he should be no color. But you see that God is white. Tarzan, King of the Jungle, was a white man. Angel food cake is white, devil's food cake is black. Man, ain't that powerful?

"Cassius Clay would not have the nerve to talk like this—he'd be afraid of what people might say or think. Ali is fearless, he's hopin', prayin' that you print this. Cassius Clay would not have the courage to refuse to be drafted for the Vietnam War. But Muhammad Ali gave up his title, and maybe he would have to go to jail for five years."

He rose again and this time brought back a plastic box, flipped up the latches, and opened the lid. It was a box of magic paraphernalia.

He took two red foam rubber balls and made them become four right before the visitor's eyes, then turned them into a box of matches, then made them disappear altogether. His eyes widened in mock shock. He still has the fastest hands of any heavyweight in history. It was a very good trick. How did he do it? "It's against the law for magicians to tell their tricks," he said. "It's a tricky world," he said. He next transformed three small unstretchable ropes of varying sizes into the same size. He made a handkerchief disappear, but, on the second showing, he was too obvious about stuffing it into a fake thumb. "You should only show that trick once," he said, a little embarrassed.

He redeemed his virtuosity by putting four quarters into the visitor's hand, snapping his fingers, and ordering the quarters to become two dimes and two pennies. The quarters obeyed. He snapped his fingers again and the quarters returned; the pennies and dimes vanished.

"It's magic for kids," he said. "It's my hobby. See how easy they can be deceived? But these aren't childish things. They make you think, don't they?"

It was mentioned that perhaps Ali's best magic trick was transforming the small house he lived in as a boy in Louisville into this twenty-two-room house with expensive antique furniture. He made more than $60 million in ring earnings and endorsements. "But the government took 70 percent," he said. He says he is financially secure. He doesn't do commercials, for example, because, he said, "I don't need the money."

He lives here in Wilshire with his two children by Veronica Ali, eight-year-old Hana and six-year-old Laila. They employ a live-in housekeeper. His six other children live with his two former wives.

"My wife likes antiques," he said, walking into the living room. He pointed to a tall clock against the wall. "It's 150 years old," he said.

Gary Catona now took his leave and arranged for a session the following morning. Ali led his visitor on a tour of the house. "I'm not braggin'," he said, "just showin'. I don't like to talk about what I have, because there's so many people hungry, homeless, no food, starvin', sleepin' on the streets."

In the dining room is a long dark table with twelve tall, carved chairs. On the second floor are the bedrooms. In the kids' rooms, toys and stuffed animals tumbled across the floor. There's an oriental sitting room, and a guest room.

The phone rang. "City morgue," he answered. He spoke briefly and hung up.

They ascended the carpeted staircase to the third floor. On a wall are a pair of red boxing gloves encased in glass. One glove is signed, "To the champion of champions—Sylvester Stallone." On an adjoining wall is a robe with multi-colored sequins that bears the inscription, "The People's Choice." In the corner of the case was a photograph of a man with his arm around Ali. It is Elvis Presley, who gave Ali the robe.

In the adjoining room is a large pool table with a zebra skin lying over it. Trophies and plaques and photographs line the wall and cover the floor.

He was asked about recent efforts to ban boxing. "Too many blacks are doin' well in it, so white people want to ban it," he said. "But how do I live here without boxin'? How would I ever be able to pay for all this? Look at Hearns and Hagler. Two poor black boys, but now they help their mother and father and sisters and brothers. It's from boxin'.

"There's more deaths in football than boxin'. Nobody wants to ban football. You see car races. 'Whoom, whoom.' Cars hit the wall, burn up. Motor boats hit a bump. Bam! Don't ban that, do they?"

Going back down the stairs, the visitor is met by a nearly life-size painting of Ali in the ring wearing white boxing trunks. He is on his toes and his arms are raised in triumph. The signature in the corner of it reads, "LeRoy Neiman, '71."

Did Ali miss fighting? "When the fight's over," he said, "you don't talk about it anymore."

The visitor asked about his health. "I don't feel sick," Ali said. "But I'm always tired." How did he feel now? "Tired," he said, "tired."

A doctor friend, Martin Ecker of Presbyterian Hospital, has said that if Ali takes his prescribed medication four times a day—the medication is L-Dopa, which in effect peps up the nervous system (the disease does not affect the brain)—then Ali's condition would be improved substantially. The medication does not cure the disease, but it increases alertness.

Ali is inconsistent in taking the medication. He believes it doesn't matter if he takes the medication because he is in the hands of Allah, and his fate is sealed. Days go by when he doesn't take the medicine. But when friends urge him to, or when he is going to make a public appearance, then he is more inclined to take his dosage.

Did he feel that after twenty-five years of amateur and professional fights, of countless hours of sparring, that he had taken too many punches? He stopped on the second-floor landing. He rubbed his face with his hands. "Uh uh," he said, softly. "Look how smooth. I very rarely got hit."

As the visitor turned from Ali and opened the door to go, he heard an odd cricket sound behind his ear. The champ smiled kindly but coyly. There was either a cricket in the house or something that sounded like a cricket in his hand.

Walking to his car in this quiet, elegant neighborhood, and then driving out past the security guard at the gate, the visitor realized he would not plumb the mystery of the cricket sound in Muhammad Ali's house. It's a tricky world, he recalled, and he would leave it at that.

[1985]

A Champ Disappears into Thin Air

❦ "HAVE WE got anything yet?" asked Lieutenant Walter Wilfinger, in his office as chief of detectives of the 61st Precinct on Coney Island Avenue in Brooklyn. He squared his black-rimmed glasses and turned to Bob Sommer, one of his detectives.

"Nothing," replied Sommer, his amber tie loosened, sitting across the desk from him. "It's going on three weeks and still not a clue. It's a total mystery."

"But," said Detective Arthur Semioli of the Brooklyn South Homicide Task Force, also seated in the room, his green velour pancake cap on a hook on the wall behind him, "we're not about to close the book. It's an active investigation, that's for sure."

Tacked to message boards in restaurants and post offices in Brooklyn, as well as in the detectives' office of the 61st Precinct, are white 4-by-6 laminated cards distributed by the New York City Police Department that tell some of the story. They say in big black letters: "Missing Person." Below this are details of the search, beginning with: "Subject: Sergei Kobozev."

For those who follow professional boxing, the name has significance. Kobozev, with a 22–1 record, including seventeen knockouts, was the United States Boxing Association's cruiserweight champion—not quite a major title in what is often an overlooked division, between light-heavyweight and heavyweight. But Kobozev, who came to the United States five years ago from Russia, had also been a captain in the Red Army and held a degree in chemistry from the Institute of Moscow—hardly common pedigrees for a prizefighter. And he had been a member of the Soviet national boxing team and was looking toward his biggest boxing payday ever in March. It was an expected $100,000 shot for the World Boxing Council title against the winner of a January match between the champion Anaclet Wamba and the challenger Marcel Dominguez.

On November 8, Sergei Kobozev was last seen leaving a garage in the Flatbush section of Brooklyn between 5:45 P.M. and 6 P.M. after having a cable short repaired in his 1988 black-and-white Chevy Blazer. He was reported missing that night by Lina Cherskikh, his dark-haired live-in companion. Five days later his car was found beside a Dumpster in the parking lot of the Petrina Diner in Bensonhurst, where he sometimes ate. The diner, open twenty-four hours, is about five miles from the garage in Midwood. No one remembers seeing Kobozev in the diner. The car was locked from the outside. There was no sign of foul play.

Kobozev had $12,000 in a bank account in his name. It has not been touched. No checks have been drawn on it. No credit cards owned by him have been used. There have been, according to the police, no ransom notes. The police have not found any connection between Kobozev and the so-called Russian Mafia in America. They have established no connection to another woman.

"It seemed he wasn't a ladies' man," Semioli said. "And there were no signs of any mental lapse by him or disorientation. Was there foul play—either random violence or planned? Or did Kobozev disappear on his own volition? We're ruling nothing out."

The Missing Person card goes on: "Description: Male, White, 6'1", 190 lbs., light complexion, Muscular, Blue Eyes, Brown Hair, 31 years old.

"Clothing: Lt. blue Levi jeans, blue & brown leather jacket, grey button down crewneck shirt, black dress shoes.

"Last seen: 11/8/95, near East 15th Street and Avenue L, 61 pct."

The background information was all on the left half of the card. On the right was a slightly washed-out head shot of Kobozev in a red shirt open at the neck. He wore his hair short and looked into the camera with a half-smile and the paradoxically kindly eyes of a prizefighter.

"The ropes really separated the two worlds of Sergei," said his assistant trainer, Peter Kahn. "He was very even-tempered, very unexcitable, very pleasant, almost shy when you'd meet him on the street. But he was a beast in the ring. He never took a step back. He really earned the right to be called tough."

"The police have investigated and can't find any enemies that he had," said Tommy Gallagher, the boxer's manager and trainer. "And outside the ring he never caused trouble."

"It is terrible," said Cherskikh, who, with her seven-year-old son, Vitaly, lived with Kobozev in their one-bedroom, fourth-floor apartment on Sixteenth Street in a working-class section of Sheepshead Bay. "I wake up every morning and see the pictures of Sergei on the wall. And every morning I cry."

Kobozev had come to America in pursuit of a dream. "All he wanted was to be world champion," she said. Cherskikh, who is also Russian, said Kobozev didn't miss Russia. "He loved here, you know."

On Wednesday evening, November 8, she had been expecting Kobozev to return home to take her son to a karate lesson. When, after several hours, he didn't show up, and didn't call—"he always call if he will be late," she said—she called the police.

Kobozev's last fight was on October 14, in Paris, where he lost a narrow split decision to Dominguez. It had been a bruising, crowd-pleasing affair in which Kobozev came back from two knockdowns to take the fight to the twelve-round distance. Some close to him reported that he was depressed by the loss, his first as a professional. And some wondered how that had affected Kobozev, a dedicated fighter who took his career seriously.

"He was very, very proud of being undefeated," said Teddy Atlas, who had trained Kobozev the first two years the fighter was in America. "It might have been working on his mind, and he might have eventually decided he just wanted to go away and be alone for a while." Still, Kobozev disappeared nearly three weeks after his last bout, long enough, conceivably, to get over any depression. And suicide was out of the question, according to everyone who knew him. They say he had too much to live for.

"He was also a man, not a boy, and he had put up such a good fight against Dominquez that he had been assured of a title fight in March," Gallagher said. "His future looked better than ever. He was looking at millions of dollars."

As no clues turned up, Cherskikh sought other means of looking for Kobozev. She went to several Russian psychics. "They all say different things," she said. "One say he is dead, another say he is alive. So now I believe nothing."

"One psychic said he was in Staten Island behind some water," Gallagher said. "But Staten Island is surrounded by water!"

Beatrice Rich, a Manhattan psychic, was consulted. In a spare room scarcely larger than a walk-in closet, she sat at a small desk and tried to get impressions from tarot cards. "I don't see that anything dire has necessarily happened to him," she said. "But I also am not sure he is alive. I see him not in a cold place but a warm place. A place like California. Normally, when someone is dead I get a very clear impression of it. But I also see another woman, a light-haired woman, though I don't know if she's a part of this. And I see two children."

There was, in fact, another woman in Kobozev's life, and another child. Apparently only those close to him knew this. According to sources, he had been married in Russia to a doctor who gave birth to Kobozev's son soon after he had come to the United States. The police say, however, that he had never returned to Russia after leaving, that he had not seen his son, and that he either was divorced or was getting divorced to marry Cherskikh.

The relationship between Cherskikh and Kobozev, the police believe, was essentially a stable one. She refers to him as her husband, and said that her son asks every day, "When is Daddy coming home?"

The 61st Precinct detectives recently cracked another case of a missing person, one Stefan Tanner, who, after two weeks, was found to have been murdered. Another missing person recently "popped up," as Detective Semioli put it, having opted for a new life with a new love interest. "There are hundreds of missing persons every year in New York," he said. "But we usually get to the bottom of them before this."

Kobozev had been working on Saturday nights as a greeter and bouncer in a Russian nightclub in Brooklyn, the Paradise, on Emmons Avenue, for $100 a night and free meals for him and Cherskikh. Friends say that she, more than Kobozev, enjoyed the night life.

There were reports of a fight at the club about a week before Kobozev disappeared, a brawl in which Kobozev was said to have acted as a peacemaker. Was there a punch thrown by Kobozev, however? Did someone get mad at him? "Right now," Semioli said, "it's something we're looking into."

Kobozev trained in Gleason's Gym, on Front Street near the Brooklyn Bridge. Inside the gym there was the sound of fighters punching bags, the scrape of boxing shoes on canvas, and the snorting of fighters throwing and taking blows. "Everyone treated Sergei with respect," said Don Diego Poeder, a young undefeated cruiserweight who sparred with Kobozev. "He had a way about him, quiet but confident. He seemed more mature than a lot of guys, maybe because he was a little older than some of the fighters here, and with that background in college and the army. And he was very strong and always very tough to fight, but nice. He didn't speak much English, but he made himself understood. He'd hit me and tell me that I wasn't dodging enough. He'd say, 'Move head, move head.'"

Last summer, a week or so after Kobozev won his title, he was celebrating at a Russian supper club on Brighton Beach Avenue in

Sheepshead Bay with Cherskikh and his Russian manager, Steve Trunov, when a friend, Sergei Artemiev, came in. Kobozev cheerfully invited him to join them. Artemiev had been on the Soviet national boxing team with Kobozev. He had fought in the lightweight division and the previous year had suffered a massive blood clot in the brain in a fight that was one step from a world championship bout. Artemiev had been in a coma for ten days before beginning to recover. He still had some health problems, and would never be allowed to fight again. Like Kobozev, he had left Russia to become a world champion. Now that dream had been dashed.

And while this was a happy time for Kobozev, he was sensitive to Artemiev's feelings. As the evening went on, Kobozev saw the sadness in Artemiev and sought to relieve it. Kobozev urged him to have more caviar and blini. "Sergei," he said, with one hand on the neck of a bottle and throwing an arm around his friend, "some champagne?"

Artemiev is currently in Russia on business. No one, though, seems to know were Kobozev is.

For those who know and care about Sergei Kobozev, there are now only questions. There is no caviar and no champagne.

A little more than a year later . . .

SOMEDAY, Detective Bobby Sommer said, in his less than tidy second-floor office in the 61st Precinct station house in Coney Island, he hopes to get a call about Sergei Kobozev. He said he was practically certain, though, that the call would not come from Kobozev himself.

"My gut instinct tells me he was murdered," Detective Sommer said. "But my main problem is that I don't have a body. And until I come up with concrete evidence, I don't have a homicide. I don't even have a crime."

For more than a year, Detective Sommer has knocked on doors

of stores and apartments in the extensive Russian community in Coney Island, Brighton Beach, and Sheepshead Bay, trying to pick up the pieces of the mystery. He has found nothing but dead ends.

"It's hard for people in the Russian community here to trust the police," the forty-seven-year-old detective said. He wore a red tie with tiny handcuffs as a tie clasp, and his feet, in grey snakeskin cowboy boots, were placed comfortably atop a sheaf of papers on his desk. He ran a hand through his greying hair. His look was direct. "From where they came from, everyone was afraid of the police. I try to tell the people here that we are not the KGB. But it takes time for them to have faith in us."

He told of the time that he and an auxiliary police officer, a Russian immigrant, were investigating a shooting in a Brooklyn apartment. They questioned a man who had been in an adjoining room when five shots were fired. "I didn't hear anything," the man told the officer in Russian. "I was sleeping."

In the Brooklyn streets where Detective Sommer has been searching, it is possible to go from a grocer to a baker to a restaurant to a gas station and never hear a word of English. The neighborhoods are home to Russians, Ukrainians, Uzbeks, and thousands of others from the former Soviet Union who, like generations of immigrants before them, have come to make their fortune, if not some fame. Sergei Kobozev was one of those with a dream, and it seemed to be within his grasp.

A former member of the Soviet national boxing team, he was the United States Boxing Association's cruiserweight champion and was a few months away from what would have been his biggest fight: a $100,000 shot at the World Boxing Council title. For five days after he disappeared, no evidence turned up in the case. Then Kobozev's car was found beside a Dumpster in the parking lot of the Petrina Diner in the Bensonhurst section of Brooklyn. Kobozev occasionally ate at the diner, which is about five miles from the garage. No one has come forth to say they remember seeing him there. The car was locked. There was no sign of foul play.

There remained $12,000 in Kobozev's bank account. It has not been touched. No checks have been drawn on it. No credit cards owned by him have been used. There were no ransom notes.

Did Kobozev have ties with organized crime? Detective Sommer says no. And there was no evidence of another woman in his life. "He apparently was madly in love with Lina," the detective said.

Tommy Gallagher, the fighter's manager and trainer, has conducted his own search. "I talked with forty million people on the street," Mr. Gallagher said. "And there's no doubt for me now. Sergei got whacked. Somebody was sending someone a message."

Detective Sommer said there was someone he suspected of having a role in the Kobozev case, a Russian immigrant whom the police and the Federal Bureau of Investigation say was involved in credit card fraud and illegal weapons sales. The man disappeared just after Kobozev did. Detective Sommer said he heard several people tell of a confrontation between the man and the boxer at the Paradise, a nightclub and restaurant in Sheepshead Bay where Kobozev worked as a bouncer and greeter on weekends.

Sergei Artemiev, the former world-class lightweight fighter who was a friend and neighbor of Kobozev, told the story this way: "I was in Russia when it happened, but I learn that it started with a big noise in the Paradise on Emmons Avenue." The man reportedly punched a musician at the club and broke his nose, Artemiev said.

Kobozev told the man to calm down, Artemiev said. "He was acting as peacemaker," Artemiev said. "He said, 'You should go away from here.' This man swore at Sergei and said, 'Who are you?' Then there were punches and of course the man fell down. And his friend fell down too. He pointed a finger and said to Sergei, 'We will remember you.'"

Artemiev shook his head grimly. "I think they remembered."

Kobozev and Artemiev had been teammates on the Soviet national boxing team, and both looked to America where, they had heard, according to Artemiev, there was "gold all over." They were brought to America with three other Russian fighters by an American manager, Lou Falcigno.

The Russian fighters had similar experiences in the ring in America. For many spectators the cold war had never ended, and one of the *Rocky* movies had presented a convenient antagonist, the Russian boxer. At first they were booed in American cities. "But when people saw how well they fought and how spirited they were," said Gallagher, "the boos turned to cheers."

Kobozev and Artemiev continued to talk to each other about their aspirations. Kobozev, Artemiev recalled, listened intently when he told him about a visit he had made to Arizona. "When I fought in Phoenix, I fell in love with the orange trees," Artemiev said. "I wanted to move there. Kobozev laughed when I told him, but he said: 'I hope to see those trees, too. Maybe we move together.'"

Detective Sommer said he felt certain there were witnesses to Kobozev's murder, or at least to his abduction, and possibly accomplices. But no one has come forward with information, let alone a confession.

"Not yet," Detective Sommer said. "But I'm going to pursue this for as long as I can. I won't let go." So he still knocks on doors and makes phone calls.

"You have to keep an open mind," he said. "Anything is possible. I mean, Kobozev could have got amnesia. But I doubt that. It's an active case, and I keep waiting for the right phone call. I'm working with authorities in Russia, and maybe one day the suspect may try to sneak back into this country. Right now, I'm trying to prove a homicide, but I could use a body."

[1995, 1997]

The LaMotta Nuptials

♈ NEITHER OF THE Las Vegas dailies, nor, for that matter, the *New York Times* reported in their society news sections the wedding of Jacob (Jake) LaMotta, sixty-three years old, erstwhile pugilist, and, Theresa Miller, younger than the bridegroom and decidedly prettier. Perhaps it was determined in some editorial conclave that to cover one of Jake's nuptials is to cover them all, for this was the sixth time he's tied the knot. But to Jake, each, of course, is unique. His first wife divorced him, he says, "because I clashed with the drapes." Another one, Vicki, complained about not having enough clothes. "I didn't believe her," LaMotta says, "until I saw her pose nude in *Playboy* magazine."

The betrothal of LaMotta, the former world middleweight champion, to Miss Miller—this was her second trip to the altar—took place last Saturday night in Las Vegas at Maxim's Hotel and Casino in a room stuffed with a wide assortment of beefy people with odd-shaped and familiar noses. They included such ex-champions as Gene Fullmer, Carmen Basilio, Willie Pep, Joey Maxim, Billy Conn, Jose Torres, and the best man, Sugar Ray Robinson, plus a potpourri of contenders, trainers, and matchmakers, all of whom were in Las Vegas to attend the Hagler-Hearns world middleweight title fight two nights later.

For LaMotta, having Robinson as his best man was a sweet and perfect touch. "I fought Sugar six times," he said. "I only beat him once. This is my sixth marriage and I ain't won one yet. So I figure I'm due."

Both the groom and the best man wore tuxedos with white corsages in their lapels. The bride was radiant in a white dress with mother-of-pearl-and-lace design and a garland of baby's breath in her auburn hair. The wedding party assembled under a white lattice arch in the corner of the room as District Judge Joe Pavlikowski of Clark County presided over the ceremony.

Despite the loud, happy chatter of the guests, the judge began a recital of the vows. "Quiet, please," a man shouted. "Quiet." When that didn't work, the man stuck two fingers in his mouth and whistled. That got their attention.

The judge continued. He asked Jake and Theresa if they would love and obey. They said they would, and Jake kissed the bride.

"Wait a minute," said the judge. "Not yet."

Jake looked up, and Theresa smiled. The judge coughed. In another corner of the room, a phone rang. Jake looked around brightly. "What round is it?" he asked. The room broke up. Theresa, laughing, said, "I've changed my mind!" Then she hugged Jake, who smiled proudly at his bon mot.

"We've got to finish," said the judge. The room settled down somewhat. ". . . With love and affection," continued the judge, speaking quicker now. In short order he pronounced them "Mr. and Mrs. Jake LaMotta."

Applause and cheers went up, and the couple kissed again, this time officially.

"Jake's ugly as mortal sin," observed Billy Conn. "He's a nice guy, though."

Shortly after, Jake and Carmen Basilio argued about who was uglier. The issue wasn't resolved. Steve Rossi, the comedian, who was performing at the hotel, was the master of ceremonies at the wedding. He brought the fighters onto the stage, where they talked and laughed and feinted and hit one another with friendly jabs and hooks. When all the fighters were on stage, Rossi said, "Let's all go eat before the platform collapses."

Teddy Brenner, the matchmaker, asked Joey Maxim, "Who was the only white guy to beat Jersey Joe Walcott and Floyd Patterson?" Maxim said he didn't know. "You, ya big lug," said Brenner. They both laughed. The story gleefully made the rounds, varying a little with each telling, until finally, ". . . and so he asked Joey, 'Who was the only white guy to beat Louis and Ali?' . . ."

Someone asked Fullmer how many times he had fought Robinson. "Three-and-a-half," he said. "The second fight, I asked my manager, how come they stopped it? He said, "Cause the referee counted to 11.'"

Basilio said he had recently retired as a physical education instructor at Le Moyne College in Syracuse. Someone asked if he had a degree. He smiled and brushed the ashes from his cigarette off the sports jacket of the person he was talking to. "I got a degree from H. N.," he said. "The school of hard knocks."

Billy Conn, who lives in Pittsburgh, was telling about the time that his brother Jackie, a noncomformist, visited Conn on a Thanksgiving Day. "We were having the Mellons over, and I told Jackie that we wanted everything to run smoothly, so here's fifty bucks and go buy a turkey for yourself. But he kept the fifty bucks and took the two turkeys we had in the stove."

What did the Conns and the Mellons eat that night? "We didn't eat," he said, "we drank whiskey all night. Oh, Jackie was a character. Jackie's dead now."

Roger Donoghue, once a promising middleweight from Yonkers and now a successful liquor salesman, was recalling the television fight days of the early 1950s. Basilio came over and handed Roger a small camera and asked him to take a picture of him and his wife. "I got hit in the head a lot," said Roger, looking at the camera, "but I'll try."

The doors of the room were opened and the clanging of slot machines was heard from the adjoining casino. People wandered in and out of the wedding party.

Jake was explaining, "You wanna go through life with someone, and she's a great kid, a great kid."

"This one," said Theresa, "is going to last until we die."

Now Jake and his bride stepped onto the dance floor. A trio, headed by a piano player wearing a black cowboy hat, played "The Nearness of You." Joey Maxim removed the cigar from his mouth as he watched Jake dance with his new bride. "Ain't that nice?" he said.

"Hey, buddy," said a man who walked in from the casino, "you know where a fella can get two tickets for the fight?"

[1985]

The G-Man Wonders
Where He Is

✌ "LISA are you there, Lisa?" Gerald McClellan, seated in a chair in his living room, called out to his sister. Lisa McClellan, in a chair beside him, leaned toward the young man in a baseball cap.

"Yes, Gerald."

"I love you, Lisa."

"I love you, G-Man."

"What?"

"I LOVE YOU, G-MAN."

"G-Man. I like that name." McClellan paused in the darkness of his world. He had given himself the nickname "G-Man" as a young fighter—a young fighter on the way to becoming a middleweight champion of the world—because it signified not only his first name but, he had said, "Green, my favorite color, the color of money." The money he spent lavishly on cars, clothes, jewelry, gifts for friends and family, and—said another sister, Stacey Cain—as much as $500 a day "just going to a mall." And the nickname also signified the money he planned to make in a bright future with million-dollar paydays. "You only live once," Gerald used to say. "So live it up."

All that ended in London on February 25 when, in a savage fight for the World Boxing Council supermiddleweight championship, he suffered a massive blood clot to the brain at the hands of Nigel Benn. McClellan, then twenty-seven, underwent an emergency three-and-a-half-hour procedure to remove the clot. The surgery saved his life but, after two months in a coma, he was left blind, hearing impaired, brain damaged, and unable to walk. His short-term memory is severely limited, and his long-term memory is selective. But he can still tease, as he once did, and has moments of good humor.

"G-Man," he said again, in his chair in the living room. And now his voice took on another tone, that of a ring announcer. "In the ninth bout, in-tro-du-cing, in this corner, wearing green, the WBC middleweight champeen of the world, from Freeport, Illinois—Ger-ald 'G-Man' Mc-Clel-lan!" And then, imagining the chant of the crowd, he said: "G! G! G!"

His smile appeared below his neatly trimmed mustache. "Puts me in a fightin' mood," he said. Then he grew serious.

"Lisa?" he said.

"Yes," she said.

"Where am I?"

"In your house, Gerald."

"Where?"

"YOUR HOUSE."

"My house?"

"YOUR HOUSE."

"Oh."

Lisa put her hand on his, and he rocked gently in his chair.

Next month the McClellans have an appointment for tests at the Mayo Clinic in Rochester, Minnesota. They hold out hope that Gerald's eyesight will be improved. They hold out hope that enough brain cells were not damaged in the fight so that, in time, Gerald will be able to comprehend to a greater capacity than he does now. He still talks about fighting again and doesn't realize he is blind. He just thinks it is dark.

On a recent evening he sat in his tidy, modest house on Wyandotte Street in a working-class section of Freeport, Illinois, a town of 26,000 that is 115 miles west of Chicago. It is a white frame house with green trim, a porch, and a backyard, one that he had proudly bought three years ago for $22,000, paying cash.

He wore the green baseball cap, green sweatshirt, green jogging pants, and white sweat socks without shoes. His right leg jiggled from a nervous condition, and his large, still-strong hands lay gently on the armrests of his chair, which is also a commode. A white towel was draped across his lap.

On the walls and end tables in McClellan's living room were numerous photographs of him as a boxer and bon vivant. He was one of the rising stars in the oddly named "sweet science," a broad-shouldered, 6-foot-1-inch, 168-pound fighting machine who could take a punch and deliver one with remarkable speed and power. Fight people termed his fists "heavy," which meant that they might fell a tree. "Pound for pound," it was said in gyms, he was up there among the best, champions like Roy Jones, Jr., Julio Cesar Chavez, and Pernell Whitaker.

After winning the WBC middleweight title in 1993, he scored first-round knockouts in each of his three title defenses. Then he relinquished the middleweight crown to take a shot at Benn.

McClellan can use his hands for everyday functions, but he cannot walk alone. He walks with the aid of two people, and generally they are his sisters. He has three sisters, all career nursing aides and all of whom, under the terms of a guardianship, rotate daily eight-hour shifts with him because he cannot be left alone for more than a few minutes. Supported by the sisters, Linda Shorter, known to the family as Auntie Lou, and who was termed "a mother figure," won guardianship.

There are no medical assurances of McClellan's getting any better, though he has made significant improvement over the last few months. After lengthy stays in hospitals in London, Ann Arbor, Michigan, and Milwaukee, he returned home to Freeport in August. He had dropped from his fighting weight of about 170 pounds to 128 pounds. Then, as he gained back strength as well as some of his hearing and comprehension, he went up to about 200 pounds. "He does like his buttered popcorn," Stacey said. "But we're going to have to put him on a diet."

McClellan's assets were determined in court to be $265,000. The money is in a trust, handled by First Bank North of Freeport. But much more money is expected to be needed for his care. And Friday night a $100-a-plate benefit dinner was held for McClellan at the Holiday Inn here to help pay some of his medical bills.

Among the more than three hundred who attended were the former world heavyweight champions Joe Frazier and Evander Holyfield and also Rachman Ali, the brother of Muhammad Ali, who was representing the former champion. Jones, the current International Boxing Federation supermiddleweight champion, who had figured on a title fight with McClellan this year, sent a video-taped message.

Holyfield spoke about McClellan the fighter, praised his courage in the ring, and held out hope for his recovery. "An injury like Gerald's can happen to any fighter," Holyfield said. "That's why I'm here to support him."

McClellan had always made a point of returning to Freeport, the hometown he loved. And Friday night the town returned that love. Freeport High School, which McClellan had attended and where he was one credit short of graduation, awarded him an honorary diploma. The family accepted it because McClellan was unable to attend.

Also conspicuous by his absence was Don King, McClellan's shock-haired, voluble promoter, who had walked ahead of him down the aisle to the ring for the fight against Benn, who was announced to the crowd with his nickname, the Dark Destroyer. King is having his own problems in a federal courthouse in New York, where he has been on trial for insurance fraud in a case involving Chavez, another of his fighters. The McClellan family—apart from, perhaps, the father, Emmite Sr.—are no longer in communication with King.

"He told me that he would take care of Gerald if we didn't embarrass him," Lisa said. "And my father told me—and testified in court—that King gave him 'hush money' not to talk to the press about Gerald. Don made a lot of promises that he hasn't kept, and now we can't even get him to return our phone calls. And we have serious questions about the purse he paid Gerald, and about an insurance policy on Gerald."

In a trial for guardianship of Gerald that ended November 3 in the Stephenson County Circuit Court House in Freeport, Mc-Clellan's three sisters and an aunt, Shorter, were pitted against the father, Emmite Sr. The father testified that Gerald told him he had a contract with King to receive $450,000 for the Benn fight but that King paid him only about $250,000. The McClellan family said Gerald's contract disappeared from his hotel room after the fight.

Charles Lomax, general counsel for Don King Enterprises in Fort Lauderdale, Florida, said he didn't have knowledge of the contract and could not immediately provide a copy of it.

Of the $250,000, King paid out $119,729.25 on a judgment against McClellan for having breached a contract with a former manager, Emanuel Steward. The sisters contend that King had promised to pay that amount out of his own pocket after luring McClellan away from Steward. King also paid other expenses after McClellan's injury, including perhaps the flight to England and a two-week stay at a London hotel by Cain, Shorter, Emmite Sr., and Angie Brown, McClellan's live-in girlfriend and mother of his one-year-old daughter, Forrest.

For his trouble that night in the devastating brawl with Benn, McClellan wound up earning $54,000. He also received from King $100,000, which King said was the amount of the insurance policy protecting against career-ending injury.

"We're looking into that," Lisa McClellan said. She is under the impression that the insurance policy was for $1 million.

Gerald Allen McClellan was born and raised in Freeport, one of six children of Genola and Emmite McClellan, Sr., a laborer in a nearby Chrysler plant. The father took pride in having been a good street fighter and wanted his sons to become professional fighters. Todd, two years older than Gerald, had talent. But only Gerald, after some reluctance when he first put on boxing gloves at the age of eight and was made to fight by his father under street lamps in Freeport, took to it with passion. "He was gifted from the start," Emmite Sr. said.

"Todd was always a little stronger," Gerald said, "but I was the more intelligent boxer. I used my head more. He'd try to do it with brute strength." And Gerald developed a single-mindedness and a remarkable focus. "He had his mind set on being a champion," said Robert Slattery, McClellan's former attorney. "And, like any subject he sank his teeth into, he was not going to be swayed."

The family moved to Milwaukee for a few years, and Gerald won the Wisconsin Golden Gloves middleweight title four years in a row (1984–1987) and the national amateur title in 1987. In one amateur fight he beat an opponent named Michael Moorer, who later rose in weight class and became the heavyweight champion of the world.

In 1988, also as an amateur, McClellan beat Jones in an Olympic trial semifinal bout. In what seemed a case of politicking, it was Jones and not McClellan who was selected for the United States team at the games in Seoul, South Korea. Jones, in fact, won a gold medal, but McClellan was infuriated by having been denied the shot.

He turned pro in 1988 and quickly moved up in the ranks. He went to train with Steward, who had trained Tommy Hearns, among other champions, in the famous Kronk Gym in Detroit. McClellan's punching power immediately impressed. "I saw him in training hit a boy on the side of the head," Steward recalled, "and that guy was so messed up he could never get his coordination back. I never saw anything like that."

In 1991, McClellan knocked out John (The Beast) Mugabi in the first round for the vacated World Boxing Organization middleweight title. In 1993, he won the WBC title from Julian Jackson. But he was getting bigger and finding it harder to make the

160-pound weight. He signed for the Benn fight, a twelve-round title shot, in the London Arena. McClellan was a 4–1 favorite. His record was 31–2, with twenty-nine knockouts, twenty-one of them within the first three rounds. He had lost two decisions early in his career.

Typically, McClellan came out smoking in the first round and within thirty-eight seconds had knocked Benn through the ropes. Benn made it back before the referee counted him out, though some ringsiders, including Ferdie Pacheco, the doctor and fight analyst, felt Benn got a break from the timekeeper.

But Benn revived, and the two fought savagely, though McClellan seemed to tire periodically, his mouthpiece coming partially out of his mouth so he could draw more air. In the eighth round McClellan floored Benn again with a vicious right. But again the British fighter got back up. In the ninth Benn reacted to a McClellan punch by throwing and missing a right hook as he lunged toward McClellan. As he did so, he apparently head-butted McClellan. It was this blow, doctors believe, that created the blood clot in McClellan's brain.

In the next round, McClellan seemed to react differently. He was blinking and held his head, and when Benn hit him with a straight right, McClellan dropped to one knee, where he was counted out. He then staggered back to his corner and, before a stool could be propped under him, slid down the ropes, where he collapsed onto the canvas. Benn—who had been behind on two of the three judges' cards—celebrated with a warrior's dance around the ring, unaware of how badly hurt McClellan was.

An ambulance and doctors took McClellan to Royal London Hospital. The British Boxing Association now provides this type of full-fledged assistance because a boxer was paralyzed last year when such help wasn't available. Benn, his face battered and bandaged, was also admitted to the hospital for exhaustion and found himself in a cubicle adjoining McClellan's.

"I spoke to him and he managed to give me the thumbs up,"

Benn said. "As I spoke, I carried on holding his hand. Then I kissed him and left. I thought, 'He's in hospital, he'll be fine.'"

At home now, McClellan receives few visitors. His mother, Genola, was found incapable of taking care of him because of an alcohol problem. His brother Todd is now in prison on a battery conviction. Two other brothers, Emmite Jr. and Vince, live in Freeport but have not taken an active role in Gerald's care, leaving it to the sisters. Angie Brown moved out of Gerald's house with their daughter when problems arose between Brown and the rest of McClellan's family. She and her daughter have not returned. McClellan has two other children with different mothers, seven-year-old Gerald Jr., who visits him from Milwaukee, and four-year-old Mandy, who lives in Detroit.

The battle over McClellan's guardianship was rancorous, but Emmite Sr. was deemed to have put his son at risk by twice leaving him alone when the two had lived together over the last two months. Emmite Sr. has left Freeport and is not in communication with the rest of his family, which has assumed the full-time job of taking care of McClellan.

Sitting in his living room, McClellan called out again for his sister, Lisa.

"I'm thirsty," he said.

"You have a soda right on the table next to you."

He reached for it and began to drink, but Lisa stopped him from poking himself by removing the straw.

"Lisa," McClellan said, "you there?"

"Yes, Gerald," she said.

"I love you, Lisa."

"I love you, Gerald."

"What?"

"I LOVE YOU, GERALD."

"G-man?"

"G-man."

"I like that name. Lisa?"

"Yes?"

"Hold my hand." She reached over and held his hand.

"I like that," he said. "Thank you, Lisa."

[1995]

An Olympic Invitation Comes Sixty Years Late

W THE ENVELOPE was postmarked Frankfurt, Germany, and bore the return address of "Der Präsident, Nationales Olympisches Komitee für Deutschland." It was delivered last month to an elderly Jewish woman living in a two-story brick house in the Jamaica Estates section of Queens.

The letter to Margaret Bergmann Lambert, eighty-two, was written in English under the letterhead of Walter Troger, president. "It is my honor and pleasure to inform you," the letter began, "that the National Olympic Committee for Germany has decided to invite you to be our guest of honor during the Olympic Centennial Games in Atlanta. This is on the grounds of our relations over the last year, and the discussion we had in New York. As you were not in a position to accept our invitation to Germany for reasons we understand and honor, we feel that this invitation might be an equivalence."

Lambert is still slender at five feet seven inches, her white hair cut short. During a recent visit she wore glasses, white sneakers, a summer blouse, and blue jeans that covered her long jumper's legs. She had opened the letter in her foyer. Close by, in a glass case, were a host of world-class track and field medals, including the one with the swastika from the meet in June 1936 when she high-jumped a winning five feet three inches, the same height that would be good enough to capture the gold medal later that summer in the Berlin Olympics. But not by her. She was not allowed to compete because she was a Jew living in Nazi Germany.

Lambert knows that she never really had a chance of making the Olympic team. That no German Jews could have competed for the country in 1936, even though she was coerced into training with threats against her family. That her training was all "a charade," as she put it, a propaganda tool to show the world an unbiased Germany.

And now the German Olympic committee was extending a hand of apology and friendship, a form of reparation. She would even be allowed to bring a guest, her husband, Dr. Bruno Lambert, a former college runner whom she had met in Germany in 1935. Margaret Lambert had not been "in a position," as the letter put it, to accept an invitation to Germany—where a gymnasium in Berlin was named for her last year—because she had sworn when she left in 1937 that she would never set foot on German soil again. And she hasn't.

Lambert, known then by her nickname and maiden name, Gretel Bergmann, has an appealing sense of humor and an easy laugh, but there is another layer beneath that. She has lived much of her life with hatred and resentment. Hatred at how the Nazi regime scarred and decimated the lives of friends and family, sending many of them to the gas chambers. And resentment for opportunities lost.

Much of this flooded back as she read the letter. Recently she watched the Atlanta Grand Prix, a major pre-Olympic track and field meet, on television. "And suddenly I realized there were tears just flowing down my cheeks," she recalled. "I'm not a crier. But now I just couldn't help it. I remember watching those athletes, and remembering what it was like for me in 1936, how I could very well have won an Olympic medal. And through the tears, I said, 'Damn it!'"

Margaret Bergmann was born in 1914 in the small farming community of Laupheim, Germany, near the Swiss border. Her father, Edwin, owned a hair-supplies factory, and she said she experienced no anti-Semitism until she was nineteen and Hitler came to power.

She had been a natural athlete, and competed and was victorious in local and national meets. "My parents thought I was a freak because I loved sports so much," she recalled. "I mean, a nice Jewish girl? They wanted me to learn to sew and cook. Which, by the way, I learned, too."

Now suddenly there were anti-Jewish edicts in Germany. Jews could not shop in gentile stores, and gentiles could not shop in Jewish stores. Jews weren't allowed in movie houses or theaters and could not stroll in the parks. There were beatings of Jews on the streets.

Gretel Bergmann had been accepted to the University of Berlin, but the admission was withdrawn. "I will never forget what that letter said—'Let's wait for this thing to blow over'—meaning, this Hitler thing can't last," she said.

But that was enough for her. In 1934 she left for England and school there. In 1935 she won the British women's high-jump championship. Her father traveled there to see her compete, or so she thought. In fact he had come with a message, one he could not risk relating by either letter or telephone.

"He told me the Germans wanted me to return and try out for the Olympic team," she said. "I said, 'I'm not going.' He said that there had been veiled threats on our family if I didn't come back. I packed my bags and sailed with him the next day."

The Nazis did not want Jews participating in their Berlin Olympics, but they tried to put on a different face for those, especially some groups in America, who protested that the Germans were discriminating against Jewish athletes. "But it was a charade," Lambert said. "The handful of Jewish track and field athletes were not allowed to be in the German Athletic Association because we were Jews, and that's where the best training and competition existed. We were forced to train in potato fields."

On the few occasions when she did train with the other German women, Gretel Bergmann made some friends, including the high-jumper Elfriede Kaun and the discus thrower Gisela Mauer-mayer. "The girls were always very nice," Lambert said. "It was the officials who were terrible. The propaganda then was that Jews were the scum of the earth. That's how the officials treated us."

On June 30, 1936, just one month before the Olympics, she was permitted to jump at Adolf Hitler Stadium in Stuttgart, the last major Olympic trial. "I remember all the Nazi flags and all the officials saluting, and I jumped like a fiend," she said. "I always did my best when I was angry. I never jumped better; I didn't miss a jump." And her mark of 5–3 equaled the German record.

When she prepared to jump for the record, she grew scared. "I thought, this would be a slap in the face to the Aryans," she said. "What would they do to me? Would they break my legs? Would they kill me? What would they do to my family? And I just fell apart. I couldn't really lift myself again."

But her earlier jump stood. And then on July 16—one day after the American team set sail for Europe, and two weeks after her outstanding jump—she received a letter from the German Olympic committee informing her that she had not made the team: "Looking back on your recent performances, you could not possibly have expected to be chosen for the team." The letter, which she has saved, went on to offer her a standing-room-only ticket, "free of charge," for the track and field events, "though ex-penses for transportation and hotel accommodations unfortu-nately cannot be supplied. Heil Hitler!"

She never replied. The Hungarian jumper Ibolya Csak won the gold medal, and Kaun, whom Bergmann had beaten during Olympic training sessions, won the bronze. Both jumped 5–3. Mauermayer won the gold in the discus. In later years Lambert corresponded with both German women, who were sympathetic. "Of course we knew you were Jewish but never treated you differ-ently because you were another athlete like we were," said Mauer-mayer. And Kaun wrote: "They told us you were unable to compete because you had been injured."

In 1937, Gretel Bergmann was able to get papers to emigrate to the United States, landing with ten dollars, all the money the Germans allowed her to take out of the country. She took jobs in New York as a masseuse and a housemaid and, later, a physical therapist.

She won the United States high-jump and shot-put championships in 1937 and the high jump again in 1938. She was preparing for another run at the title in 1939 when war broke out in Europe. "And since my family was still in Europe, I stopped competing," she said. Her mother, father, and two brothers escaped to America in 1939. Many others in her family, including her grandparents, and her husband's family, including his parents, were murdered in concentration camps.

"We feel that Mrs. Lambert was not treated adequately at the time of the Berlin Olympics," Troger, the president of the German Olympic committee, said by telephone from Frankfurt last week. "She was an Olympic candidate who did not get a fair chance. We wanted to do something for her, we felt she deserved it. And since she was not coming back to Germany, the idea that the Games were taking place in her country now seemed very appropriate."

Though Lambert did not return to Germany last year, her two sons, Glenn and Gary, did. "They told me, 'You know, Mom, we only knew about the Nazis,'" she said. "'These people are different. They have a different way of looking at things.'

"I don't hate all Germans anymore, though I did for a long time. I can't even speak German too well anymore. I had tried to forget the language. But I'm aware of many Germans trying to make up for wrongs as well as they know how. In recent years I've gotten a bunch of letters from Germans saying how sorry they are.

"And I thought, yes, the young people of Germany should not be held responsible for what their elders did. And I decided to accept the invitation to go to Atlanta. I felt that there would be publicity in Germany—there has been already—and the young people should always be aware of what happened to innocent people so many years ago.

"And while I know I could never root for the German team—

I'll be cheering for the Americans—I thought that going to Atlanta as the guest of honor of the German Olympic committee would be good for my mental outlook. It will make the ghosts of the past a little less unfriendly."

[1996]

Wilma Rudolph: Black Cinderella

SHE BECAME America's black Cinderella. But her early dreams were not to find Prince Charming, or to be queen of the Debutante's Ball. Or even to be adored, as she would be, and cheered lustily and mobbed around the world, with her fans sometimes even stealing off her shoes—while she wore them.

"The only thing I ever really wanted when I was a child," Wilma Rudolph once said, "was to be normal. To be average. To be able to run, jump, play, and do all the things the other kids did in my neighborhood."

Wilma Rudolph's life, however, became the stuff of fairy tales: the crippled girl at age eleven who became an Olympic sprint champion at twenty, whose charm and elegance captivated millions.

She was born in 1940 in a small house in Clarksville, Tennessee, the twentieth of twenty-two children from the combined two marriages of her father, Ed Rudolph, a railroad porter, and her mother, Blanche, a domestic.

And yesterday, early in the morning in Brentwood, Tennessee, not far from her birthplace, Wilma Rudolph died, having succumbed to a malignant brain tumor.

"She was beautiful, she was nice, and she was the best," said Bill Mulliken, winner of an Olympic gold medal in swimming and teammate of Rudolph's on the 1960 American team in the Rome

Olympics. "I can still see in my mind's eye a photograph of her gracefully crossing the finish line first in the two-hundred-meter dash in Rome, her head back, her outside leg raised. To me, that picture symbolized what Wilma Rudolph was all about—the epitome of athletic femininity."

When Wilma was four, suffering simultaneously from double pneumonia and scarlet fever, her left leg became paralyzed. At age six, she was fitted with a special shoe, which enabled her to walk haltingly. She wore that shoe until she was eleven.

"I remember the kids always saying, 'I don't want to play with her. We don't want her on our team,' she said. "So I never had a chance to participate. And all my young life I would say, 'One day I'm going to be somebody very special. And I'm not going to forget those kids.'"

Whatever spurs are needed to drive a champion, one of those must be a need continually to prove oneself to others, as well as to oneself. Talent, while significant, is not enough. "I was competitive from the very first moment I heard that girls were allowed to run track," she said. "And from that moment, that was my world. I trained daily. I was forever skipping class and would climb over the fence and be the only girl in the stadium."

Tall and slender—she grew to 6 feet and 130 pounds—she was also greatly gifted. She became a track and basketball star in high school and then at Tennessee State University in Nashville. As a high school star she won a bronze medal in the relays in the 1956 Olympics in Melbourne. Good, but perhaps not enough to make those kids in her old neighborhood never forget her.

Four years later she won three gold medals, in the one-hundred-, the two-hundred-, and the four-hundred-meter relay, the most track and field gold medals won by a woman since Babe Didrikson in 1932. "The '60 Olympics was my greatest thrill," Rudolph said. "And when I think back on it, I still get frightened to remember a capacity crowd in the stadium all standing and chanting my name."

She returned to America and earned a teaching degree from

Tennessee State. Her life took on a frequently mundane quality. She tried a few jobs, from teaching school to coaching. She was human, sometimes self-involved, and making decisions that turned out poorly. Had tax problems. Was married twice and divorced twice.

But she remained Wilma Rudolph, Olympic champion. She set up the Wilma Rudolph Foundation for minority youngsters. She gave speeches, she reaped honors for long-ago achievements. And, like other black Olympic champions, she returned to an America that could be hostile. When, once, she went for a bank loan, she experienced rejection because, she believed, of her color. And while she might not have had the same reaction to racial slights as her fellow 1960 American Olympian, Cassius Clay, who threw his gold medal into a river, she remained aware that, in effect, the playing field outside of the playing field was uneven.

But none of that diminished her beauty or her stature. When she entered a room, she commanded it immediately, walking straight and tall, invariably wearing a stylish hat and a generous smile, all warmth and majesty.

She retired from running in 1962 because, she said, she wanted to be remembered "at her best." And her legacy, her inspiring story, is a model of all the clichés turned truisms in sports. For boys as well as girls. For any color. From any culture. With any handicap.

"When I was running," Wilma Rudolph said, "I had the sense of freedom, of running in the wind. I never forgot all the years when I was a little girl and not able to be involved. When I ran, I felt like a butterfly. That feeling was always there."

[1994]

The Rides and Falls of an Emperor Named Cordero

EVERYTHING was bright orange. The horses were orange. The sky was orange. The other jockeys were orange. The stands and crowd and track were orange. Then everything went black.

"For five nights in a row in the hospital, I had this nightmare," Angel Cordero, the jockey, said last week. "All I could remember was orange, because I was wearing orange silks when the spill happened, and I went somersaulting through the air. I don't remember anything else for days afterward, not being hit by the horse, not slamming into the pole, but later I was told that I kept calling out, 'Doctor, give me something for the pain.'"

"For the first two days," his wife, Marjie, had said, "we thought we were going to lose him. He had all the support systems, the tubes going in and out of his body and nose and mouth. It was terrifying."

At home now, Cordero sat in a chair in the recreation room beside a large picture window that let in the grey light from the winter's day. "I know I look like someone who hasn't eaten in two weeks," he said. At 5 feet 3 inches, Cordero normally rides at about 114 pounds. "I'm 98 pounds now," he said. He wore a blue robe and a pair of oversized white woolly house slippers into which his dark-complexioned, thin-as-pipestem legs sank.

Cordero's house is situated in Greenvale, Long Island, just a few miles from Aqueduct where, on Sunday afternoon, January 12, he was the most seriously hurt of four jockeys in a chain-reaction accident.

In his thirty-one years as a professional jockey, this was Cordero's most serious injury. His right elbow was broken, four ribs were broken, he had massive internal injuries, particularly to his small intestines and kidneys, and he underwent surgery to remove his spleen. He was in intensive care for nine days, and in the hospital for thirty-one days overall. These new injuries were just the latest in a long riding career in which he has broken, among other things, both ankles, both knees, both elbows, his collarbone, assorted vertebrae, four ribs on his left side (plus the four ribs now injured on his right side), and nine fingers.

Despite the occupational wounds and mutilations, Angel Tomas Cordero, Jr., born and raised in Puerto Rico, has been one of America's best jockeys, and, arguably, the finest ever to ride regularly in New York. He has ridden 7,054 winners, third on the career list behind Bill Shoemaker and Laffit Pincay, Jr., and his triumphs include three victories in the Kentucky Derby, two in the Preakness, one in the Belmont Stakes, and four in the Breeders' Cup races. He has led the nation in winners and money earnings—his total purses coming to nearly $165 million—and has twice won the prestigious Eclipse Award as the nation's top jockey. In 1988 he was elected to the Racing Hall of Fame.

At the age of forty-nine, Cordero had been one of the oldest jockeys still riding, and riding effectively, when he was injured in January. Last year, in fact, he was sixth in the nation in money winnings, earning close to $7 million in purses. After expenses, he said, he cleared about $300,000 to $400,000. It was close to the most he has ever earned in one year.

"My wife says she doesn't want me to ride again," said Cordero. "She's seen this before, like in '86 when I had another spill and shattered my liver in seven places and was in a cast and crutches for two months. My mother says that if I ride again she'll kill herself. But she's said that before. Any time I even hurt my pinky she's wanted me to retire." He smiled, which was difficult, because it caused pain in his neck and back and shoulders. "And my doctor doesn't want me to ride again, says I'm crazy if I do."

Cordero gently readjusted his body in the chair, which was beside the pullout bed that Cordero sleeps on when he hurts too much to climb the stairs to the second-floor bedroom. "But I can't even think about it for a while," he said. "The doctor tells me it'll be four or five months until I'm healthy again. Right now I have no energy. Right now I feel like a hundred years old."

He recalled, though, that there have been jockeys about as old or even older than he who have ridden successfully. He mentioned Eddie Arcaro, who rode till he was forty-six, and Shoemaker, who rode until he was fifty-six, and Johnny Longden, who rode into his sixties.

"Every time you go out, you know it's a big risk," said Cordero. In the accent he retains, "big" came out "beeg." "But every time I go out, I also think I can win. I don't always say this to people. Sometimes when I have a horse that's a real long shot, I tell my friends, 'Don't bet it.' But I think in my heart, I can win. If a horse has four legs, and I'm riding it, I think I can win."

Cordero recalled how he had grown up around racetracks in Puerto Rico, with his father and both grandfathers and several uncles being both jockeys and trainers. He became an apprentice at age seventeen in 1959, and three years later tried his luck in America. Cordero idolized Arcaro and copied the way Arcaro rode the horse—"very low on the seat"—and studied on film how Arcaro switched the whip from one hand to the other, as swiftly as a magician. He met Arcaro in 1959 at the El Commandante racetrack in San Juan, and the boy said to the man, "I want to be just like you."

"When I came to America I couldn't speak English, I had no money, and I got lost every time I went into the subway," Cordero said. "But I just had a dream to become the top rider in New York." He remembers sleeping on friends' sofas and walking hots around the barns and galloping horses for trainers. He failed to make a mark as a jockey and returned to Puerto Rico three different times. Then he tried again, in 1965. "A few people gave me some chances, especially Laz Barrera, the trainer," he said. "He was a friend of my father's, and my father asked him to look out for me. I called him my white daddy. I called him Papa."

Soon people at the track began to take notice. "I rode cheap horses and won on 'em," said Cordero. "Then they started to give me better horses." He was a hard rider, an aggressive rider, and angered some rivals who said that in his combative style he would do anything to win. He was suspended on numerous occasions, but he kept coming back, kept winning. In 1967 he became the top jockey in New York, and in 1968 he was the leading jockey in North America with 345 victories.

"He learned all the tricks," said Sammy Renick, the former jockey. "He learned where to go and how to do it, how far to carry out his horse, how to drop in when someone's trying to pass him inside. He's about as close to a perfect rider as you can find."

Cordero recalled his first Derby victory, aboard Cannonade in 1974, and pointed to a picture on a nearby wall of him in the winner's circle with a garland of roses draped about the horse's neck.

The second Derby victory, in 1976 on Bold Forbes, was even better. "It was more emotional to me because Barrera was the trainer and Rodriguez Tizol owned the horse. My father used to ride for Mr. Tizol, and the first horse I ever rode in a race, at the old El Commandante, was for him."

The crunch of a car pulling into the driveway made Cordero turn his head to the window. It was his wife, returning from Aqueduct.

Marjorie Clayton Cordero had been a jockey in the mid-1980s, when she met Angel, and is now a trainer. This is Cordero's second marriage, and he and Marjie have three children—Julie, five, who had been with her at the track, and Canela, three, and Angel III, one and a half. From his first marriage Cordero has two children in their twenties, and is a grandfather of two.

Marjie, in jeans and riding boots and sporting a long ponytail, came into the room and kissed her husband. Marjie had asked Angel to accompany her to the track for the workout, but he said he couldn't get up. He'd had a bad night from the pain and finally fell asleep at about the time she left, at 4:30 A.M.

"I want to get him out of the house," she said. "I think it's depressing for him to just sit here looking out the window at the bare trees."

"And the squirrels," he said lightly.

"And the squirrels," she agreed.

She also hopes that getting him to the track in the morning will whet his interest for horse training. "It's time to forget about riding," she said. Eventually, Cordero says, he does plan to go into horse training. "Horses is all I know," he said.

"But he's scared," said Marjie, sitting down on the edge of the bed. "Not scared of riding again, because he'll go back on a horse in a race in a second, without flinching. That's Angel. But he's scared of starting something new."

"If I start as a trainer," he said, underscoring her point, "I have to start at the bottom. But they are two very different careers, riding and training. One you can get very wealthy, but it is dangerous. The other, you are not as wealthy and it is not as dangerous."

Money, he said, is a concern. Even though he has made millions from riding, he says he is not financially secure. "For a few years, yes, but not for my whole life," he said. "I don't have nearly as much as I should have. And I have nine dependents—my family, my mother, some nieces and a nephew, and my alimony. The money can go fast."

Marjie Cordero shook her head. "You'll do fine as a trainer," she said. "You know horses mentally and physically. You know how they think. Owners would love to give you horses."

"I don't want to go through what I've gone through in the last month," she added. "Not knowing whether Angel would live or die or be paralyzed."

Yet Frank Sanabria, Cordero's agent, said that Angel wants to continue riding. "He still has the fire," said Sanabria. "It's what he does best. Athletes hate to ever have to leave the stage. And when he got hurt last month, he was riding great. I know in the back of his mind he's thinking of Saratoga in August."

When his latest injury occurred, Cordero seemed to be riding as hard as ever. Complaints about his tactics still exist among some jockeys, though some view him with affection, like Julie Krone, who now calls him "Papa."

Cordero has a videocassette tape of his last race and played it for a visitor, rewinding, stopping, flicking it to slow motion as he watched himself coming around the far turn on Grey Tailwind, then the tumble. He seemed almost spellbound watching it. On the first showing, Cordero observed himself fly head over heels through the air and then hurtle against one of the small steel shafts that hold up the rail. "Look," he said, still amazed. "I'm wrapped in there like a horseshoe."

Marjie had viewed that scene once too often. She stood and left the room without a word. In a few minutes, Cordero clicked off the video recorder. He invited his visitor to follow him into another room, which looked like a playroom for his children.

On a shelf circling the room were hundreds of small plastic horses. And in the middle of the room stood what looked like a broad wooden rocking horse, but with just a torso and head, no rocker and no legs. It was covered with a worn beige rug and equipped with a small red riding saddle, stirrups, a green bridle, and a white "5" on the black number cloth. It had a black, narrow wooden face with big, round eyes, like a cartoon character or a Picasso sculpture.

"This is Johnny Dance," explained Cordero. "It was made by a jockey friend of mine, Frankie Lovato. He calls it an Equisizer. He gave it to me when I got hurt in '83, and I've used it a lot. You can see, the stuffing's coming out of the neck."

It's good exercise on days he doesn't ride, he said, or when recovering from an injury. Cordero demonstrated, carefully climbing aboard and pulling the stirrups high. "You got to ride really short," he said, his knees touching his chest. "Your heels are back and you see only your toes in the stirrup."

"Oohh," he said, wincing. "I can't bend—the incision." He took a breath and gripped and bunched the reins. "You're supposed to put your neck back and look through the ears of the horse, like a radar. Then you whip it—and ride the hell out of it."

Crouched in his blue robe and woolen slippers, the veteran jockey swayed in the saddle ever so gently and peered between the ears of the wooden horse. For a moment Angel Cordero seemed transported, back to the thrill of the track, racing to win, to the scent of danger even, his heart and the hooves of his horse pounding, and a huge crowd cheering him on.

[1992]

The Changing Faces
of Arthur Ashe

❦ THEY WERE SEATED around the kitchen table—Arthur Ashe;
his wife, Jeanne, and their daughter, Camera, now six years old.
This was a short time ago, and the conversation was unremark-
able, about what Jeanne and Arthur had done that day, and what
Camera was doing in school. Jeanne looked at Camera and then
casually turned back to Arthur, and saw that he had begun to cry.

"Camera didn't question it, because she knew that her father
had been troubled, though I don't think she was quite sure of the
depth of it," Jeanne Ashe recalled. "Then Arthur reached over and
held her hand. And I rubbed his back. It was one of the few times
I have ever seen Arthur cry.

"Nothing was said."

As the gauzy cloudscape outside the airplane window slipped
by, Arthur Ashe thumbed through his appointment book. He was
flying from New York City to a speaking engagement upstate at
Niagara County Community College, where posters on the small,
rural campus in Sanborn, New York, read: "Today at 12:30 in the
Fine Arts Auditorium/Arthur Ashe/U.S. Tennis Champion and
AIDS Victim/Discussion on AIDS and the Right to Privacy."

These are new and very trying times for Ashe—in a lifetime
that has been full of new and often trying times. But it is also a
life that has been, by any account, extraordinary.

At forty-nine years old, Ashe, as the world knows, found him-

self last April feeling virtually compelled to reveal that he had contracted AIDS. The disease was apparently transmitted through a
blood transfusion that Ashe received after he underwent heart-
bypass surgery in 1983. After overcoming his anger over the belief
that his privacy had been invaded, that he had been pushed to go
public because a newspaper, *USA Today*, was pursuing the story
that he had the disease, Ashe, as he has done with virtually everything else in his life, made adjustments. He has become a leading
spokesman for education about AIDS, a man as consumed by
helping those who will come after him as he once was determined
to live his life on his own terms. He talks frequently on college
campuses and elsewhere, and he does so openly, and patiently,
about what he knows and what he has learned, both about himself
and the disease.

"I'm amazed at Arthur," Seth Abraham, the president of Time
Warner Sports, and a close friend, had said earlier. "Barriers just
don't exist for him. They don't impede him, don't block him, don't
hem him in. He feels that there's just too much in life that he
must do. And time is an element." So Ashe has quit asking certain
questions.

"When I first learned that I had contracted this supposedly
terminal illness, in 1988," Ashe said, "I used to ask my doctor every
few months if I had time enough to plan to take my daughter to
Disneyland, or to play in a celebrity golf tournament, or to take
part in a seminar on race, or some other matter. But I don't anymore. I've fallen into a kind of routine. I know I'll be sick with di-
arrhea and fatigue about once every five or six days. And this has
been going on for several years. So I've learned not to panic when
I feel bad. When the symptoms change, when I'm sick two or
three times a week, then I might again have to bring up the subject of longevity with my doctor."

Arthur Ashe has always been lean, and he is thinner now,
down to 147 pounds from 153 when he was playing tennis and con-
founding observers who wondered how he summoned so much
power into a serve that could whistle at 115 miles an hour. That

serve helped propel him to become the first black man to win the United States Open, in 1968, and Wimbledon, in 1975, and to be ranked number one in the world.

"I weigh a little less than I used to, but I know I look even thinner because the muscle mass has diminished," Ashe said. "It happens with most retired athletes. I play golf now and have given up tennis completely. I love golf. I'll play golf in a minute. I'd miss a meal to play golf." His eyes, behind aviator glasses, twinkled. "Sometimes I have."

He remains surprisingly active for someone who has suffered three heart attacks—the last, a relatively mild one, only six weeks ago—undergone two heart bypass operations, one a quadruple and the second a double, and is coping with AIDS. Ashe takes two drugs regularly, AZT and DDI, to try to slow the breakdown of his immune system. He takes a larger quantity of natural vitamins. In all, for his heart and because of AIDS, he consumes about thirty pills a day. His prescription drug bill is $18,000 a year.

As the lone black male tennis star in the 1960s and 1970s, Ashe carried a burden that sometimes made him uncomfortable, but he carried it with dignity. He was a role model and a source of inspiration to blacks as well as whites. The story is by now well known: how a youth from segregated Richmond rose swiftly through the ranks, sometimes being refused entry in junior tournaments held in the South, to triumph in the nearly all-white tennis world.

Since the de facto end of his tennis career in 1979—after he suffered a heart attack, while ranked seventh in the world, at age thirty-six—Ashe had been involved in numerous social causes. Now that his condition is known, his life, his schedule have become even fuller.

In his window seat in the airplane, Ashe mentioned that he had a dentist's appointment the following day. Arthur Ashe's going to the dentist is different from most people going to the dentist. "The dentist comes out like he's going to war," Ashe said with a little smile. "He wears a long green surgical gown, a mask, goggles, latex gloves—well, he's always worn gloves—and his assistant is dressed the same way. No, it doesn't bother me. That's the way they should dress. I mean, he's going to poke around in there, and he might draw blood and he'd be foolish not to use all the health precautions he can. But he's been great. And he's shown courage. I don't mean just physically because he still treats me, and some doctors would not. I mean that because he still treats me, he's lost business. A number of his patients have left him because of me."

Ashe looked down at his appointment book, which is brimming: there is a function for the Arthur Ashe Foundation for the Defeat of AIDS; one for the Safe Passage Foundation, which he founded to deal with problems in inner cities, and one for a black athletic organization that he has recently helped organize with the former Knick guard Dick Barnett.

Ashe handed his companion an article on AIDS in which it said that people with the disease feel an odd sense of liberation, that they can pursue activities and say things with candor that might have inhibited them before.

"Absolutely true," he said.

As an athlete, Ashe had transcended the sport, taking a stand for the end of apartheid and in 1973 becoming the first black athlete to play in an integrated sporting event in South Africa. When a delegation of Americans assembled to visit Nelson Mandela in October 1991, the black leader requested that Ashe be among them.

And just a day before the most recent heart attack, Ashe was arrested, handcuffed, and placed in jail for a few hours in Washington while taking part in a demonstration in front of the White House. He was protesting the administration's policy of restrictions on Haitian immigrants.

Now, en route to his speech upstate, he was pursuing another cause, the one of helping educate people about AIDS.

Ashe has known that he has AIDS since 1988. It was then that he underwent brain surgery after his right arm became paralyzed. The surgery revealed a parasitic infection that quickly led to a diagnosis of AIDS. But Ashe had not planned to reveal his illness until, he said, the time came when he would be noticeably changed by the disease physically, and then would have to confront obvious questions.

He said that he thought it was a private matter because he was no longer an active athlete whose performance would be affected by his having AIDS. But when *USA Today* asked him to confirm or deny a rumor that he had AIDS, he decided it was only a matter of time before the word was out, and he scheduled a news conference the next day to make his own announcement. He wanted, as much as he could, to control the dissemination of the information.

"Rumors and half-truths have been floating about concerning my medical condition," he said at the news conference April 8. He then made his announcement.

After the plane landed in Buffalo, Ashe was met by a Niagara County Community College student who took him into his confidence. "Mr. Ashe," said the student, "my brother has AIDS, and he's dying. But my parents don't know it. He's told me, but he doesn't want to tell them."

"How did he contract it?" Ashe asked. "I mean, what was the opportunistic infection that revealed it?"

"He's gay," said the student. "I think it was a liver problem he had been in the hospital for."

"Do your parents know he's gay."

"Yes. Yes, they do."

"I think they can handle that he's dying," said Ashe. "He's probably afraid to tell them because he feels he'd be rejected by them. But I don't believe he would be. And he'd feel unbelievably good, knowing that he was being supported. People in this situation need as much support as they can get to bear up under it. It would be a big relief for him."

"He's afraid that my mother's health couldn't take it."

"Mothers hold up suprisingly well," Ashe said, evenly. "Their love is almost unqualified. I'm not one to give advice, but I think you should tell your parents about it. Does your brother work?"

"No. He gets a welfare check."

"I think he should try to get a job," Ashe said. "Otherwise he just sits around collecting a check and watching the clock tick away. If he felt useful, he'd feel much better. It's important to be productive."

Some three hundred students and faculty members—close to capacity—appeared for Ashe's talk in the college's auditorium. Much of the talk was about the most basic aspects of living with AIDS.

"I've had a religious faith, growing up in the South and black and having the church as a focal point of your life," Ashe said. "And I was reminded of something Jesus said on the cross: 'My God, my God, why hast thou forsaken me?' Remember, Jesus was poor, humble and of a despised minority. I wasn't poor in that my father was a policeman, but we certainly weren't rich. And Jesus asked the question, in effect, of why must the innocent suffer. And I'm not so innocent—I mean, I'm hardly a perfect human being—but you ask about yourself, 'Why me?' And I think, 'Why not me?'

"Why should I be spared what some others have been inflicted with," he continued. "And I have to think of all the good of my life, of having a great wife and daughter, and family and friends, and winning Wimbledon and the U.S. Open and playing for and coaching the Davis Cup team, and getting a free scholarship to UCLA—all kinds of good things. You could also ask about this, 'Why me?' Sometimes there are no explanations for things, especially for the bad."

Sometimes, he said, paraphrasing a bumper sticker, stuff happens.

Ashe believes he contracted HIV, the virus that causes AIDS, when he underwent heart-bypass surgery in 1983 and was given a blood transfusion. At the time, hospitals were not checking blood samples for HIV. That test began nationwide two years later.

"Just yesterday," Ashe went on, "literally, just yesterday, my daughter, Camera, who is six years old, asked me, 'Daddy, how did you get AIDS?'

"To use a sports analogy, this came out of not deep left field, but deep center field. But I was glad to hear she was asking. The more open the better. I know that she had asked her mother questions about me, and we've talked to her about my illness in a way that we hoped would penetrate a six-year-old's mind. And so now I told her what had happened, how the blood they gave me in the hospital was someone else's blood and it was 'bad.' She immediately perked up. 'And the person had AIDS?' I said yes. She sat a little longer. 'Are you sure?' I said, 'Oh yes, that's how I got it.' And then she mercifully went to sleep."

It was recalled that earlier Ashe spoke about his wife and his daughter, and how doctors have said that he posed no danger to them. Each has tested negative for HIV. "But one day," he said, "my daughter may be a danger to me. I couldn't go near her if she got a communicable disease."

In that earlier conversation, recalling the April news conference and her husband's starting to cry as he made his announcement, Jeanne Ashe had pointed out that "it was only when he came to the part about Camera."

"I think a lot of things flashed through his mind," she said. "They're really close, and he wanted to be able to see her graduate—from elementary school, from high school, from college. And he wanted to be around to be a grandfather, too. I think his mortality really hit him at that moment."

Back at Niagara Community College, Ashe said he remembered with anger that the Reagan administration had said that the "nation's blood supply was safe." "And it wasn't," said Ashe. "The medical community was slow to react. If it had been a more mainstream sickness, they would have been quicker."

In the question-and-answer period, he was asked about the rights of privacy in his case. "Just because it's newsworthy doesn't mean it should be printed," he said. "Sometimes the media goes too far." At that moment, the April news conference was recalled. At one point as he made his announcement, the often stoical-appearing Ashe had been forced to stop while reading his message—pausing at the part about his daughter—and put his fingers to his temple to prevent himself from sobbing. His wife had risen from her chair and had begun to read his statement where he had left off. After a few moments, Ashe resumed his reading.

In the community college auditorium six months later, Ashe was asked, "What about your daughter, and the cruelty of other children?"

"That was also a grave concern of ours," Ashe said. "But there has been no problem at all, not at her school or anywhere else. Camera is never without supervision from adults. And people have been wonderful."

Does he ever need counseling?

"I remember sitting on my hospital bed when I was told I had AIDS," he said. "It was the day after I'd had brain surgery, and I'd experienced a paralysis in my hand, and as it turned out it was all related to AIDS. It was hard to believe, of course. But I never needed counseling. I'm able to function normally. I told myself, 'Just adjust and deal with it.'

"I wasn't trying to be macho. When you've gone through all I've gone through, like the heart operations, you learn that if someone can help you, damn it, get help. But emotionally I've been able to deal with a lot of things in my life. I viewed this as just one more challenge.

"There have been tons of these things in my life. And here's another one. I've learned to be self-reliant. It was kind of forced on me. The first moment that comes to mind in this regard was when I was twelve years old. And I went with my first tennis instructor, Ron Charity, to enter a USTA-sanctioned tournament for twelve-and-under at Byrd Park in Richmond. Byrd Park was a white park. It was a nice, warm, sunny spring day. And I remember the head of the tournament—a white man named Sam Wood—he's long gone now, but he was a nice, kindly gentleman.

And he was apologetic, but he said, 'No.' There was no integration in Virginia then and he said, 'I'm sorry, but a law is a law.'"

Ashe continued: "I began to learn that I couldn't rely on others, that I had to take charge of my life. If I wanted to be a tennis player—and I did, passionately—that I'd have to leave there. In my senior year of high school, it was arranged for me to go to St. Louis. I knew that if I couldn't play indoors in the winter, the white kids would pass me by. I'm not bitter about any of that now. It's all in the past. But I learned that I couldn't let circumstances dictate my life for me. I have a minister—he's more of a friend—whom I'll talk over some personal things with. But in effect, I've become my own counselor."

Did he see himself as a victim?

"No," he said, "I see myself as a patient."

His lecture had consumed an hour and a half. After he answered the last question, the audience in the darkened theater rose and began to applaud—standing and clapping for long minutes, moved by the candor, warmth, and strength of the man under the lights, in front. Arthur Ashe stood listening to the applause echo through the auditorium, then gathered up his notes and left the stage.

[1992]

Martina at the Top

❦ IT WAS near the end of a three-hour workout, and Martina Navratilova, the champion tennis player, was serving to Gregg Manning, a young professional just starting on the men's tour. They were indoors in the green and white Brookhaven Tennis Club here.

"Match point," she called. They had not been keeping score but had been working on various points of Miss Navratilova's game as she prepared for the Avon Championships in Madison Square Garden starting Wednesday. If she wins the $100,000 first prize—and she is favored—it would put her over $3.7 million and she would pass Chris Evert Lloyd—not entered in the tournament—as the career leading money-winner among women tennis professionals.

"Match point" now simply designated that this would conclude the exercise. But she wanted to simulate game pressure. "Whenever you call 'match point,'" Manning warned from his base line, "don't ever hit it to my forehand." Navratilova, her thin blond hair caught up in a ponytail, nodded. She looked at him for a moment, her angular eyes narrowed. Her high cheekbones and long chin appeared set.

Then she drew together her body, muscular at 5 feet 7 1/2 inches tall and 145 pounds, and served. Gripping her racquet in her left hand, she pulled her arm back, highlighting the network of veins. Then she whipped the racquet forward, met the ball squarely, and propelled it toward Manning's forehand. The ball struck the net and bounced back.

"Tempting fate," she said, with a little smile. Manning laughed at the fact that she had taken the challenge and hit to his strength. He had expected she would.

Martina Navratilova is no stranger to living dangerously. As a fifteen-year-old in 1972, she had traveled the two hundred miles by train from her home in Prague to Ostrava to play in the Czechoslovak national championships. She was unseeded, unheralded, and poor. No expenses were paid unless the participants made it past the first round. If she didn't, she would not have enough money to stay overnight and play in the doubles competition.

Not only did she win in the first round, she captured the title, and repeated for the next three years as well. She began to represent her country in international tennis, and in September 1975, at the United States Open, Navratilova, one month short of nineteen, announced that she was defecting to the United States.

It was a difficult and painful decision to leave her home and family, perhaps never to return and possibly never to see her parents and her sister again. She defected to play tennis in an atmosphere not dominated by the Czechoslovak government. "The sports club in Czechoslovakia kept putting more and more restrictions on me," she said at the time. "They said I would not be able to leave Czechoslovakia so freely."

She rose to the top level of her profession, becoming the number one rated player in the world in 1978 and 1979. She is second now to Lloyd, but seems likely to pass her soon. Navratilova has won most of the major tournaments and championships, including Wimbledon twice. But she had never won the United States Open. Last year she made it to the final against Tracy Austin before a packed crowd at the National Tennis Center in Flushing. It was a sunny Saturday afternoon, September 12, and the moment was emotional for Navratilova.

Two months before, she had been granted United States citizenship papers after a five-year wait. "I was trying very hard," she would say later. "It would have meant a lot to win here, being an American now." The crowd seemed to sense that.

Her appearance had changed a little as well. She no longer wore her customary headband; now her hair was drawn back with a yellow ribbon. Her tennis blouse and skirt were white with multi-colored piping. She said she had wanted to look "prettier, more feminine." She had also been involved in other personal problems that had sapped some of her spirit, and she went into the Open having played poorly in several previous tournaments.

Playing well, she took the first set from Austin. But Austin didn't fold, returning shots that Navratilova was certain were winners. Navratilova began to press. Austin came back to take the next set.

Navratilova went ahead in the third, but Austin broke her service and went on to win the championship. "When the match was over," the *New York Times* reported, "Miss Navratilova collapsed in a courtside chair, biting her lip and shaking her head in disgust, and buried her face in a towel. But she was roused by a loving ovation that lasted several minutes."

Soon she accepted the runner-up award, a silver ball. At courtside she brushed away tears and looked at the ball. "It took me nine years to get the silver ball," she said to the crowd over the public-address system. She had learned English so well that she spoke with virtually no trace of an accent. "I hope it doesn't take me nine years to get the championship cup."

More applause rang out, and she waved and departed. The Open experience seemed to give her more confidence. "It's great to feel people are behind you," she said. As an alien, she had gone through emotional turmoil about being in a foreign land, often suffering bouts of loneliness. "I would call my parents and talk to them for maybe an hour at least once a week," she said. "And, especially in the beginning, it would end up in tears—on both ends of the phone."

Two weeks after the Open, she again met Austin, this time in the final of the United States Indoor championships, in Minneapolis, and she won by 6–2, 6–0.

This year Navratilova has won five straight tournaments, the best she has done since 1978 when she won seven in a row. But because of the ratings that go back to last March, she is placed second to Lloyd. "And Chris has played only one tournament this year—she says she is injured," said Navratilova. "But a champion should defend her crown. She should make a special effort to play in more tournaments. It's frustrating for me. I feel I'm the best right now, and I want to prove it."

Neither Lloyd nor Austin, the other top-rated women's tennis professional, will be competing in the tournament at the Garden. Austin is suffering with a bad back, and Lloyd has a muscle strain.

Much has changed in Navratilova's life in the last year—and, she said, all for the better. She has a coach, Renee Richards, who works with her on technique, strengthening the parts of her game that had been flawed. "There were things I knew but wasn't sure how to change," said Navratilova, "like getting more top spin on my shots, to keep from missing so much. You have to be constantly reminded about that. And in tournaments, Renee helps me with strategy. She has watched the other players and has an idea of how I can beat them."

Navratilova's family situation has also settled down, and that has eased her mind. In 1979 her parents—Miroslav and Jana—and sister, also named Jana, who is six years younger than Martina, came to live in Dallas. "They wanted to live with me," said Navratilova, "but I didn't want my parents dictating my life-style. I've grown beyond that. I bought them their own house—about three hundred yards away from mine."

It didn't work. Her father, a finance minister for a large industrial firm in Prague, never learned to speak English. He had coached Martina when she was young and now wanted to resume that role, as well as be her manager. Navratilova, with difficulty, thought that would not be a good idea.

And her parents watched her closely. "When I was sick, they said, 'Don't drink a cold Dr. Pepper,' and when I was getting ready to play a tournament in another city, they said, 'How come you're leaving again so soon?'"

Finally, after about a year of much discussion and fluctuation, her parents and sister moved back to Czechoslovakia. "I was unhappy to see them go, despite everything," she said. "But my father insisted. We still talk on the phone, and I hope to get a visa to go back there this summer—for the first time since I left—and my family seems happy again. They are home, they have their friends and life-style again. They had missed that."

Despite the large amounts of money Navratilova was earning, there was a great financial drain on her with her family here and her father not working. In fact, although she has investments that should see her comfortably through for the rest of her life, her cash flow was ebbing. Now her financial situation is again balanced.

Navratilova shares a modest, three-bedroom, two-story townhouse on the south side of Dallas with Nancy Lieberman and Rhonda Rompola. Navratilova and Lieberman, the red-haired, green-eyed, five-foot-ten-inch basketball star, have a special relationship. They are close personal friends and, for want of a better phrase, athletic associates. They encourage each other in their mutual endeavors, sometimes goading, sometimes biting, always concerned. At the tennis club, Navratilova hits serves to Lieberman, a tennis novice, after Gregg Manning has gone. There is a towel placed at the corner of the front court, and Martina tries to hit it, often doing so. When she missed, she said, "Well, pretty good."

"Fair," replied Lieberman. "Fair?" said Navratilova, her husky voice rising. "Fair." And she shook her head. Then Lieberman laughed, and so did Navratilova. Later, though, on the basketball court, in a two-on-two game with a man and another woman, Navratilova seemed too passive for Lieberman. And Lieberman urged her to get more aggressive with the woman she was playing against. Navratilova's eyes grew a little red around the edges, but she began using her strong, agile, low-to-the-ground body to physical advantage.

"You'd think that a great champion like Martina would have the killer instinct," said Lieberman later, "but she defies all the laws of champions. Too often she's too passive. And she beats herself. Martina is such a great athlete, but in tennis she would get down on herself, lose patience and confidence, and then get beat."

Navratilova agreed and said that basketball has helped her get "meaner." "It's exciting," she said, "it adds an entire new dimension." With Lieberman, Navratilova trains about six hours a day—playing tennis for three hours (she says she used to practice only about one and a half hours a day), then jumping in either her white Rolls-Royce convertible or Lieberman's white Mercedes convertible, then taking off—truly, they are speedy drivers—to a gym, generally at Southern Methodist University, where they lift light weights and play basketball. Later, at home, they will go out for a two- or three-mile jog. Physically Navratilova brings exceptional attributes to women's tennis. She is very fast; she runs the sixty-yard dash in 7.3 seconds, with an exceptionally good first-step acceleration that allows her to get to many balls a slower player could never reach—and she is strong—her serve is as good or better than any of the women.

She is also more content, she says, than in the past. In fact, in the last year there has been a tremendous change. Last April she split up with a woman with whom she had lived and, she has publicly admitted, had a romantic affair. The breakup and the subsequent publicity jolted Navratilova, with the result that her tennis suffered.

"It was important to have Nancy's friendship after that," said Navratilova. "I don't know where I'd be now without her." Navratilova helps Lieberman with her attempts to resurrect women's professional basketball after the Women's Basketball League folded last season. Lieberman is engaged in a campaign to get sponsors for it, and last Sunday night, after Navratilova won the Avon tournament in Dallas, Navratilova tried to type out a letter for Lieberman.

"She's a hunt-and-peck typist," said Lieberman. "And so am I. Martina was getting frustrated. So I sat down, and we typed the letter together. It worked out perfectly. She's left-handed and I'm right-handed. We split up the keyboard. It was like a duet."

"What Nancy's doing is very important," said Navratilova, "she is in basketball where Billie Jean King was in tennis about ten years ago."

"Times are changing," Navratilova added, "people are coming to respect female athletes more. People used to think it wasn't natural for a woman to be an athlete. And that's how the homosexual aspects surface. Sportswriters will ask a woman, 'Is it true that you're sleeping with other women?' They'd never ask a man whether he's sleeping with other men—and God knows there are baseball players and football players and basketball players who are sleeping with other men. But if a reporter asked that question of a man, he'd get a knuckle sandwich, and he wouldn't wake up for a week.

"But me, I was gullible and naive, and I tell every stranger my life story. But you live and learn. It's stupid to talk about it, and all that's behind me now. I'm going out with some guys, but nothing serious. And that's really all I want to say about my private life."

The last time Navratilova played in the New York area was last December at the Toyota championship in the Meadowlands. She had sent a message to Katharine Hepburn, then appearing in *West Side Waltz*, and invited her to the tournament. Katharine Hepburn, said Navratilova, is her idol, and has been since she saw *The African Queen* as a young girl in Prague.

"But an assistant of hers called and said Miss Hepburn was sorry but she couldn't make the tennis matches," said Navratilova. "But I'll try again this year.

"I've always admired how strong she was inside, and her calm, and I understand she was once a very fine golfer and tennis player.

Did you see *On Golden Pond*? She does a back-flip dive into a lake. She's seventy-three years old. Imagine. I hope I can have that courage and that inner peace. Really, the lady has me psyched out."

Navratilova says she is gaining strength as a woman. "I'm twenty-five years old, but sometimes I feel like I've already lived about ten lives. I feel good, I feel like I'm soaring now, like I'm up in a balloon. And I'm not planning to run out of air."

[1982]

Chuck Norris: The Ninety-seven-pound Weakling Grows Up

❦ ALL RIGHT, if Chuck Norris is such a tough guy, I decided, let's see how he handles Lutèce.

Norris, the great martial-arts, action-adventure, karate-wheeling movie star, was in town recently promoting his new film, *Sidekicks*. The title refers to the asthmatic teenage boy Norris befriends and inspires in the movie and to his own swift foot-in-the-belly predilections.

Before picking a place for dinner with Norris, I did some research on him.

It happens that in *Return of the Dragon* (1973), the first movie he ever made, he played a small, villainous role. The plot revolves around its star, Bruce Lee, the first of the famous barefoot bashers, who saves the owner of a Chinese restaurant in Rome from Mafia scum. *Sidekicks* has some important scenes set in the Frying Dragon, a fictional Chinese restaurant in an unnamed city in Texas. Norris has found himself in Chinese restaurants in some of his other nineteen films, and you have to figure that by now he is fed up with Chinese restaurants. Scratch them. I also saw his new CBS series, "Walker, Texas Ranger," in which he beats up about a dozen desperadoes in maybe fifteen seconds in a Mexican restaurant. The tacos there might have left a bad taste in his mouth. So forget Mexican too.

Then I recalled something Goose Gossage told me when he was with the Yankees and, with his blazing fastball and curling mustache, was the most feared pitcher in baseball. "Goose," I said, "you intimidate everyone in baseball. Who intimidates you?"

"New York waiters," he said.

That's it! What better test of the mettle of Chuck Norris than to take him to the most formidable restaurant in New York?

Tieless in a brown checked sport jacket, black knit sweater-shirt, and black slacks, Norris, with his trademark neatly trimmed blond mustache and beard and quiet smile, entered the restaurant, a former town house on East Fiftieth Street, and was led into the "défense de fumer" section. Norris moves with an easy gait, as befits a man whose diligent daily workout routines keep him, he says, in the kind of condition that helped him win seven straight world middleweight karate championships, the last in 1974.

"Oh, hello, Mr. Norris," said one waiter in black tie, standing aside and letting Norris follow the maître d'hôtel to a table in a far corner of the garden dining room. "Hello," said another waiter, and a captain or two. "Hello, Mr. Norris," came a chorus from cooks leaning out of the open windows of the kitchen.

"Hi, guys," Norris said, smiling and shaking a hand. "Good to see you."

There wasn't a single "Bon soir," which most guests get. Suspicious.

We sat down in front of the white latticework, like a high fence against the pink walls. Three fresh sweetheart roses in a thin vase greeted us.

The guy's a phony, I concluded. Everyone knows him. He was born in the prairie town of Ryan, Oklahoma, moved when he was nine years old to Torrance, California, now owns a home in Tarzana, California, and a ranch outside Houston, but the guy's got to be a regular here.

"You come to this restaurant often?" I asked.

"Nah," Norris said. "Never been here before."

"Never?"

"They know me from my movies—they've been on television a lot lately," he said. "I think I was on twenty times last week alone. TNT recently had a Chuck Week." He laughed. "I get the same thing all over. It's like I'm part of the family."

Shortly, the chef and owner of the restaurant, André Soltner, in whites and a chef's toque that seemed to reach the ceiling, appeared at the table. He had a small pencil and a small pad of paper in hand. "Good evening, Mr. Norris," he said. "The waiters, they are all scared. They don't want you should beat them up. So I come myself to take the order."

"Aw, I'm not here to hurt anyone," Norris said gently, smiling. "I'm here to eat."

I glanced around and saw a handful of waiters watching in awe, at a respectful distance. Soltner was smiling.

"For appetizer," he said, "our specials today we have the gambas—the fresh shrimp—with scallops in light Nantua sauce, and we have halibut on puree of eggplant and, um, the salmon stuffed with mousseline of pike in pastry with sauce Choron."

"I don't eat appetizers," Norris said, politely.

Soltner cleared his throat. He looked slightly mournful.

I said quietly to Norris, "Maybe you ought to at least try one of them."

"Uh, okay," he said, agreeably. "Halibut."

"And for the main dish," Soltner said, "we have beef, veal, seafood, chicken, sweetbreads—"

Norris stopped him at sweetbreads. "I'll have the chicken," he said.

"We have a nice baby chicken, roasted crisp in natural juice and herbs, and with vegetables."

"That'll be fine."

"And to drink? We have an extensive wine list."

"Iced tea," Norris said.

"Iced tea," Soltner said. "Yes, certainly, iced tea." He wrote this down dutifully. "Thank you," Soltner said.

"My pleasure," Norris said.

Norris said that he rarely eats in French restaurants. "Don't go in much for sauces," he said. And he doesn't eat hearty dinners. "I eat my big meal at lunch, and that's usually pasta and vegetables," he added.

The 5-foot-10, fifty-three-year-old Norris watches his weight carefully and remains in fighting trim at about 160 pounds. His workout routine—he spends nearly six hours a day, six days a week—goes from tromping up the Stairmaster to tangling with ju-jitsu.

"I identify with the kid in *Sidekicks,*" he was saying, as he took one bite of the complimentary onion tart and casually inched it away. "I grew up a dreamer, like he did. John Wayne was my hero." In the movie, the boy idolizes Chuck Norris, who plays himself. "But I was shy, unathletic and only a C student," Norris continued. "I did make the football team, but I was second string. The coach wanted those aggressive types. I just wasn't one of them."

Norris also grew up poor, with an alcoholic father, a Cherokee Indian, who was gone from home much of the time. He and his brother Aaron, who directed *Sidekicks,* and a third brother, Wieland, were raised for the most part by their Irish mother. "There were taunts by kids about being a half-breed," Norris said. "I had very low self-esteem. And I used to daydream about being strong and being able to handle myself. To beat up the bullies."

He went into the army right out of high school and was stationed in Korea. That was when he took up karate. "Four months later my coach told me I was ready to break cinder blocks with my hand," he said. "You have to strike at the middle of the blocks and hit them with the knuckles of your first two fingers—because they can take a lot of pressure—and follow through. And you have to have your mind focused solely on the task at hand. It's an exercise in discipline and teaching you to focus in life.

"So I got all ready, staring, concentrating hard, and then

brought down my fist. But just at the point of impact, I got scared, and turned my hand just a little. Wound up in a cast for six weeks."

He later broke the hand again, and his nose, too, in karate fights. But he persevered, another lesson not lost in his movies.

The baby chicken in natural juice and herbs arrived. Norris checked it out, without comment. The waiter checked out Norris in a similar wary fashion. And departed.

Norris said he never had any intention of becoming an actor. His plan was to be a karate instructor. Upon leaving the army, he opened a karate school in Los Angeles, then added five more. He sold them to a conglomerate, which mismanaged them, and when he was brought back to run them, he went broke.

Norris, married (he's now divorced) and the father of two boys, had to start over again. He opened another karate school, and one of his students happened to be the son of Steve McQueen.

"Steve thought I might have a shot at the movies," Norris said. "He said, 'You've got this intensity in your eyes when you fight that audiences might find appealing—could be profitable for you.'" It has been, making Norris one of filmdom's top box-office draws, putting him up there with such knock-'em-down heroes as Clint Eastwood, Charles Bronson, and McQueen.

"But none of it came easy," Norris said, picking at the chicken. "I remember going for a casting call. There were about fifty of us for one small part, and some jerk in charge is screaming at us, 'Get in line, you slobs!' I got so mad, I grabbed him by the collar. Needless to say, I didn't get the part. I thought: 'This just isn't going to work. I have to find another way.'"

He and a friend then wrote the script for *Good Guys Wear Black* and took it to about thirty producers, all of whom turned it down. He finally found one who loved the script and filmed it in 1977. Despite some terrible reviews, Norris was on his way to stardom.

McQueen had one piece of advice: "Next time, not so much dialogue." And Norris has hewed to that line of the strong, silent type, letting his punches and boots, often in lyrical, balletic sequences, do the talking.

"All I wanted to do in movies was be a positive image," he said. "I wanted to be likable, as I do in real life. I don't like violence for violence's sake. I hated the movie *Blue Velvet,* for example. I liked *Aladdin,* because it has a positive message. In my movies I never attack anyone. I don't cause trouble, but I end it.

"I never wanted to be Dustin Hoffman or Al Pacino. I mean, I never dreamed of being an Ac-tor." He said the word slowly. "I do what I do."

Among other things, he has written several books on karate and an autobiography, *The Secret of Inner Strength: My Story,* with Joe Hyams (Little, Brown, 1988).

"Are you finished, Mr. Norris?" asked a waiter, with circumspection. About half the chicken in its bright yellow sauce remained uneaten.

"Yeah, thanks," Norris said.

Desserts were suggested. Norris declined. For the sake of reportorial thoroughness, I went for the tarte au chocolat with the caramel ice cream.

"Do you mind?" I asked.

"No, go ahead," Norris said, reaching for his iced tea.

On another subject he recalled a time when he himself was in awe, when he met George Bush when he was running for president in 1988. "But he made me feel comfortable right off the bat," Norris said. "This was at a time when people were calling him a wimpy candidate, and I was asked to emcee a rally in Riverside, California, for him. And I was asked to travel with him, and I did for a little while. It was funny. His image had changed. You'd read in the papers, 'Two macho men have just arrived in town. . . .'" He laughed.

"This 'macho man' stuff is strange. You know, some people get things into their heads and make you bigger than you are. I'm not Superman. If a guy comes up behind me and puts a gun to my back and tells me to give him my wallet, what I'd do is reach back, pull out my wallet, and give it to him. Absolutely. You'd be foolish to gamble your life for money."

At the next table a woman leaned over and said, "Excuse me, Mr. Norris, but I just have to tell you that you have saved our marriage, numerous times."

"Oh?" Norris said.

"My husband"—here the woman half-turned to the man shyly smiling at her right—"always goes down to our den when we've had a fight and puts on your films. I think his favorite is *Delta Force*. He gets his aggressions out that way."

"Glad to be of service," Norris said.

As Norris departed, the waiters and the captains and the cooks in the kitchen said: "Goodbye, Mr. Norris." "So long, Mr. Norris."

André Soltner shook his hand with a little bow. There was not one "Au revoir, monsieur."

Incredible! Without delivering a single blow, not by fist and not by hoof, Norris had brought Lutèce to its knees. No contest. The winner and still champ, Chuck Norris.

[1993]

The Quad Squad

✿ THE SUN had dipped behind steel-wool clouds, darkening the trodden-green field and the newly bare limbs of fall trees. A wind picked up, and some of the spectators standing along the sidelines or seated in the small bleacher section last Tuesday at Rocky Hill High School near Hartford, Connecticut, shivered from the chill and the tension.

The chance to go to the Connecticut girls' high school soccer final could come on the next penalty kick. In the semifinal between New Canaan High School and Woodstock Academy, the score had been tied at 1–1 in regulation time, had been tied after two scoreless overtime periods, and was still tied after a five-kicks-each shootout.

Now it was a sudden-death shootout, with the weather adding to a moment of drama. In her New Canaan white-and-red jersey, black shorts, and white knee socks, Jennie DeMichele, age seventeen, ponytailed and with a senior athlete's mask of dispassion, began her approach to the ball. In front of the net a short distance away, the Woodstock goaltender hunkered in a defensive position. The two were alone on the field, as on the set of a western.

On the New Canaan bench, one of Jennie's teammates, Julie DeMichele, age seventeen, could not watch and stared at the ground. Another of Jennie's teammates, Chrissie DeMichele, age seventeen, covered her face with her jacket but peeked with one eye. A fourth DeMichele, Brian, age seventeen, in a white baseball cap, stood along the yellow restraining rope on the sideline, shouting: "Visualize! Visualize!"

"It was like I was trying that kick, like Jennie and I were one," Chrissie recalled later. Julie said the same thing. So did Brian.

In fact they were once as close as one, and in many ways remain so. They are quadruplets, born within thirty seconds of one another on May 30, 1980, to June and Bob DeMichele. At the time, according to Mrs. DeMichele, quadruplets occurred once in every 650,000 births. The DeMicheles, who had had no children, were told three months into June's pregnancy that they were going to have quadruplets.

"We had wanted a family," she said. "Suddenly we were going to have more family than we knew what to do with."

The kids grew up known from birth as "The Quad Squad," and have been virtually inseparable as friends, teammates, schoolmates—they are all honor students—and siblings. Occasionally they are competitors as well, for grades, in sports, or, for the girls, for which one gets to use the hair dryer first. Mostly, though, they remain a support quartet for one another. As was the case when Jennie kicked.

"Jennie, take it in!" called her mother, standing beside Brian, and clutching her brown woolen-gloved hands to her forehead.

Jennie and the team had practiced penalty kicks for the last two weeks, and now she turned her foot so it would look as if she were kicking to the right, but would boot to the left. She met the ball squarely and sent it hard on a line. But the goalie was not tricked. The ball landed in her stomach with a soft thud. Jennie hung her head. Chrissie, with difficulty, called out, "It's okay, Jen." Julie said, hugging her, "It's not over." Brian said he had "a sinking feeling." Their mother clapped softly to try to pick up everyone's spirits, including her own.

The next Woodstock girl, clad in yellow, missed her kick, then Sarah Scholl, a New Canaan sophomore, converted her penalty kick. Woodstock missed, and New Canaan won, improving its record to 17-2-1. Tomorrow the team will play in the M division final (for midsized schools, based on enrollment) against Holy Cross Academy of Waterbury (15-2-3) at Willow Brook Park in New Britain.

Bob DeMichele, who is usually a regular at games, was unable to attend the semifinal because of business but will be at the final. He is president of a financial consulting firm in Saddle Brook, New Jersey. Even though the family lives in a large house in a manicured setting in an affluent town, he still feels financial pressures. The girls will be going off to college next year, and he has established a fund for their education.

Brian, the last of the quadruplets, and the smallest at birth by a couple of pounds—he weighed about 2 1/2 pounds—is now the biggest, at 5 feet 8 inches, 140 pounds. Chrissie, the firstborn, is 5–7, 135; Jennie, who was born third, is 5–6, 128; Julie is 5–4 1/2, 123. They are fraternal, having come from four eggs. Mrs. DeMichele, who had a cesarean section, had taken no fertility pills, but twins had been born in both her and her husband's families.

"I knew I had to be organized," said Mrs. DeMichele, who had been an executive assistant for a pharmaceutical company in Manhattan, "so I kept daily charts on everything so I wouldn't miss anything: feeding time, bathroom time, bath time. I ran it like a little business. Never got boring, I can tell you."

The bills, to be sure, were staggering. But there was another problem. "Girls mature quicker than boys," Mrs. DeMichele said, "and by the seventh grade it was clear that Brian was having trouble keeping up with his sisters." So, with advice from professionals, the DeMicheles decided to keep Brian back one year.

"It was the best thing we could ever have done," she said. "It gave him a sense of being independent and able to find himself without competing with his sisters."

The quadruplets were enthusiastic about most sports, and good at them. The girls took particular interest in basketball, lacrosse, and soccer, in which all three have been starters at New Canaan since their sophomore year. Jennie is captain of the basketball team, Chrissie is captain of the lacrosse team, and Julie is captain of the soccer team. Brian was especially good in ice hockey and started on the high school team as a sophomore. "And so we determined that that would be Brian's sport," Mrs. DeMichele said. "The girls wanted to play it, but they understood. Ice hockey would be Brian's domain, and Brian's alone."

While they value their closeness, the girls seek assiduously to be different from one another. In the Woodstock game, for example, Julie wore a red ribbon in her ponytail, Chrissie a tawny-colored one, and Jennie a black one. "This was by design," Jennie said. "We never wear the same clothes on the same day."

"But," Julie added, "we do wear the same clothes. We borrow each other's on different days."

Later that day as they spoke in the living room of their home in New Canaan, the girls, each dressed in different style and color shirts, sweaters, and pants, were seated together on a couch. Brian sat on the floor across from them, keeping what seemed a respectful but bemused distance. Jennie and Chrissie are blondes; Julie and Brian have brown hair.

"When we were growing up," Brian said, "we met another set of quadruplets living in Stamford. It was just like us, three sisters and a younger brother. They were six years older. And the boy gave me a piece of advice. He said, 'I learned that the best thing to do is just stay out of their way.'" All of the DeMicheles laughed, including their mother. So it may not be a coincidence that the girls' three bedrooms are at one end of the house and Brian's is at the other.

There are three areas in which the girls have particularly competed with one another and learned early on to resolve whatever conflicts arose. "It was academics, sports, and social life, in that order of importance," Mrs. DeMichele said.

In sports the girls find a way not to compete directly with one another. On the soccer team, for example, each plays a different position: Jennie is a center midfielder, Chrissie an outside back, and Julie a forward.

And the social life: "When they were about twelve or thirteen years old, I saw that there was going to have to be a resolution about boys," Mrs. DeMichele said. "In the beginning, it was cut-throat. I said: 'Look, if you fight over boys now, you'll lose each other's friendship and trust. And for what? A boy that in a month will be dust in your interests?'"

Jennie said: "So now we just ask each other. 'Do you like him?' 'Do you?' 'How much?' 'Okay, then you go for him.'"

"It works," Julie said, "though sometimes there have been tears."

At the Woodstock game, Mrs. DeMichele had said that being mother to quadruplets has been "an incredible experience, with having four times the joy of one child, but also four times the stress, four times the anxiety, four times the work—especially now with four teenagers in the house." And so she has sought her outlets, like the soccer game.

When the game came down to the frenetic, closing minutes of regulation time, Mrs. DeMichele turned away from a friend she was speaking to. "Excuse me," she said, "but I've got to go scream."

[1997]

Woody Allen, from
Defense to Offense

❦ "JIMMY CANNON'S New York is my New York," Woody Allen said recently, sitting in his home-away-from-home, the suite at the Beekman Hotel on Park Avenue where he edits his movies. "My whole feeling of New York City as a black-and-white Gershwin town comes from reading the late Jimmy Cannon," Allen said. "I never missed him."

Allen, fifty-nine, who plays a sportswriter in his new movie, *Mighty Aphrodite,* can still recite passages from Cannon's sports columns in the *New York Post* during the 1950s: the time he described "the serene dependability of Stan Musial," or "the bookmaker who took a guy's money all year and then gave him a ball-point pen for Christmas." And he still remembers Cannon describing how he had been in a New York apartment late at night where Frank Sinatra was singing at a piano, and then how he walked home alone through the melancholy New York streets as the sun was coming up.

That dream of Manhattan is harder for Allen to sustain today. On the streets of his New York, he knows that he is viewed by some as everything from a dirty old man to a child molester, he said in an interview with no ground rules. "When I go into a public place, like a restaurant or a ball game, I know some people are looking at me and thinking that I'm a terrible person," he said. The custody case with Mia Farrow over their children—Moses, seventeen; Dylan, ten, and Satchel, seven—and his romantic relationship with Ms. Farrow's adopted daughter Soon-Yi Previn, has cast him for many in a negative light.

And so Allen finds himself using a self-defense technique he learned while watching Jimmy Cannon interviewed by Mike Wallace on a television talk show in the 1950s. "Wallace was this tough interviewer, and he said to Cannon, 'Why were you never married?' And Cannon, in that New York way, shot back, 'For the same reason you were married three times.' It completely intimidated Wallace, which was not easy."

Allen now employs that kind of reversal in his encounters with the public. "So the question for me is, not how everybody feels about me, it's how I feel about them. I'm the one who was suddenly smeared." His voice rose slightly. His hands went up in his familiar shrug to make a point, but there was none of the customary Woody Allen humor in the eyes behind the glasses.

"I seriously considered whether I still wanted to entertain, to work hard at whatever gift I had to offer these people," he said. "Then I told myself that not everyone was that way, that some still believed in me. And so I went on—it's also the way I earn my living."

He has always denied the charges that he sexually molested Dylan, which were brought by Ms. Farrow in January 1992, when Dylan was seven. Allen has been denied custody of the three children as well as visitation rights with Dylan. "I haven't seen my daughter in three years," he said. "I haven't spoken to her on the phone. But I keep fighting vigorously to be allowed to."

She has chosen not to see him, and social workers believe any connection with Allen at this time could be traumatic for her. Allen's appeals on visitation have twice been turned down by the New York State Court of Appeals. Moses, a high-school senior, also refuses to see his father.

He is allowed to see Satchel six hours a week, supervised by a social worker. The court stated that it was not concerned for Satchel's physical safety but that it was concerned by Allen's "demonstrated inability to understand the impact that his words and deeds have upon the emotional well-being of the children."

His situation was complicated by the revelation that he was having an affair with Ms. Previn, then a college student and the adopted daughter of Ms., Farrow and her former husband, the conductor André Previn.

Allen and Ms. Previn, who is around twenty-four (she was orphaned in Korea, and her exact age is uncertain), remain romantically linked. Last summer she graduated from Drew University with a degree in English and has applied to graduate school in social work. "We love each other," he said. "It's one of the best relationships I've ever had. Maybe the best. It's a firm relationship, and a lasting one—on my end, anyway.

"It's amazing the misconceptions. People think Mia and I were married and living together, and we weren't. I never spent a night in their home. I never felt like and I thought I never acted like the father of any of Mia's other children, even though, yes, I was around the house a lot and we did go away together on occasion. One night someone at Madison Square Garden stopped me with Soon-Yi and asked, 'Can I take a picture of you and your daughter?' People think I was sleeping with my daughter! She's not my daughter. She's never been my daughter. It's so crazy."

He said he admired her bravery under pressure. He continued: "She's had to withstand finding reporters in her dormitory room and facing such dishonest things written about her, everything from she's retarded to she's disloyal and terrible. She's a marvel. And she laughs at all my jokes. She thinks I'm hilarious, and that doesn't hurt the relationship one bit, I can tell you."

Some people think he simply doesn't understand, or can't bring himself to admit, the hurt he inflicted on the family. "Maybe it wasn't all anyone's fault, but Woody was the adult," Eleanor B. Alter, who was Ms. Farrow's lawyer in the custody case, said last week. "Whatever hell was created, was created by him. And yet I truly believe that Woody feels he didn't do anything wrong."

"But is he a great artist? Yes," she conceded. "Is he a brilliant writer and filmmaker? Yes. And when you see his movies, should you compartmentalize the art from the artist? If you can, the answer is yes."

Allen, wearing black-frame glasses, appeared a little tired during the interview, a not uncommon look for him. He had just returned from Nyack, New York, where he was making his next film, a musical. Strands of his thinning hair were askew. He had on a tan sweater, brown corduroy pants, and plain black shoes that would seem an appropriate fashion statement for a detective. The peach-colored walls of the editing room were bare, the lights were soft, and a portable movie screen stood at one end. He sat in a cushy blue armchair and talked again of Jimmy Cannon.

"He was the most meaningful writer for me in my early years," said Allen, who grew up in the Midwood section of Brooklyn. "I felt comfortable using a sportswriter as a basis for my character. I mean, I love sports. I'm a writer. And I had always thought about being a sportswriter. I've fantasized about spending a year writing sports for a newspaper—if a newspaper would be interested—but then I just would want to do home games. And that would probably be impossible. When I imagined being in locker rooms in Seattle or Philadelphia—or Houston, my God!—I thought being a sportswriter wasn't such a great idea."

In *Mighty Aphrodite*, Allen's character, a sportswriter named Lenny Winerib, and his wife, played by Helena Bonham Carter, adopt a baby boy. When they discuss naming him, Allen's character suggests names like Sugar Ray, for the former boxing champion Sugar Ray Robinson, and Earl the Pearl, for the former Knicks basketball star Earl Monroe. In real life, his son, Satchel, was named for the pitcher Satchel Paige. "I'm constantly thinking of sports," said Allen, who for four decades has been a regular at the Knicks games at Madison Square Garden.

"Those Knicks championship teams, for example, were everything you'd want in the theater and don't usually get. In the theater you're usually a step ahead of the play or movie. But in sports it's almost never that way. And those old Knicks—they played such a cerebral, satisfying game. You knew the players, you cared about them, and the drama and tension in the games was fantastic down to the last second."

He holds a particular affection for Monroe. Allen once wrote an adoring yet remarkably insightful magazine piece about him, drawing, surely, on artistic qualities with which he was familiar: "Some kind of diabolical intensity comes across his face when he has the ball . . . and yet he has enough wit in his style to bring off funny ideas when he wants to."

Some athletes transcend their sport to become artist-performers, he said. Earl Monroe is one, and Sugar Ray Robinson and Willie Mays were others. He compared the effervescent quality of Mays—his "poetry of motion"—to certain actors in the theater.

"Marlon Brando has it," he continued. "And Humphrey Bogart, who wasn't a great actor, had that star quality. Jack Nicholson, too. There's some fire in them that you respond to. But Lawrence Olivier, who was a great, great actor—he could play ten different characters and you'd believe in all of them—wasn't a star in that other sense."

Allen says he watches almost any sports on television he can find. "I watch timber-cutting, and rodeos when they try to catch the Brahman bulls—I even know all the rules," he said. "I guess in sports it's the combination of competition and athleticism that makes it so interesting to me."

Allen grew up playing all sports. "I was a good ballplayer when I was young," he said. "Nobody believes that because I'm small, I wear glasses, and they can't associate my movie characters with being an athlete. But I played baseball from dawn to dusk growing up, and even thought about making a career of it."

What position did he play and with whom? "I was mostly a second baseman, and I played in the Police League for the 70th Precinct," he said. "I was also a good schoolyard basketball player and won medals in track meets. I was very, very fast. And to this day there is no deadness in my arm. I can still throw hard."

The last ballplaying he did in public was in a few celebrity soft-ball games some twenty years ago. "One of my biggest thrills was playing in one of those games in Los Angeles with some major league ballplayers, and I made a catch on a high fly ball by Willie Mays," he said. "Some people were surprised I could make the play, but it was nothing, a can o' corn," he added, using an old baseball expression. Then he shrugged with what seemed a ballplayer's touch of bravado.

"One of the announcers—I think it was Ralph Kiner, who had seen me bat and field—said, 'Hey, he's got a good motion,'" he continued. "That meant as much to me as winning the Academy Award." (Allen won an Oscar for directing and co-writing the screenplay of *Annie Hall* in 1977, which was named best picture.)

Allen says he often dreams of sports and sports figures. He makes up all-poetry-in-motion basketball teams (Monroe, Michael Jordan, Julius Erving, Isiah Thomas, and Hakeem Olaju-won are on his first team) and sundry all-star and "dream teams" in other sports.

Allen remembers seeing Sugar Ray Robinson, at the height of his career, driving with an entourage through Times Square in his canary-yellow Cadillac convertible and waving to people. When Allen was a young writer for the Pat Boone Show in the early 1950s, he met Robinson, a guest on the show. "The studio was on the twenty-third floor of this building, and Robinson was nervous about taking the elevator up," Allen said. "He was claustrophobic. Like I am. It's the only thing we had in common.

"He told me he was serious about show business and about singing. He said that one day he was going to sing opera. I thought, Ray, you're never really going to sing opera. And he never did.

"He was the most magical guy I've ever seen, but unfortu-nately the world is not magical, and there are limits."

[1995]

The Strongest Man in the World

V TED SOBEL won the "grand salami," as he calls it, in the United States Power Lifting drug-free national championships in December in Ossining, New York, while "grunting like a piglet." And Karen, his onetime fiancée, probably didn't know a thing about it.

Sobel, in his red-white-and-blue wrestling singlet, lifted 760 pounds in the squat, 545 pounds in the bench press, and 733 pounds in the dead lift, for a total of 1 ton 38 pounds to better his own world records in the bench and the total. Not only did he capture his weight class—242 pounds—but he also won the over-all title of best lifter, and with it the distinct possibility of being the strongest man in the world. This is the fourth straight time he has won power lifter of the year, and this time he couldn't call Karen to tell her about it.

After Sobel had won his first world title in the World Natural Power Lifting Championships, in 1989, and set records in each event, the muscular, five-foot-eleven-inch Bronx resident with long, curly dark hair and a size nineteen-inch neck, went home to Pelham Parkway and, after a few days of soul-searching, decided to phone Karen to share the news. Sobel referred to her as his "unofficial fiancée" because they had broken up several months before the competition. The problem was not a new one among lovers: one wanted to get married—she—and one didn't. He had become just too absorbed in his training. He had, at around age thirty, come out of a kind of six-year retirement from lifting to enter that competition.

"You love your weights more than me," she said before the breakup. "This isn't exactly my idea of the perfect Yuppie romance."

"If I quit now I'd always wonder if I could have done it, particularly since I'm gaining momentum," he said. "I'm just trying to lasso a miracle."

"I think I'm going to start seeing other men," she said.

There was a long silence, about six months' long. And then Ted dialed Karen's number after winning the title. She wasn't home. He left a message relating his happy news on her answering machine. One month later, Karen returned the call and left a message of her own on Ted's answering machine.

"Ted," she said, "congratulations on winning your contest. I'm really happy for you. Please forgive me for not answering sooner, but I just got back from my honeymoon. And, by the way, my husband—who's earning a lot more money than you—eats quiche! Bye."

This was a disappointment as well as a shock for Sobel, but he overcame that one as he has overcome other obstacles. He is now involved in another relationship, a relatively smooth one, although she has some trouble relating to his getting up at 3:30 every morning to lift weights in his basement.

Sobel, who doesn't like to reveal his age, has been nicknamed the Derrick by his colleagues for the weight he can pick up. "He has to be about the strongest drug-free lifter in the world," said Jimmy McCree, a onetime Olympic weight lifter and a current power-lifting competitor. But Sobel's interests extend beyond power lifting, which has brought him to the top rank in a sport that has fifty thousand competitors in the United States and more than a million around the world, a figure substantially greater than for weight lifting.

The difference between power lifting and weight lifting is that in weight lifting the snatch and clean-and-jerk are lifts in which the barbell is raised over the head. In power lifting, the barbell is never raised above the head—and in the dead lift, it is brought up to the waist.

Sobel lives alone with his four dogs in his two-story red-brick house on a quiet street near the park. "Kind of a monastic existence," he said, "like an Oscar Madison with dogs." The dogs are all strays. He picks up lost animals and keeps some and gives others away to friends. He even had a pet pigeon that he found with a broken leg and nursed back to health.

And just when one might think that Sobel is, perhaps, distantly out of the mainstream, you learn that he has earned a master's degree in American literature from Fordham University, taught English at Lehman College, is the national chairman for the power-lifting program for Special Olympians and for physically challenged athletes, has been a magazine editor for, among other publications, *Muscle & Power* and *Military Electronics*, and is currently a freelance writer, head of his own desktop publishing business, and recent founder of *The Throgs Neck Dispatch*, a community newspaper.

But his particular passions remain his dogs—especially Chingo, his chocolate-colored Labrador retriever, of whom, he says, he is "absolutely enamored"—and his lifting in the natural, or drug-free, competitions, a relatively recent phenomenon.

When he heard about the World Natural Power Lifting Championships in 1989, the first of its kind, he decided to come out of retirement. "I'd quit about five or six years earlier because I didn't want to take drugs, and I knew that I couldn't compete with those freakazoids who were on drugs, and most were," Sobel said. "In my teens and early twenties I'd been a kind of lifting phenom, but as time went on, and I stayed drug-free, I realized I just couldn't compete with the freakazoids. A normal person just can't."

Sobel sat on a couch in the living room of his house, Chingo sleeping at his feet. He wore a white sweatshirt, blue jeans, and white sneakers, with his long hair framing what he describes as a cherubic face. "And you can tell the drug users from just looking at them," he said. "They've got gunfighter jitters, they've got these skeletal features, weird eyes, and strange bodies—extremely protruding elbows and these marine-cable arteries. Sometimes you see pimples on their stomachs from needle injections."

Sobel says he never drinks, takes drugs or caffeine, or smokes. "And I only curse when I drive," he said. He thinks he became a kind of pariah in the lifting world because he was so adamant against drug-taking, and, as a freelance writer and editor, he says he lost jobs on various muscle magazines because of his unwavering stand.

"It's not even that I was such a moral person," he said. "But it was unfair competition because of the money involved. Guys I know who got into steroids told me that it cost as much as $50,000 a year to keep up. I have other things I want to spend my money on even if I had that kind of money."

When Sobel heard about the drug-free competition he was stirred. He had envisioned great things for himself, the kind of fame and fortune that Arnold Schwarzenegger achieved, perhaps, but didn't want to go the steroid route that Schwarzenegger has acknowledged he took. Sobel thought this was his chance to overcome his frustration and become what he felt should be his due. "I wanted to be muscledom's King Biscuit," he said.

So back to the weights he went.

There are some who doubt that such a thing as a natural, or drug-free, competition exists at all, that virtually every lifter in the weights or the power contests is or has been on some kind of body-enhancing drug, from steroids to caffeine supplements. And while many competitions from the Olympics to other international events seek to test diligently—and Sobel says this began seriously only in 1988—there always seems to be some way for eager competitors to mask drugs.

"One of the most effective ways found to test for drugs, strangely enough, is the polygraph test," Sobel said. "But that's only when everyone speaks the same language—or are considered to—like in the United States. The World Natural Power Lifting organization, the United States Power Lifting organization, and the National Athletic Strength Association do as good a job as possible in keeping the competitions drug free with the polygraph and with careful urine testing. I feel comfortable competing in them."

Power lifting, meanwhile, is not, like its brother sport, weight lifting, an Olympic sport. Sobel thinks it has not been granted Olympic status because the Eastern European countries, such as Bulgaria and Russia, excel at weight lifting and not power lifting, as the United States does, and through political means have kept power lifting on the outside. Another reason, according to Jim Schmitz, president of the United States Wrestling Federation, is that "power lifting worldwide is a relatively new sport—going back about thirty years while weight lifting was in the first Olympics in 1896—and there have arisen several national and international federations," which has led to disorganization among the groups.

The sport of power lifting is also growing rapidly because of the increased appreciation for building muscle that coaches in other sports, such as football, wrestling, and track, have found so beneficial.

While Sobel has been both a power lifter and a body builder, he has rarely competed in the better-known weight lifting. "The usual feeling about power lifting is that it takes more brute strength to succeed while weight lifting combines strength with more technique and quickness and agility," Sobel said. "And that's true to an extent, but power lifting also requires technique. Otherwise every power lifter would be walking around with a slipped disk and a hernia."

The major reason that Sobel chose power lifting over weight lifting was that he could lift in his home and didn't need a coach. "I lived in an apartment with my mother, who was very sick for years, and my brother, who suffered from Marfan's syndrome, and I had to spend a lot of time taking care of them. The burden fell on me because my father had died when I was six years old," he said.

"My mother and brother died within six months of each other two years ago, but the one thing I could do in the apartment to develop myself during my years with them was lifting. I could lift in my room and not risk having to bring the barbells over my head, because if I had to drop them fast, I'd not only make a lot of noise, but I'd have put a hole through the floor."

Sobel continues to lift, for fun and for competition, and for the rewards. "No money, the prizes are mainly trophies," he said, "but sometimes I get invitations to compete in other countries. Like I have one now to go to New Zealand in a few months. I've always wanted to see that country, and the Maori tribesman. And I'd stop off in Bora Bora and see the Great Reefs. That would be fantastic. When I told my girl friend, Jeanette, about it, she said, 'Let's make it a honeymoon.'"

Sobel told her he had to be honest, that she is a great woman but that he didn't know if he was ready for marriage just yet. "But I'm thinking about it," said Sobel, as Chingo barked beside him. "I'm thinking about it."

[1994]

Index

Index

Index

A NOTE ON THE AUTHOR

Ira Berkow has been a sports columnist and feature writer for the *New York Times* for more than twenty years. In 2001 he shared the Pulitzer Prize for National Reporting with his article on "The Minority Quarterback." His work has appeared in numerous sports and literary anthologies, and he is the author of almost two dozen books, including the best-sellers *Red: A Biography of Red Smith* and *Maxwell Street: Survival in a Bazaar,* as well as a recent memoir, *To the Hoop,* a *New York Times* Notable Book of the Year. Born in Chicago, he studied at Miami (Ohio) University and Northwestern University's Medill Graduate School of Journalism. Before coming to the *Times,* he worked for the *Minneapolis Tribune* and Newspaper Enterprise Association. He lives with his wife, Dolly, in New York City.